ENGLISH GRAMMAR
A complete introduction

Teach® Yourself

ENGLISH GRAMMAR
A complete introduction

Ron Simpson

First published as *English Grammar* in Great Britain in 2001 by Hodder Education.

This edition published in 2019 by Teach Yourself, an imprint of John Murray Press, a division of Hodder & Stoughton Ltd. An Hachette UK company.

British Library Cataloguing in Publication Data: a catalogue record for this title is available from the British Library.

ISBN 978 1 529 39310 1

Ebook ISBN 978 1 444 13145 1

The publisher has used its best endeavours to ensure that any website addresses referred to in this book are correct and active at the time of going to press. However, the publisher and the author have no responsibility for the websites and can make no guarantee that a site will remain live or that the content will remain relevant, decent or appropriate.

The publisher has made every effort to mark as such all words which it believes to be trademarks. The publisher should also like to make it clear that the presence of a word in the book, whether marked or unmarked, in no way affects its legal status as a trademark.

Every reasonable effort has been made by the publisher to trace the copyright holders of material in this book. Any errors or omissions should be notified in writing to the publisher, who will endeavour to rectify the situation for any reprints and future editions.

Typeset by Cenveo® Publisher Services.

Printed and bound in Great Britain by Clays Ltd, Elcograf S.p.A.

John Murray Learning policy is to use papers that are natural, renewable and recyclable products and made from wood grown in sustainable forests. The logging and manufacturing processes are expected to conform to the environmental regulations of the country of origin.

Carmelite House
50 Victoria Embankment
London EC4Y 0DZ
www.hodder.co.uk

Contents

Meet the author

WELCOME TO *ENGLISH GRAMMAR: A COMPLETE INTRODUCTION*!
Having spent my schooldays having English grammar drilled into
me as an unchanging monolith, I felt a sense of liberation when
the tutors on my university English Language course suggested
that correct English is what *is*, not what *should be*. It's a dictum,
however, that presents the writer of a book on English grammar
with a dilemma. Should he or she simply give up any attempt to
lay down norms of correctness on the basis that they are subject to
constant change? Or should he or she take the opposite approach
and resist change in the interests of a historical correctness?

It seems to me that neither of these extreme positions is necessary.
People wishing to use English correctly in the 21st century can only
benefit from a guide to what is currently perceived as correct, and
so my intention in this book has been to be descriptive, rather than
prescriptive, and to explain what is currently acceptable rather than
look for infringements of age-old principles. Rules are helpful, and
an explanation of the historical background to modern English
can aid understanding (and, of course, entertain), but the function
of studying these is to facilitate confident use of the language as it
currently exists.

Of course, for some years pessimists have been predicting the total
demise of English grammar, syntax and orthography thanks to the
dominance of emails and texting as methods of communication and
to the irresistible spread of the use of social media. This is clearly an
extreme position, but there is, perhaps, a nugget of truth within it.
The grammar school-educated 40-something who regularly emails
me with such phrases as 'Thanx, m8' doesn't think for one moment
that this is correct written English. The danger lies with the young,
unfamiliar with life before email: can they distinguish between the
informal register (level of language) found in emails (which in reality
are a curious hybrid of oral and written forms) and the register
required for more formal written communication? It is a trend that
needs watching, but in reality there are no grounds for panic. Those
who think that English grammar is in terminal decline have little
reason for their opinions except their own misplaced nostalgia for
a golden age of literacy that never was. Interestingly, a publishing
boom in the last decade has been in books that, often with a light
touch, take a zero-tolerance approach to English grammar. This no

doubt is fuelled both by the nostalgia already mentioned and by the public's perceived need to be able to understand the rules of English.

Anyone who approaches the 2019 revised edition of *English Grammar: A complete introduction* thinking it will all be about emails, texts and tweets will be disappointed. It's perfectly reasonable that a form of English outside the rules of grammar should exist, but, as anyone applying for a job or university place will know, the demands of formal English have changed very little, even if that application is made via email. I can't predict what form English will take in 2050 (though I suspect correct formal English will be surprisingly similar to that found in 2019), but I hope I have managed to describe the state of the language today, with a little explanation of how it got here.

Ron Simpson, 2019

The history of the English language

In this chapter you will learn:

- ▶ *how the English language began*
- ▶ *how to tell the difference between Old English, Middle English and Modern English*
- ▶ *the ways in which language is still changing.*

English as a hybrid language

We are all familiar with the notion that English is made up of elements from many different languages, just as the British are descended from many different tribes. In particular the language is seen, correctly, as based mainly on German, Latin and French sources, with, of course, distinct elements from Scandinavian languages, other Latin-derived languages (Italian and Spanish) and, in terms particularly of vocabulary, the languages of nations explored or colonized by the British – most notably, the ex-colonies of North America, which continue to transform our language slowly day by day.

We need, however, to be careful of the inference that we draw from these different elements. It is tempting (and wholly wrong) to think that the Romans invaded us and brought Latin with them; then came the Angles, Saxons and the rest, with their German dialects, and finally the Normans completed the mix by adding French.

Insight

It is possible to find traces in vocabulary of the language of conquest. It has become a truism that the words for animals in the field, where they are tended by peasants, are English in origin (cow, sheep, calf, pig, etc.), while their names when carved at table by the nobles are French: beef (Modern French *boeuf*), mutton (*mouton*), veal (*veau*), pork (*porc*). Of course this does not apply with all animals, but there is certainly a pattern. However, the use of French by nobles was, by no means, all due to the Norman Conquest.

The sources of modern English

In fact there is no point in considering any connection between the Latin of Roman Britain and modern English (a few place names like London from *Londinium* are direct survivals), though all the European languages mentioned above, dead and living, are connected by a common ancestor in the Indo-European language of 2000-plus BC. The history of English starts with Old English, but the ways in which the influences of other languages have occurred may be surprising.

For example, the influence of Latin has occurred mainly through religion and scholarship. Remember that Roman Catholicism was the only faith in Britain until the 16th century. Through all the Middle Ages the Bible in use was the Vulgate in Latin; the first attempts at an English translation did not occur until the late 14th century. Until the reign of Henry VIII (1509–47), much teaching and learning was centred on monasteries. International scholarship (science, philosophy, medicine, etc.) depended upon the common language of Latin. As late as the 17th century scientific works were still being written in Latin by Englishmen. In the more personal field of poetry John Milton, famed for *Paradise Lost*, wrote poems in Latin as well as in English, also in the 17th century.

The clear distinction between France and England as countries was not there in the Middle Ages. The first Norman kings ruled over parts of France as well as England; the Plantagenet royal house was also known as Angevin (from Anjou in France where the family originated); Henry V, in the early 15th century, married the King of France's daughter and tried to merge the crowns. At times the English court was as French as it was English, so that the three languages had their own niches in England, with French the tongue of courtiers (it later became the language of diplomacy), Latin framing the law and expressing the consolations of philosophy, and English, sadly, something of a rough country cousin.

Insight

The above are only a few examples of how deeply England was in touch with the wider European community so that the language was constantly subject to that influence. The celebrated last words of Mary Tudor, Queen of England from 1553 to 1558, were, 'When I am dead and opened, you shall find "Calais" lying in my heart.' As recently as her reign England lost the last of her possessions in mainland France, Calais, though the Channel Islands still remain.

Old English

The term 'Old English' is applied to the language spoken between the Germanic invasions of the 5th century and the 12th century, by which time the language had been transformed into what is known as **Middle English**. Old English was formerly called **Anglo-Saxon**, and you may find this term in older books or used archaically in the present day. While there may be two terms, there was only one language – or, rather, group of languages and dialects.

Old English changed form on two main bases:

1 Time: Over seven centuries there were many changes in the language to the extent that language scholars can date (or argue over the dating of) a manuscript on the internal evidence of its language. Reputedly the last document of Old English is the 1154

annal of the *Anglo-Saxon Chronicle*, but clearly the population, including the monkish chroniclers, did not suddenly say, 'It's time we spoke and wrote Middle English.' A stage was reached in the transformation of the language which makes it convenient for scholars to define it by a new name.

2 Place: At any one time different versions of Old English were in operation in different parts of the country (in the earlier period, they were actually different countries). Kentish English and Northumbrian English, for instance, were not the same thing. Change comes more quickly in what is largely an oral language and change tended to come from the south-eastern part of the country, so scholars still argue about whether a document or poem was written at an early date in the south or later in the north.

Insight

The ways in which language changes can vary considerably depending on whether the changes are influenced by speech or writing. A good example, though from a much later era than Old English, is our borrowing from the French word *gentil*, meaning much the same as our 'gentle', originally in the 'noble' sense (as in *gentilhomme/* gentleman). 'Gentle' appeared first as a word either from French or direct from Latin, but gradually changed its main meaning (to 'mild and considerate'). 'Jaunty' (bold and vigorous) comes direct from the French pronunciation, with no hint of the French spelling, and 'genteel' (aspiring to gentlemanly manners) comes predominantly from the written form, though '-eel' hints at the French pronunciation. Thus we have three words and at least four meanings from one French root.

Old English Grammar

Though it is well outside the scope of this book to explain Old English grammar, it is worth noting that Old English was an **inflected language**; that is to say, word endings showed whether, for instance, a verb was in the 1st, 2nd or 3rd person or whether a noun was the subject or object of a sentence. Many, but by no means all, of these forms would be familiar to us, for example:

▶ Some nouns indicated plural and possession by *-s*. *Stan* (stone) took the forms *stanes* (possession) and *stanas* (plural) – pretty familiar – but others, as in Modern German, used *-n* for this purpose.

▶ Verb forms like the 2nd person singular *-est* and the 3rd person *-eth* (spelled *-eþ*) suggest rather old-fashioned Modern English, as does *thu* (spelled *þu*): *þu drincest* is clearly thou drinkest – you drink.

Insight

Old English contained a number of letters based on Runic script of which thorn, ash and wynn are the best known. Ash was written æ and represented the *a* sound. Thorn was written þ and, as it represented the *th* sound, was widely used. It also survived much longer than the other Runic characters, later becoming confused with *y* in writing. Hence the influence of Thorn is still with us. In Old English *The* was written *þe*. Later that turned into *Ye* (still pronounced *The*) and even today many of our popular tourist centres are graced with 'Ye Olde Englishe...' signs. The extra *e* on *old* and *English* is an equally misguided borrowing from a later phase of English: the medieval French influence.

CAN YOU READ OLD ENGLISH?

When we attempt to read Old English, two things become immediately apparent:

1 It is a different language from English;

2 It is related to English, possibly a great-great-great-grandfather.

See how much sense you can make of the following lines from the Old English poem *The Battle of Maldon*. The battle was fought in 991 with Byrhtnoth, the 'ealdorman' of Essex, making a heroically unsuccessful stand against the Vikings. All the Runic characters have been replaced by their nearest modern equivalents:

> *Byrhtnoth mathelode, bord hafenode,*
> *wand wacne aesc, wordum maelde,*
> *yrre and anraed ageaf him andsware:*
> *'Gehyrst thu, saelida, hwaet this folc sageth?'*

Much of this is probably incomprehensible, but, in the first three lines, as Byrhtnoth raises his shield (*bord*) and brandishes his spear (*aesc*) before speaking, you can identify the Old English equivalents of 'words', 'answer', even possibly 'angry' (*yrre*) and 'gave' (*ageaf*). Then suddenly the fourth line reads almost like old-fashioned modern English (the 19th century, perhaps):

> *'Hearest thou, sailor [seafarer/Viking] what this folk [people]*
> *sayeth?'*

Middle English

'Middle English' is the term used for the language in the period after the effects of the Norman Conquest had been absorbed (mid-12th century), up to the mid-15th century. Though Middle English contains some of the most beautiful poetry of the pre-modern period, the changes in the language are more for the dedicated linguist than a book of this sort. In simple terms:

▶ the French influence became stronger;

▶ the language steadily became less inflected;

▶ separate dialects still prevailed in different parts of the country, plus, of course, Welsh and Gaelic elsewhere in what is now Britain;

▶ the English language was still in the shadow of French and Latin in scholarship, the court and the law;

▶ by the end of the Middle English period, it is possible for the modern reader to find the language intelligible.

LATE MIDDLE ENGLISH – EARLY MODERN?

By the 15th century, with the *Agincourt Carol*, the modern reader has little difficulty if he/she is prepared to read it aloud – or, better still, sing it:

> Owre kynge went forth to Normandy
> With grace and myght of chyvalry;
> Ther God for hym wrought mervelusly;
> Wherfore Englonde may calle and cry,
> 'Deo Gracias.'

You will have noticed the influence of Latin (the refrain, *Deo Gracias*, 'Thanks be to God') and the odd spelling. Otherwise there are just a few rather archaic words: for example, *wrought* for 'worked' or 'did' (like *wright* in such trades as *shipwright*, *wheelwright*, etc.). It is interesting that standard spelling, even in one manuscript, was not yet established: elsewhere 'our' is spelled *oure*, not *owre*, 'through' is spelled *thorwe* and *throw*, 'field' appears as *felde* and *feld*. For all this, you can sense a language on the brink of Modern English.

EAST MIDLAND, CHAUCER AND STANDARD ENGLISH

The process by which English became a single language rather than a series of closely related dialects was particularly active in the 15th and 16th centuries. Since the great poet Geoffrey Chaucer died in

1400 and wrote copiously in the East Midland dialect, which became
the basis for modern English, it is tempting to see this process as the
result of Chaucer's influence after his death. What is certain is that
the centralization of power at court and the invention of the printing
press did much to establish 'standard English'. Not that it was totally
standard by any means: Sir Walter Ralegh, the late 16th/early 17th-
century courtier/poet/explorer/politician, reputedly spoke broad
Devonian and Shakespeare's different signatures are famous.

Insight

Much of the research into Old and Middle English language and
literature in the early middle years of the 20th century (including such
matters as the dating of poems like *Beowulf* and *Sir Gawain*) was done
by Professor J.R.R. Tolkien, still to be heard declaiming *Beowulf* in
the lecture theatres of Oxford in the 1960s. The professor had another
part-time career, as the author of *The Lord of the Rings*, and readers of
that saga of Middle Earth will easily find hints of Norse and Old English
in his linguistic inventions.

Modern English

Already, by about 1450, English had settled into what scholars call
Early Modern English. By the Elizabethan Age the language reached
a state where it can both seem totally modern and yet surprise us by
occasionally proving blankly incomprehensible. Think of the famous
speech of Elizabeth at Tilbury, the plays of Shakespeare (written
between approximately 1590 and 1612) and the Authorized Version
of the Bible (prepared at the behest of Elizabeth's successor, James I,
in 1606). However, we must remember that, if we find Shakespeare
at his most metaphorical difficult to understand, the problem is no
worse than that presented by, say, Dylan Thomas (died 1953) or some
of the denser passages of Ted Hughes, the former Poet Laureate. To
blame all difficulties on 'old-fashioned English' is misleading.

CODIFYING THE LANGUAGE

By the 17th and 18th centuries scholars and students were ready to
explain the English language, to tidy it up and put it in order. It was
no longer a second-rate language in its own land, but 'the language
of Chaucer and Shakespeare'. Ben Jonson set to work producing
an English grammar in the 17th century, a hundred years later
his near namesake Samuel Johnson produced the first dictionary,
and so on. Correctness became, for the first time, essential. Thus

the fundamental changes in modern English have involved such matters as codifying sentence construction (read a learned work of the 17th century and you will find mighty sentences that defy analysis), standardizing spelling, punctuation and the use of capital letters, removing such illogicalities as the double negative, etc. By and large these changes proved helpful, but they gave rise to some nonsensical rules. The split infinitive (*to boldly go*) was banished and prepositions banned from the ends of sentences. In both of these there is an element of sense: it is ugly, for instance, to split an infinitive with a lengthy phrase (*I would like to before eating my dinner wash my hands*). However, as general rules, they can be safely ignored.

NEW WORDS, NEW SUBJECTS

The main developments in the language in the last 300 years have been in vocabulary. A visitor from the 18th century would find formal English of today only slightly unfamiliar in its form and constructions, but desperately confusing in its vocabulary, in precisely the same way as he/she would struggle to understand the changes in science, politics, sport, medicine, society, industry, fashion, etc., that have brought about this new vocabulary: from astronauts to socialism, from snooker to motorways.

REAPPLYING EXISTING WORDS

Many of the neologisms (new words) have been applied by inventors, discoverers, etc., but many more are compounds of existing, often very simple words. For instance, what should we call the new horseless carriages (too cumbersome a phrase to survive long) that began to appear at the end of the 19th century? *Automobile* was rather good (from the Latin for 'moves by itself'), but, in Britain, the simple *motor-car* (*car* meaning a wheeled vehicle, a cart or chariot) won the day. With the subsequent abbreviation to *car*, our 18th-century visitor would find the word totally familiar, but would be surprised to see the horse replaced by the internal combustion engine. *Football* is a good example of a different type of confusion. From medieval times, a game involving kicking a ball has been known as *football*. The problem is that there are many different ways of playing ball-and-feet games. Originally a whole community rough-and-tumble, football came to mean different things to the pupils of Rugby and Eton in the 19th century and today still refers to a different game in the USA from in Britain. Bizarrely, the old-fashioned public-school slang, *soccer*, has found a home in the democratic Land of the Free!

PREFIXES, SUFFIXES AND CLASSICAL ROOTS

Of course not all new words are formed by putting together two existing words. Some may be named after the inventor/discoverer: daguerrotype photographs (from Louis Daguerre) and the saxophone (from Adolphe Sax) are two 19th-century examples where the capital letters of the proper nouns have long disappeared. Or it may be a forgotten association of place: *denim* (a fabric 'from Nîmes': 'de Nîmes') or *hamburger* (from 'Hamburg steak').

Very often, however, new words are created by turning to Latin or Greek roots and/or existing prefixes with known meanings: just think how many words are now being coined using *super*, *hyper*, *mega* and *multi*, a sign of the increasing scale of much in our current lifestyle, though, at the other end of the scale, *micro-* (*microelectronics* and *microbiology*, for example) fills more dictionary pages year by year. Similarly *tele-* is a prefix whose day has come: from the Greek for 'afar' or 'at a distance', it now has a huge field of telecommunications to frolic in. It is interesting that there are two words which both mean 'seeing at a distance': *telescope* (from two Greek words) and *television* (with a mix of Latin and Greek that one pedant said would never come to good).

Sphairistike. The game, but not the name, caught on, so the term *lawn tennis* (on the old principle of combining existing words) became common. Since *real tennis* is played by few people, the other is usually referred to as *tennis*. As so often happens, an inventor has been unable to impose his chosen name on the public and a word has changed meaning for totally non-linguistic reasons.

SLANG AND FASHION

The most rapid changes in language (of grammatical form, but particularly of vocabulary) occur in spoken English, especially slang, and in accordance with the dictates of fashion. Very often, of course, the two go together, fashion dictating the latest slang. Equally, fashionable slang is the least permanent element in language. For instance, the language of a Restoration or 18th-century comedy now seems most out of date in those features which were then considered most fashionable. What can the would-be man of fashion, Sparkish, in Wycherley's *The Country Wife*, mean when he says, using a series of common monosyllables, 'We wits ... make love often, but to show our parts'? Surprisingly, the answer is, 'We wits pay court to [*chat up*, in more recent slang] ladies simply to show our abilities [*wit/cleverness*].'

A striking modern example of the fashionable rebranding of a word is *cool*. As well as relating to temperature, the word has long referred to unflappable characters (*cool* customers), a style of jazz and a social attitude and lifestyle that is indefinable (if you have to ask, you're just not cool). In the last years of the 20th century its lifestyle implications were very un-coolly hijacked for political purposes: 'Cool Britannia', etc. What does the future hold for *cool*? The one certainty is that, as usual, it's a case of 'last in, first out': when *cool* still applies to mountain streams, intrepid explorers, Miles Davis's trumpet and screen icons like James Dean, the politicians already view it with the amnesia associated with yesterday's slogan.

RULES AND TRENDS

Currently language is undergoing rapid innovations in vocabulary and developments in jargon, the technical language of a particular trade, skill or profession, from plumbing to the Stock Market. At the same time, the diversity of dialect has reduced and changes in the form and structure of 'correct' English grammar are happening, but at nothing like the same speed or in the same quantity. Vocabulary designed to dignify the humble and routine is now so common that old jokes about 'rodent extermination operatives' (rat catchers) have been overtaken by reality and political correctness throws up absurdities ('Winterfest' for Christmas in order not to offend non-Christians) alongside very welcome developments. Politically, too, the use of language to obscure meaning is becoming ever more common.

However, the major change in our language has been brought about by the use of emails and texting. Essentially, emails have created a form of English that falls between spoken and written, combining the instant communication of a telephone conversation with (if the recipient wishes) the permanence of a letter. The first result of this is that elements like capitalization, punctuation and spelling lose their importance. With texting deliberate misspelling appears in the abbreviated form of words. Essentially, this has no bearing on mainstream English grammar, just as chatty telephone conversations have nothing to do with formal written English, though many of us may be a little worried about the spread of such features as *u* (you), 4 (for) and 2 (to) into advertising and tabloid headlines – possibly the thin end of the wedge.

? Test yourself

1.1 Read the two extracts following and see if you can translate them into modern English. Also decide which you think is the earlier piece. The translation appears in the 'Test yourself answers' section at the end of the book.

a The first is part of a poem about King Arthur and uses the letters þ (thorn – equivalent to *th*) and ȝ (yogh – equivalent to *y* or *gh*):

> Þis kyng lay at Camylot vpon Krystmasse
> With mony luflych lorde, lede of Þe best,
> Rekenly of Þe Rounde Table all Þo rich breÞer,
> With rych reuel oryȝt and rechles merÞes.

b The second is a mock-serious meditation on murder from a comic fable of the cock and the fox:

> Mordre wol out, that se we day by day.
> Mordre is so wlatsom and abhomynable
> To God, that is so just and resonable,
> That he no wol nat suffre it heled be,
> Though it abyde a yeer, or two, or thre:
> Mordre wol out, this my conclusioun.

1.2 Read the following brief extracts and consider the ways in which they use English:

- ▶ What do they mean?
- ▶ Do you notice anything unusual?
- ▶ Have you any idea when and where they were written? (Not necessarily precise: 'earlier than the last one' is a sensible response.)

a The Skies gan scowle, orecast with mistie cloudes,
When (as I rode alone by London way,
Clokeless, unclad) thus did I sing and say.

b Him se yldesta andswarode,
werodes wisa, wordhord onleac.

c Hain't we got all the fools in town on our side? and ain't that a big enough majority in any town?

d It was at Rome, on the 15th October, 1***, as I sat musing amidst the ruins of the Capitol, while the barefoot friars were singing vespers in the Temple of Jupiter, that the idea of writing the decline and fall of the city first started to my mind.

e In a somer seson when soft was the sonne,
I shope me in shroudes as I a shepe were,
In habite as an heremite unholy of workes,
Went wyde in þis world wondres to here.

f – But is this the law?
– Ay, marry, is't – crowner's quest law.
– Will you ha' the truth an't? If this had not been a
gentlewoman, she should have been buried out a' Christian
burial.

g I struggled through the alphabet as if it had been a bramble-
bush; getting considerably worried and scratched by every
letter. After that, I fell among those thieves, the nine figures,
who seemed every evening to do something new to disguise
themselves and baffle recognition.

h Ichot a burde in boure bryht
That fully semly is on syht,
Menskful maiden of myht,
Feir and fre to fonde.

Dividing the word: syllables and morphemes

In this chapter you will learn:

▶ *how a word can be divided into smaller units*

▶ *how these units differ in spoken and written form*

▶ *the variety of forms of morpheme (the smallest grammatical unit).*

Minimum free form?

The following units will deal with different types of words, their functions and properties and their relationships with each other in linguistic units. However, it is worthwhile first to reflect on what distinguishes a word and how we can define the smallest units of meaning.

We assume that a word has a meaning that is free-standing: the American linguist Bloomfield defined it as **minimum free form**; in other words, the smallest unit of language that can occur by itself. By the same token we assume that anything less than a word has no meaning on its own. Both these assumptions are, to some extent, misleading.

A **word** on its own in written English generally means nothing until it takes its place in a sentence or phrase, though a note consisting of the word 'Help!' could serve its purpose so long as the recipient knew where it had come from. In spoken English there is more chance of an isolated word conveying meaning:

'Where is this train going?' 'Exeter.'
'Is this your English or History notebook?' 'History.'

However, in the same way, if rather less frequently, units smaller than a word can provide answers to questions:

'Is this inclusive or exclusive of insurance?' 'In-.'
'Are you pro- or anti-fox hunting?' 'Anti-.'
'Are you confident of doing well?' '-ish.'
'Is this the priority or non-priority queue?' 'Non-.'

HOW MANY WORDS?

The word is not a fixed unit, established for all time. Two words, at first used side by side, may become a **compound word** (one made up of two or more other words), possibly initially joined by a hyphen, then, as they become more and more familiar with each other, merging into a single word. Think, for instance, of the single word *homework*, made up originally of the two words *home* and *work*, with the same relationship to each other as *garden* and *seat* which are written separately or, possibly, hyphenated. Eventually the concept of *homework* became so familiar that the two became one.

The word is clearly the most familiar **lexical unit** (one or more words that function as a unit of meaning, such as can be defined in a dictionary). However, the above suggests that regarding it as the only base unit, as somehow having a fixed and unique role, is misleading. It is, of course, even more misleading in speech when words are not individually wrapped with their own space before and after, as in written English.

Speech and syllables

We are used to regarding the atoms that make up a word as syllables. A syllable consists of a single **vowel** sound and any consonant sounds that go with it. Remember that we are dealing with a vowel **sound**, not a written vowel. Therefore a syllable may include *y* (or *w* in words of Welsh origin like *cwm*) as well as *a*, *e*, *i*, *o* or *u* as a vowel sound. Similarly, two vowels joined together (what is called a **diphthong**) make up only one syllable.

So, for instance, the most simple words consist of one syllable and can be described as **monosyllables**: *that, den, kick, shot, bun.* But *you, their* and *bait* are also monosyllables, although they contain two vowels. A word like *di-et*, however, has two syllables because the *i* and the *e* are sounded separately.

Look at the following examples of long words divided up by syllables:

can-tank-er-ous (4 syllables)
in-cred-i-ble (4 syllables)
bi-o-chem-ist-ry (5 syllables)
in-des-truc-ti-ble (5 syllables)
un-pre-med-it-at-ed (6 syllables – 7 if you add *-ly*)

It must be emphasized that syllables refer purely to sound. Three examples will suffice to prove this:

1 How many syllables are there in *-ious*? There are three vowels and *ou* clearly functions as a diphthong, so most of us would regard it as consisting of two syllables. However, if you listen to someone saying the word *pretentious*, there is every chance that it will be pronounced 'pre-ten-shus', three syllables, including one for *-ious*. But is the precise, old-fashioned, somewhat pretentious speaker who says 'pre-ten-shi-us' wrong? Clearly not. As a grammatical unit, applied to words on the page, the syllable is inadequate to explain the form of *-ious*. *Conscientious* creates even more problems. Many people would be tempted to see it as a five-syllable word; many others pronounce it as nearer to three syllables 'con-shen-shus'.

2 The ending *-ed* applied to a verb to show the past tense has the same grammatical function in all such cases, but sometimes it is a syllable and sometimes not. In such cases as *walked, fixed* and *hampered* it is not: the words remain of one syllable (in the first two cases) or two syllables (in the third). In *attempted, diverted* and *protected* it is a syllable in itself, turning two-syllable words into three-syllable words.

3 *Comparable* is a word which has two alternative pronunciations, each with a different number of syllables. The normal 'correct' pronunciation is 'com-pra-ble' (three syllables). In recent years 'com-pa-ra-ble' (four syllables) has become the more usual pronunciation and is widely accepted.

Thus it is necessary to find a way of breaking words down into their constituent parts which is relevant to their meaning and grammatical form, not just their sound.

What are morphemes?

As the smallest grammatical or syntactical unit, the **morpheme** has one single quality: it cannot be divided into smaller units. It is like the grammatical equivalent of prime numbers, those that are not divisible by any number except themselves and 1. Just as many small numbers (e.g. 4) are not prime and many larger ones (e.g. 23) are, so the length of morphemes cannot be predicted.

Many are single syllables, whether complete words or not: *the*, *see*, *pre-*, *-dom* (as in *kingdom*), but, just as there is no certainty whether a morpheme will be a complete word or not, so there is no normal length. For instance, the short word, *died*, consists of two morphemes (the verb *die* and the ending *-d*). The much longer word, *chimpanzee*, consists of one morpheme because there are no smaller units within it, *chimp* being merely a **diminutive** (or shortened form) of the word itself.

Before turning to types of morpheme, it is worth illustrating the difference between a morpheme and a syllable. In many words the syllables and morphemes are identical: *un-friend-ly*, for instance, *ship-ment* or *shoot-ing* (plus all monosyllables). In these cases the blocks of meaning (morphemes) and the vowel sounds (syllables) coincide. But look at the following:

rhino-ceros (2 morphemes)	*rhi-no-ce-ros* (4 syllables)
dynam-ic (2 morphemes)	*dy-nam-ic* (3 syllables)
un-attain-able (3 morphemes)	*un-att-ain-a-ble* (5 syllables)

TYPES OF MORPHEME

Many morphemes can stand on their own as whole words; for instance, 'attain' in the above example. These are known as free **morphemes**. You will find it easy to think of examples of free morphemes, from whole words such as *live, suggest, rare* and *resist* to their use in longer words like *live-li-hood, suggest-ion, rare-ly* and *ir-resist-ible*. Usually the free morpheme will provide the root for the meaning of a word, though, of course, a word may contain more than one free morpheme: *drumstick, outhouse* or *handicap*.

Morphemes which serve a particular purpose and usually serve to modify the meaning of a free morpheme are known as **bound morphemes.** So, for instance:

> *un-, in-* and *dis-* and many others indicate negatives;
> *-s* indicates plural or present tense or, usually with an added apostrophe, possession;
> *pre-* and *ante-* both mean 'before';
> *-ed* indicates past tense, etc., etc.

Bound morphemes can be again subdivided, if you wish:

Inflectional morphemes add additional information about the existing free morpheme, but it remains the same lexical unit (there is no need for an extra dictionary entry): *look-ed* (past), *give-n* (past participle), *shoe-s* (plural), *friend-'s* (possession).

Derivational morphemes create a new word, though one linked to the free morpheme in meaning: *free-**dom**, **un**-kind-**ness**, quick-**ly**, **dis**-continue*.

PREFIXES AND SUFFIXES

Many bound morphemes are also **affixes** or **prefixes** and **suffixes**. There is nothing unusual in finding words or parts of words which are examples of more than one grammatical form. Prefixes and suffixes are dealt with in Chapter 11 and are morphemes which can be placed at the front (**prefixes**) or at the end (**suffixes**) of words with a fixed meaning. So, in the above examples, we find the negative prefixes (*un, dis*), suffixes creating an abstract noun (*dom, ness*), and a suffix indicating the adverb (*ly*).

FURTHER READING

This is a fairly brief and simplified account of the role of morphemes in the structure of language. Those of you who wish to study the nature of language, rather than just the correct forms of English grammar, are advised that *Aitchison's Linguistics* (also in this series) contains a more detailed and academic examination of morphemes.

2.1 Some of the following words are compounds; some are not. Try to identify which are compounds:

glucose	pirate	headstrong
housewife	timekeeper	discernible
footing	footman	helpful
milkmaid	milky	hypochondriac

2.2 Decide which of the following words are single morphemes, then divide the others into their constituent morphemes, suggesting which morphemes are free and which are bound:

indigestible	turned	prunes
oral	recall	embarrassment
distaste	flying	cobra
foreman	forest	misdirection
wearily	condensation	elephant

2.3 In this exercise you are asked to distinguish between morphemes and syllables. Write out the following words, first separating them into syllables, then into morphemes:

departure	inaccessible	postscript
poster	infirm	disarm
diseased	unappealing	dreadful
wickedly	attempting	kettles
walking	refreshing	recollect

Nouns

In this chapter you will learn:

▶ *how to identify the different types of noun*
▶ *how to form the plural of nouns*
▶ *the various functions of nouns within the sentence.*

What is a noun?

Whatever method of explaining English grammar we adopt, **nouns** and **verbs** are the basic building blocks of the English language. In traditional terms the noun is a 'naming word' and the verb a 'word of doing or being'. Hence the simplest of statements consists of a name and what he/she/it did: 'Jesus wept.'

According to more modern explanations of **function** (i.e. what words do), we can explain words and phrases according to **processes, participants** and **circumstances.** Of these the **process** (the happening or state) and the **participants** (who or what is taking part in the happening or state) are essential – and, of course, the process is a verb and the participants nouns or pronouns.

However defined, understanding nouns and verbs is central to our knowledge of English grammar and many other parts of speech (**pronouns, adjectives** and **adverbs**) can only be explained in relation to nouns and verbs.

Types of noun

COMMON AND PROPER NOUNS

The definition 'naming word' has potential for confusing the unwary student. You are familiar with 'name' as something individual, the name of a city, person, club, association or firm. Nouns are more often the name not of an **individual**, but of a **species**, **genre** or **type.** You have a name that applies to yourself individually (*Margaret, Mr Rowley* or whatever), but there are many other nouns that can be applied to you as a type or member of a group. Take your pick from such words as: *student, woman, youth, sportsman, driver, worker, painter, cleaner, campaigner* or *couch-potato.*

A **common noun** is one that applies to the group or type: it is common to all. For example, *singer, town, sword, tea, politician, regiment, actor.*

A **proper noun** is one that applies to the individual. For example, *Callas, Weymouth, Excalibur, Typhoo, Churchill, Grenadier Guards, Olivier.*

▶ All proper nouns begin with a capital letter

A slight exception occurs in the case of names (proper nouns) that consist of more than one word. The tendency in such cases is not to use a capital letter at the start of any 'unimportant' word. So both words in Menai Strait have capitals, but not every word in Straits of Gibraltar. Or compare the titles of two Graham Greene novels: *Brighton Rock* and *The Power and the Glory.*

▶ **emails and www**

The whole structure of punctuation and capitalization is, of course, apparently undermined by the working practices of emails and the World Wide Web (or www, not W.W.W.) which are all about the instant communication of ideas and knowledge, unhindered by the use of the shift key. It is comparatively easy for us to adjust to different habits when emailing or surfing the net. The question is whether email practices are spreading into ordinary usage. The main sign is in company names: an existing tendency towards lower case (small letters) or the insertion of capitals in the 'wrong' places is rapidly increasing, as in a company such as easyJet (with subsidiaries like easyRentacar). But this has little relevance to normal written English. It would certainly be dangerous to use emails as the justification for omitting capital letters from a job application or a report.

Insight

Long before capital letters were endangered by the internet, American poet e. e. cummings virtually banished them from his verse. If you are a whimsically original poet, then it is fine to write:

*and eddieandbill come
running from marbles and
piracies and it's
spring
when the world is puddle-wonderful*

Similarly American humorist Don Marquis wrote the upper-case-free adventures of 'archy the cockroach and mehitabel the cat', secure in the knowledge that cats and cockroaches cannot work the shift key.

COLLECTIVE NOUNS

A **collective noun** is the name of a group comprising several (many?) individual parts. It is very straightforward to think of words such as: *class, team, herd, committee, association, collection, staff, fleet, flock, group* (of course) or (in some senses) *party.*

The difficulty is that, strictly speaking, a collective noun is **singular** (i.e. refers to one thing only), but sometimes our instincts are to regard it as **plural** (referring to more than one) because of the many individuals involved. It is natural to say, 'The fleet's in', but it is equally natural to say, 'The class *have* had enough of English grammar.'

ABSTRACT AND CONCRETE NOUNS

Another broad distinction is between abstract and concrete nouns.
Concrete nouns are described as 'material', **abstract nouns** as
'immaterial'. This means, simply, that concrete nouns exist in a
physical form, are there to be seen, touched or tripped over, while
abstract nouns have no existence that can be determined by the
senses of sight, touch or even smell.

Take the sentence, 'We crossed the meadows in hope, expecting soon
to see the beauty of the daffodils.' There are four nouns there, two
concrete referring to things with a physical form (*meadows, daffodils*),
two **abstract** referring to emotions or concepts (*hope, beauty*).

NUMBER: SINGULAR AND PLURAL

Like so much in English grammar, the question of **number** becomes
a problem only in the exceptions to the rule. Modern distinctions
between **count nouns** and **mass (non-count) nouns** need not worry
the general student of English grammar. Certainly some nouns
can form a plural (count nouns) and some cannot (mass nouns).
However, many nouns can operate as either. A recent book cited
homework as an example of a mass noun, unable to form a plural,
but how many schoolteachers have said to their students, 'You've
missed *three homeworks*!'?

What matters is the correct formation of the **plural**. The majority of
nouns form the plural by adding *s*, but there are many exceptions.

▶ *s* and suchlike

To make them easy to say, words ending in a sibilant (*s, z, x, sh, ch*,
etc.) add an *e* to make an extra syllable: *mass/masses, quiz/quizzes,
fox/foxes, marsh/marshes, church/churches*, etc.

▶ *y* into *ies*

A rule that is easy to learn and almost without exceptions is to replace *y*, if it follows a consonant at the end of a noun, with *ies* in the plural: *factory/factories, story/stories, country/countries*. Note that this does not apply if the *y* follows a vowel. In particular, be careful with *-ey*: *story* (a tale) becomes *stories*, *storey* (the floor of a building) becomes *storeys*.

▶ *-ves* or not

The practice concerning words ending in *f* or *fe* is rather more difficult. Some form the plural by changing the ending to *-ves*; some form the plural in the normal way; in some cases, both versions are correct. Unfortunately it is simply a matter of learning which are which and being sensitive to pronunciation. The way in which we say *knives, loaves, halves, lives*, etc., tells us the spelling. *Chiefs, griefs, proofs* and *gulfs* are similarly straightforward. With *roofs/rooves, hoofs/hooves, scarfs/scarves* and *dwarfs/dwarves* you must decide for yourself where you stand.

▶ *o* for an ending

Words ending in *o* can also cause confusion. Many like *potatoes* and *tomatoes* add an extra *e*, but many others form the plural in the normal way: *pianos, folios, cameos, solos, cellos, concertos*. Interestingly many of these are of Italian origin and the plurals end in *i* in the original. You will find *celli, concerti*, etc., in English, but usually only in specialist music writing: 'Handel wrote many *concerti* grossi', but 'The *Emperor* is one of my favourite piano *concertos*'.

Insight

Sometimes forming the singular, not the plural, can be the problem. Famously a former Vice-President of the United States, Dan Quayle, visiting a school, encouraged a pupil to add a missing *e* to *potato*. In fact, though we do not think of English as having many words ending in vowels except *e*, *o* endings are more common than *oe*.

▶ No change

In some cases nouns have **zero plural**; in other words, they remain unchanged in the plural. These are, most notably, nouns referring to animals, maybe because we often see animals in both number and mass. We may eat/keep as a pet/be attacked by an individual animal, but we also make our living by breeding *cattle* or order *salmon* for a meal. Other cases include *sheep*, *deer*, *cod*, *grouse* and *trout*.

▶ Foreign origins

If a foreign word is taken into the English language without change, there is a tendency to use the original foreign plural (often *a* for *um* words derived from Latin). The soundest advice is:

▶ When a word is so fully absorbed that we think of it as an English word, it is probably wiser to form the plural with *s*: *stadiums* and *gymnasiums* now seem more natural than *stadia* and *gymnasia*, though the latter two are not wrong.

▶ When the original plural becomes established in its own right, then use it. The best example is *data*, much more widely used than *datum*. Anyone using *datums* to mean 'given facts' would simply spread confusion.

▶ There are many cases where personal choice is all that matters. You may use *radii* because *radiuses* sounds cumbersome; *addenda* may continue to be used because it has little currency in ordinary conversation, but *radiuses* and *addendums* are perfectly acceptable words. The plural of *genius* can be *genii* or *geniuses*. Many people use *geniuses* for astonishingly gifted people and *genii* for spirits. In the same way the context can have an effect. For instance, what word do you use for more than one cactus? Usually, looking at them as a mass in a garden centre, we would say, 'That's a fine display of *cacti*.' Singling them out individually and in the tough world of the Hollywood Western, the besieged leader of the wagon train would perceive the Apaches hiding behind the *cactuses*.

Insight

Use of foreign plurals can produce confusion. A good example is the word *phenomenon*, a Greek word meaning, in its present use, a remarkable thing or event. It is a matter of choice between the plurals *phenomenons* and the original *phenomena*. Sadly, it is not uncommon for *phenomena* to be used as the singular, resulting in the plural *phenomenas*, both of these wrong. 'Criterion' and its plural 'criteria' suffer the same fate: how often have you heard phrases such as 'the sole *criteria*', a self-evident contradiction?

Phenomena and *criteria* do not exist as singular nouns. However, we must face the possibility that a few more generations of inaccurate usage by the educated and powerful might establish them as such.

▶ *en* plurals

The *en* ending for plurals is an ancient and once common form. Appropriately enough, apart from *children*, it tends to be used in rather old-fashioned contexts. *Oxen* and *brethren* are two such examples. *Brethren*, of course, means the same as *brothers*, but the situations where it is used are quite different. *Brethren* usually has a biblical or religious context: *Joseph and his Brethren* or *The Plymouth Brethren*.

▶ Change the vowel

Derived from Old English, the plural of several common nouns involves changing the central vowel rather than adding an ending. Many of the irregular and old-fashioned plurals apply to nouns which were staples of existence before the regular *s* ending became common. Just like the zero plural, the **vowel change plural** applies to several animals *(goose/geese, mouse/mice)*, plus parts of the body *(tooth/teeth, foot/feet)* and, of course, *man/men* and *woman/women*. A variation on this is the archaic plural of *cow* (*kine*) which you may still find in old Bible stories.

▶ Compound nouns

Some nouns are made up of two or more words (**compounds**). Which one is turned into the plural? It is impossible to lay down an exact rule, but it is probably best to focus on the main noun in those cases where hyphens are used (*daughters-in-law, lords-lieutenant*; in ranks such as *Major-Generals* the second word is the more important) and to place the *s* at the end where they have become one word (*cupfuls, bucketfuls*).

Insight

What are you to do when the plural has completely taken over the function of the singular? For instance, *news*, apparently a plural, has a precise meaning of its own, though connected to the adjective *new*: similarly *politics*. These words have now obtained a life of their own as 'singular' nouns, so we write, 'The news is bad' or 'Politics is a dirty business.' *Data*, at this moment, is undergoing that change: you will find some writers and speakers referring to *data* as singular, others treating the word as plural. Which is correct? Usage dictates that both are.

Functions of nouns

The roles that nouns play within a **clause** or **sentence** are more fully examined in Chapters 8 and 9, but it is worth noting here that most of the main constituents of a clause are filled by **nouns** or **noun substitutes**, the main verb being the chief exception. The **subject** (noun) performs an action (verb). This action may be directed at someone or something (**direct/indirect object** – noun). Alternatively the **subject** may be related to a name, state or condition (**complement** – noun). It is essential to maintain **agreement** between these various parts. Hence the emphasis on **number**. If the subject is singular, the verb is singular – and this can also affect the object or complement.

This can be difficult with **collective nouns**. The *committee*, a collective noun, is therefore technically singular:

> The committee *is* due to finish *its* deliberations before lunch.

That sounds natural as well as being correct, but what if we refer to something more personal?

> The committee is expected to have pizza for its lunch.

The answer to this awkwardness is twofold. In informal situations the statement that the committee *are* having pizza for *their* lunch is normal. There is always the possibility of personalizing a collective noun, though it may take longer: in this case, *members of the committee*, followed, of course, by *are* and *their*.

NOUNS IN APPOSITION

Nouns in any part of the sentence can be modified by the addition of adjectives, adjective phrases or adjective clauses. However, the information given about a noun can also be enlarged by placing another noun, noun phrase or noun clause **in apposition**. This term is used when two or more nouns or noun equivalents are placed next to each other, each of them referring to the same person or thing so that the sentence would still make sense if one of them was removed. Let us imagine that Mrs Lindley is the Chair of Governors at a school. The secretary could tell the Head:

> *Mrs Lindley* (proper noun) *has arrived.*

or

> *The Chair of Governors* (noun phrase) *has arrived.*

If the two were combined in the sentence

> *Mrs Lindley, the Chair of Governors, has arrived.*

they would be in apposition.

To take another example, here are two ways you could tell the reader more about Charles Dickens' novel *The Mystery of Edwin Drood*:

> The Mystery of Edwin Drood, *set in a fictional version of Rochester*, was never finished.
> The Mystery of Edwin Drood, *Charles Dickens' final novel*, was never finished.

In the first example the section in italics is an adjectival phrase; in the second it is a noun phrase in apposition. Note that the sentence would make sense if the title of the novel was omitted.

Insight

It is possible to leave out the definite or indefinite article before nouns in apposition, though this is not universally popular. You would write *The President of the United States* or *a courtier and (a) poet*, but you could, if you prefer it, put *Donald Trump, President of the United States*, or *Sir Walter Ralegh, courtier and poet*.

NOUN EQUIVALENTS: NOUN CLAUSES

Pronouns, noun phrases and noun clauses can all be considered as **noun equivalents** and all are dealt with in Chapters 4 and 8. However, it is important to your study of the noun to remember that noun clauses are often not built around a key noun. A noun clause carries out the same function as a noun. In the sentence 'Why I am leaving is none of your business', the subject is the noun clause, *Why I am leaving*. There is a pronoun in it, but there is no noun that relates to the meaning of the subject: my *reasons*.

We might write:

> I found it hard to understand *his methods*.

In this case the direct object is *methods*, but we could replace that with a noun phrase with no equivalent word:

> I found it hard to understand *how he did it*.

? Test yourself

3.1 First of all you need to check that you can identify nouns and also work out which are proper, common and collective. In the following passage there are 40 nouns. See if you can find them all and arrange them under the headings Proper, Common and Collective:

> The new hotel on the site, the Edison, will have 105 rooms all meeting high standards of comfort. All will be en suite and air-conditioned and have television, telephone and minibar. For added luxury the Clarendon Suite will offer a welcoming and stylish set of rooms furnished in Regency style. Special rates will be available for groups and parties from firms on the hotel's Welcome List. Apart from formal meals at the Oak Tree Restaurant, residents can expect varied menus in the Grapes Bistro, plus a wine list of outstanding discrimination. Full English breakfast will be served from 6.30 until 10.00 and for early or late risers Continental breakfast will be available at the discretion of the management team.

3.2 Which of the common nouns above do you think are abstract nouns?

3.3 Applying the rules and advice of this chapter, what do you think the plurals of the following nouns are?

friend	match	fish
cargo	valley	enemy
memorandum	spoonful	lady-in-waiting
bonus	brass	elephant
trousers	moose	army
journey	reef	census
catch	soprano	hoof
toy	theory	ditch
swine	louse	brother
auditorium	monkey	tax

3.4 Each of the following sentences contains a noun or noun phrase in italics. Decide whether the phrase or clause which follows it is adjectival or in apposition:

    a When we were on holiday we bumped into *the Schofields* from next door.

    b When we were on holiday we bumped into *the Schofields*, our neighbours in Priestfield Drive.

c In the story Dr Jekyll becomes *Mr Hyde*, a monster of depravity.

d In the story Dr Jekyll becomes *Mr Hyde* who is hideous and cruel.

e *The gentle breeze*, blowing from the West, just stirred the flags.

f *The gentle breeze*, the merest zephyr, just stirred the flags.

g *The Great Charter*, what we usually call Magna Carta, was signed in 1215.

h *The Great Charter*, which we usually call Magna Carta, was signed in 1215.

i In the Antarctic Scott's expedition endured *great suffering*, privations we can barely imagine.

j In the Antarctic Scott's expedition endured *great suffering* which we find hard to imagine.

Pronouns

In this chapter you will learn:

▶ *how to distinguish a noun from a pronoun*
▶ *the forms and functions of personal pronouns*
▶ *how to identify the many other forms of pronoun.*

Nouns and pronouns

In terms of function, pronouns are the same as nouns – or, indeed, as noun phrases. In the following example, all the words in italics have the same role in the sentence:

> *Mrs Robinson* used to collect house-to-house for Oxfam.
> *The woman living next door* used to collect house-to-house for Oxfam.
> *She* used to collect house-to-house for Oxfam.

Each is the **subject** of the sentence: that is to say, the doer of the action. In the first case the subject is a **noun,** in the second a **noun phrase,** in the third a **pronoun.** The prefix 'pro-' in this case means 'in place of', so a pronoun is simply a word that can take the place of a noun. Very often replacing nouns with pronouns is simpler and less monotonous; sometimes (as we shall see) it can be confusing.

What makes the following paragraph so boring?

The policeman examined the document carefully. At first the policeman seemed convinced that the document was genuine, but then the policeman noticed the alteration to the signature. The policeman turned the document over and revealed the false serial number. The policeman pushed the document toward the prisoner.

Certainly some names, wider vocabulary and rephrasing would help, but above all the repetition of *policeman* and *document* is monotonous: the use of *he* and *it* (pronouns) is desperately needed:

The policeman examined the document carefully. At first he seemed convinced that it was genuine, but then he noticed the alteration to the signature, etc.

Personal pronouns

Personal pronouns take the place of personal nouns, though you must remember that the neuter *it* is also a personal pronoun. Additionally they form the only way of referring to certain people. Personal pronouns can relate to two different persons or groups of persons not normally covered by nouns:

> the person speaking or writing or the people of whom he/she is one;
> the person(s) being spoken or written to.

These are known as the **first person** (*I, me, we, us*) and the **second person** (*you*). The other pronouns are in the **third person**.

All nouns are customarily thought of as in the **third person**. Situations where a speaker/writer may refer to him/herself by a noun are few, sometimes suggesting arrogance: e.g. Shakespeare's Julius Caesar: 'Shall Caesar send a lie?', 'Caesar doth not wrong', etc. You might find a journalist referring to him/herself as 'your correspondent', blurring the distinction between 1st and 3rd person, but this is rare.

Insight

The awareness of 1st, 2nd and 3rd person is important to your enjoyment and understanding of fiction. Most novels are written in the 3rd person (by an omniscient narrator – i.e. one who knows about all the events) or in the 1st person (with one of the characters telling the story – and therefore unaware of other characters' actions).

These types of narrative produce very different effects. You would not, however, expect to find novels in the second person, though it might be possible!

CASE IN PERSONAL PRONOUNS

English is a language that has virtually done away with **case**. In Latin and many of the languages derived from it, a noun takes a different form if it is used as the subject of a sentence or the object or in a certain type of phrase or showing possession. These different forms are known as **cases**: the **nominative** if the noun is the subject, the **accusative** if it is the object, the **genitive** if indicating possession, etc. Pronouns provide one of the few examples in English of the continuing use of cases. In the following chart the terms nominative and accusative are replaced by the more familiar **subjective** and **objective**:

	Singular	
	Subjective	**Objective**
1st person	I	me
2nd person	you	you
3rd person masculine	he	him
3rd person feminine	she	her
3rd person neuter	it	it
	Plural	
1st person	we	us
2nd person	you	you
3rd person	they	them

The subjective is used when the pronoun is the subject of the sentence ('*She* went on holiday'). The objective is used when the pronoun is the object of the sentence ('The receptionist called *her* to the phone') or of a preposition ('Her children ran to *her*'). Because the case is identified by the word itself, it means that word order is less important than is usual in English. Though it sounds very old-fashioned, you could write '*Him* smote *I* with my mighty sword' and it would make sense. This is not possible with nouns where the word order indicates who is striking the blow. Just imagine a sentence like, 'Goliath killed David with a stone from his sling'. The meaning is reversed, but 'Goliath killed *he* with a stone from his sling' retains the correct meaning, though it does sound old-fashioned and awkward.

GENDER IN PERSONAL PRONOUNS

One of the problems in the use of personal pronouns can arise because of the identification of gender. Where the person is identified, there is no difficulty: *he* or *she* is used. Sometimes, when the person is not identified, the context removes all (or nearly all) doubts:

> When the manageress appeared, *she* sorted out the bill.
> The actor said *he* thought that playing Hamlet was the greatest challenge of *his* life.

Though there have been female Hamlets, both of the above are fairly safe, as are all cases in the plural (*they/them*). But what are you to do with the following sentence?

> When an inexperienced teacher starts work, * * * must expect to be confronted by a range of problems.

They is ungrammatical (singular turned into plural), though its use is becoming more accepted. *He* is possibly inaccurate and probably sexist. *He or she* is accurate and would fit here, but constant use throughout the following sentences would become monotonous. *He or she/him or her* have their uses (certainly in documents, reports, circulars, etc.), but they seldom sound or read like natural idiomatic English. In the above case you can turn the whole thing into the plural:

> When inexperienced teachers start work, they must expect to be confronted by a range of problems.

See also Chapter 12 for more on gender in grammar.

YOU IN SINGULAR AND PLURAL

Three or four centuries ago, our chart of the cases of personal pronouns would have contained one very large difference: the 2nd person would have been much more varied. Up to that time *you* referred to plural only (with *ye* an alternative for the subjective case). In the singular the correct form was *thou* (subjective) and *thee* (objective). What effect does this have on English grammar today?

▶ **Archaic/romantic/poetic**

Certainly until the 19th century it was common to use this already archaic (i.e. out-of-date) form in heroic and romantic poetry, hymns and sacred pieces, and operatic and parlour ballads. Lord Macaulay's famous poem, *Horatius*, for instance, has the lines:

> Lo, I will stand at thy right hand,
> And keep the bridge with thee.

This is not normal Victorian usage, but the use of an archaic term to impress the reader with the solemnity of the events. We still find *thou* and *thee* in such traditional forms as Valentines and In Memoriam verses. If used, *thou* should be followed by the *-(e)st* form of the verb:

> In all life Thou livest
> (from the hymn 'Immortal, invisible, God only wise')

▶ **Regional speech**

Much regional speech preserves archaic forms, such as the use of *tha, thee* and *thysen* (*yourself*) in Yorkshire. This continuance of the old 2nd person takes various regional shapes, as readers of Thomas Hardy's 19th-century Wessex fiction or Barry Hines's 1960s *A*

Kestrel for a Knave (set in South Yorkshire) will be aware. This is not the preservation of some 'correct' form and it would be unrewarding to set out a correct table of cases. It is essentially an oral survival, perfectly valid within a given community, but unlikely to travel well and sometimes without a single 'correct' written spelling.

AMBIGUITY IN PERSONAL PRONOUNS

Care needs to be taken with the use of personal pronouns when writing about more than one individual of the same gender. *He*, *she* and *it* cannot be modified to indicate two or three separate boys or women or garden sheds. The following examples show the possibilities for confusion:

> The Branch Manager told the salesman that he had left early last Thursday.
> Mrs Tate told her daughter to ask the teacher if she would mind if she brought the reply slip in to her just before she went to London.

It may be that, in context (the phrases and sentences surrounding them), these examples may become clear. This is purely a matter of judgement, not rules. If you think that the meaning is ambiguous, there are various ways of solving the problem. The most obvious is to replace some of the pronouns with nouns. If you are writing a report where clarity is the only requirement, you might write, 'she (the teacher)', but in ordinary writing you would look to be a little more subtle. Remember that it is always possible to recast the whole sentence:

> Mrs Tate planned to bring in the reply slip just before her daughter went to London. She told Louise to check with her teacher that this was not too late.

PERSONAL PRONOUNS IN PHRASES

Generally, in written English, there is not much difficulty in using the correct case for pronouns. The one exception is when the pronoun, especially in the 1st person, is linked with a noun: *Me and my dad* or *my brother and I*. The problem comes from two sources:

1 the use of *me* as the subject in such phrases, frequent in informal spoken English: 'Me and our kid are off to the match' is normal in informal speech, but to be avoided in formal oral situations and most forms of written English;

2 a confusion of good manners and snobbery, based around the idea that the other person should come first and a supposed version of the Queen's English, 'my husband and I'. This usage is perfectly correct in the subjective case, but the belief that *I* is always more correct than *me* in such phrases is misleading.

The most frequent error, therefore, is the use of *I* in the objective case: 'When two players dropped out, the manager brought John and *I* into the team' or 'I'm sure they saw my sister and *I* in the restaurant' – in each case, *I* should be replaced by *me* and could, if you wish, precede *John* or *my sister.*

The situation is governed by two rules:

1 Politeness and grammar are two different things. It may well be a good thing to put I or me second, but it has nothing to do with correct English.

2 Imagine that the pronoun is there on its own. Use the same form as you would in that situation. You would write 'The manager brought me into the team', so you should write, 'The manager brought John and me (or me and John) into the team.'

POSSESSIVES: ADJECTIVES OR PRONOUNS?

You will find that many modern grammar books list a third case for personal pronouns, the possessive, equivalent to the genitive:

1st person singular	my
2nd person singular	your
3rd person singular	his/her/its
1st person plural	our
2nd person plural	your
3rd person plural	their

The connection of these with the personal pronouns already listed is very evident, but strictly speaking these are not pronouns, but possessive adjectives, because they are add information about a noun, rather than taking its place: 'That is *my book*' or 'She lost *her place*' in the queue' or 'They rose to *their feet*'. In these examples *book*, *place* and *feet* are nouns and *my*, *her* and *their* tell us something about them.

If actually used as pronouns, these possessive adjectives in most cases take a slightly different form, usually adding *s*:

1st person singular	mine
2nd person singular	yours
3rd person singular	his (unchanged)/hers (no equivalent for neuter)
1st person plural	ours
2nd person plural	yours
3rd person plural	theirs

So, in modern English, we write, 'Here is *your* wallet' (adjective referring to *wallet*), but 'This one's *yours*' (where *yours* takes the place of the noun and is therefore a possessive pronoun). Remember that the *s* in possessive adjectives or pronouns is never preceded by an apostrophe. Words like *yours* and *theirs* never include an apostrophe; *its* does so only when it is an abbreviation for *it is* or *it has*.

It's about time we visited the new supermarket with its special offers.

Reflexive pronouns

Though personal pronouns are the most frequently used of pronouns, there are several other common types. The most similar in form to personal pronouns are **reflexive pronouns**:

1st person singular	myself
2nd person singular	yourself
3rd person singular	himself/herself/itself
1st person plural	ourselves
2nd person plural	yourselves
3rd person plural	themselves

Once again there are many regional variations in speech, with *theirself* or *theirselves* having national currency: not surprising, since *ourselves* and *yourselves* both use the possessive form (i.e. *our* and *your*, not *us* and *you*) and *theirselves* simply extends that to the 3rd person (*their* instead of *them*). Despite that, it is not correct in written English.

You should also note that, unlike personal pronouns, reflexive pronouns do make a small distinction between 2nd person singular and plural: *yourself* and *yourselves*.

Reflexive pronouns have two functions. Their main task is to indicate that the action is 'reflected' back on the doer, that the subject has done something to him/herself:

I've hurt myself quite badly.
The Managing Director gave herself a huge pay increase.

However, reflexive pronouns (sometimes referred to as **emphasizing pronouns** in this use) can also emphasize a noun or a personal pronoun. What is the difference between the following sentences?

The Queen is due to visit the factory.
The Queen *herself* is due to visit the factory.

There is no difference at all, except that it is rather impressive that the reigning monarch is coming, so *herself* emphasizes the surprise, delight, awe or even fear that the visit brings. Alternatively the emphasis may be due not to the status or importance of the person, but his/her significance in the story being told or the fact that he/she has been the main focus of interest:

Jane laid on three goals with her clever stick-work before she *herself* scored the fourth.

The use of reflexive pronouns for emphasis is purely a matter of taste and should not be overdone.

Relative pronouns

Relative pronouns establish a relationship between objects or people in different clauses: in other words, the same noun is involved in both clauses. The **relative pronoun** serves to join the clauses into one sentence and combines the functions of *and* and the noun or pronoun in question. For example:

> Mrs Brown took her children to school every day. She was worried by the traffic on the main road.

In linking those two together in one sentence, you could emphasize her reason for taking the children to school:

> Mrs Brown took her children to school every day because she was worried by the traffic on the main road.

Equally, though, you could use the fact that Mrs Brown is the subject of both clauses and link them with a **relative pronoun**:

> Mrs Brown, *who* was worried by the traffic on the main road, took her children to school every day.

The same applies when the noun or pronoun is not the subject of the clauses/separate sentences:

> The director cast Kirsty as Juliet. I had met her at audition.
> The director cast Kirsty, *whom* I had met at audition, as Juliet.

The relative pronouns are:

Subjective	Objective	Possessive	Referring to non-human nouns
who	whom	whose	which

Though there is a separate relative pronoun of possession for humans, possession with non-human nouns is correctly indicated by *of which*, as in the following:

> I shouted to Kerry, *whose* distinctive red hair could just be seen through the window.
> We discovered the car the front *of which* had been badly damaged.

However, *whose* is so much simpler that it is often acceptable to use it in place of *of which*. This is a matter of personal judgement, but many of us would feel happier applying it to an animal or something which can be treated personally (a ship, for instance) than to something solidly inanimate, like a shoe or a kitchen:

> We sat on the deck of the ship whose bow nudged against the quay.
> I stared into the kitchen whose walls were stained by the floodwater.

Technically each of these is wrong (*of which* is correct), but only the most pedantic of people would dispute the first one.

THE USE OF *WHOM*

The aspect of relative pronouns which needs most care is the use of *whom*. The easiest way to remember how to use *whom* is to take note of the *m* at the end. This can remind you of *him* and *them* (though admittedly not *her*). Like *him* and *them*, it refers to the objective case. If the relative pronoun is the object of the clause it introduces, then *whom* is required. Look at the following separate clauses:

> The referee sent off the player. The player had committed a dangerous late tackle.
> The referee sent off the player. He had booked the player earlier.

In both cases *the player* is the object of the main sentence, but only in the second one is he the object of the second clause as well, the one being introduced by *who* or *whom*, so the correct versions are as follows:

> The referee sent off the player *who* had committed a dangerous late tackle.
> The referee sent off the player *whom* he had booked earlier.

Whom is becoming less common, but it is still regularly used in formal situations. However, it is far more embarrassing to use *whom* wrongly than to fail to use it correctly.

What are determiners?

Words which are used to determine or demonstrate which things or people are being referred to are now commonly known as **determiners**.

Possessive pronouns/adjectives can be used as determiners: '*my* house' or '*her* car' determines which object we are writing or speaking about.

The definite and indefinite articles (*the*, *a/an*) are now categorized as determiners. These words have always been subject to grammatical dispute and may be best seen as a category on their own. The rules governing them are very simple:

1 *The* is always used for the only example of something: '*the* Managing Director', '*the* Principal' or '*the* defendant' may not be the only person to take on this role, but within this firm, college or court case there is no other. *The* also refers to something or somebody already identified. After 30 minutes at a bus stop you are pleased when '*a* bus' appears, but then furious when you see that '*the* bus' is out of service.

2 *A* or *an* (in front of a vowel) is used for a non-specific or unidentified person or object when there are several or many of the same type: We saw *a* walker on *the* cliff path. You have not previously identified the walker, but you know which path you are on. Later, now that you have identified whom you are writing about, you will refer to '*the* walker stopping to speak to us'.

Demonstrative pronouns and adjectives

However, the most specific group of determiners are the **demonstrative pronouns/adjectives**. These consist of:

▶ two singular pronouns, one indicating presence or closeness (*this*), one indicating absence or distance (*that*);

▶ two plural pronouns, on the same basis (*these* and *those*).

These are very straightforward, except for a warning not to replace *those* with *them* in standard English: 'in them days' and 'just one of them things' are strictly for informal conversation.

It is worth noting that, as with possessive pronouns, the modern tendency is to refer to these as **demonstrative pronouns** at all times. Traditional grammar makes a distinction between their use with nouns and on their own. *This*, *that*, *these* and *those* can be used singly in place of a noun (demonstrative pronouns) or modifying a noun (demonstrative adjectives):

Show me *that* book. – modifying a noun (*book*) – **demonstrative adjective**.
Show me *that*. – in place of a noun – **demonstrative pronoun**.

This matter of detail should not be a cause for concern. Whichever terminology you prefer will be acceptable to most people and you should not find it difficult to understand a textbook whichever definition it employs.

Other forms of pronoun

The above account does not cover every possible example of a pronoun, but further definition would be unhelpful. You might, however, wish to note:

a The relative pronouns (*what*, *who*, *whom*, *whose* and *which*) can also be used in question (**interrogative**) form:

What did you find in the cupboard?
Who was that lady?

In the example, 'Which book did you choose?', *which* is strictly an interrogative adjective, telling us about the noun *book*.

b There are also two linked groups of pronouns which often cause difficulty because they are always **singular** even though they might refer to more than one person or thing. *Each*, *every*, *either* and *neither*, plus *everyone* and *everything*, can be called **distributive pronouns** because they separate items whereas *all* and *both* (which are **plural**) bring together persons or things. This is easy to see in a sentence like:

Either of them is likely to get the job.

In that case, you know that, though both have a chance, only one will be appointed. The meaning of 'Both of them are likely to get the job' is quite different. In the second case we expect two people (not one) to be employed.

On the other hand, things are rather more complicated in:

Each has passed the examination.

In this case many people (4, 30, 200?) have passed the examination, but the grammatical justification is that the sentence is making the statement about each candidate individually. If you feel ill at ease with this, you can recast the sentence:

All of them have passed the examination.

This time, the meaning of *each* (singular) and *all* (plural) is effectively the same and the distinction between the whole lot passing and each separate individual passing is merely technical.

c *Any*, *anyone*, *anything*, *someone*, *somebody*, *nothing*, *nobody* and *no one* (two words) can be referred to as indefinite pronouns and also take the singular:

Anyone is capable of understanding the situation.
Somebody has to take responsibility for the loss.

d *Any*, however, which is often used as an adjective, can take either singular or plural nouns:

Any difficulty is to be reported to the manager.
Any difficulties were of her own making.
Have *any* been found? (if you are referring to separate things – any screws or any cigarette ends)
Has *any* been found? (if you are referring to a quantity of a substance – any cement or any evidence)

4.1 Insert the correct personal pronouns (including possessive adjectives and pronouns) in the following sentences:

a I presented ... report at the same time as the secretary and the treasurer presented ....

b When my friends and .... went to the zoo, we took my brother with ...

c He enjoyed the day out with my friends and ....

d Yesterday the team met ... new manager.

e We need at least two phones, so, even if Jane brings ..., you'll have to bring ....

f We'll play doubles: you and your sister against my brother and ....

g The dog wagged ... tail.

h Mr and Mrs Brewer resisted every attempt to direct ... towards ... destination.

4.2 Each of the following sentences has a problem in relation to the gender of personal pronouns. Identify the problem in each case. At the moment every one uses *he, his* or *him:* would you replace that and with what?

a A novelist is bound to find that his first novel is difficult to place with a publisher.

b Any member of the staff committee must make sure that he attends all meetings.

c Attending his first interview is an ordeal for anyone.

d Every entrant in the competition must print his name in block capitals.

4.3 The following short passage contains examples of ambiguity in the use of personal pronouns. How would you alter it to make it completely clear? You will have to make your own decisions about who did what:

> Marian saw Kate as she was turning the corner in the market. She called out to her and she caught her up just as she reached the Market Hall. At this moment Jamie and Chris came out of the burger bar: they looked amazed to see them. They waved, but they were in a hurry and, calling out 'See you later', ran to the bus station.

4.4 In the following sentences there are gaps left to insert reflexive pronouns, either used reflexively or for emphasis. Decide what pronoun to insert – or, if you think it would be better, decide to leave it out.

- **a** Playing in the park, the children really enjoyed....
- **b** The General ... took responsibility for the prisoners' safety.
- **c** David cut ... on the broken glass.
- **d** My family and ... enjoy giving our opinions on radio phone-ins.
- **e** We needed no second invitation: we helped ... to the drinks and snacks.
- **f** You're so conceited you're always praising ....
- **g** It was Sue ... who raised the alarm.

4.5 Use relative pronouns to join together each of the following pairs of sentences:
- **a** We bought a dog. It was a German shepherd.
- **b** The girl came to see us yesterday. We met the girl on holiday.
- **c** The shopkeeper went to the police. His premises had been raided.
- **d** We wanted to see the church. Its tower dated back to Saxon times.
- **e** I arranged to photograph the model. She had been featured in the new magazine.
- **f** The police arrested the woman. They found her at the scene of the crime.

4.6 Each of the following sentences gives you a choice of two possible answers. The decisions relate to various points made about pronouns in this chapter:
- **a** Each step she takes bring/brings recovery closer.
- **b** Years ago I used to have a/an MG.
- **c** A polite term for something unpleasant is known as a/an euphemism.
- **d** You should not express yourself in them/those terms.
- **e** Either of them is/are capable of doing the job.
- **f** Either vandals or rough sleepers is/are to blame for the damage.
- **g** The paramedics did that/what they could.
- **h** The paramedics did everything that/what they could.
- **i** The road was blocked by a lorry whose driver/the driver of which seemed to be missing.
- **j** Neither assistant were/was much help in finding what we wanted.

Verbs

In this chapter you will learn:

▶ *the importance of verbs within grammatical structures*

▶ *how to identify the types of finite and non-finite verbs*

▶ *the form and functions of tenses, moods and voices.*

The importance of verbs

In its simplest form language may consist of indicating and naming things or persons or expressing feelings of pleasure, disgust, fear, etc. However, as language becomes more sophisticated, it needs to state what is/was/will be happening and when, or make statements about the nature of things. These requirements place **verbs** at the centre of language expression and grammar.

The analysis of the forms of verbs can (indeed, will) become complicated, so it is extremely important to hold on to the simple, but most essential, facts. **Verbs are words of doing or being**; in other words, they express the actions being carried out or enable us to comment on the state of things. There are many different ways of classifying verbs. First let us divide them into three main types.

VERBS OF DOING: TRANSITIVE AND INTRANSITIVE

Two of the categories are different types of **verbs of doing**. There are some actions that are complete in themselves: *sleeping, waiting, screaming*. The reader may be interested in where you are sleeping, what you are waiting for or why you are screaming, but such information is not necessary to make sense of the statement:

> In a corner of the room the guard was sleeping.

This is a fuller statement than the simple 'The guard was sleeping', but the shorter statement still makes sense in its own right. *Sleep* is an **intransitive verb**.

Other verbs do not make complete sense until you add an object: the 'done to' person or thing. It makes no sense to say that you *poured* or *opened* or *appointed* unless you say who or what you poured, opened or appointed:

> Yesterday we appointed a new office manager.

Manager is the object of *appointed*, a **transitive verb**.

Many verbs can be transitive or intransitive, but you should be able to work out which way a verb is being used. For example:

> She *runs* in the park every morning. (intransitive)
> She is planning to *run* a half-marathon. (transitive – object *half-marathon*)
> She even finds time to *run* the guide troop. (transitive – object *guide troop*)

> The waves *are breaking* on the sand. (intransitive)

Make sure you don't *break* my favourite bowl. (transitive – object *bowl*)

I must admit he always *tries* hard. (intransitive)
He does *try* my patience sometimes. (transitive – object *patience*)
Won't you *try* a piece of my birthday cake? (transitive – object *piece*)

I don't like to *sit* in the most comfortable chair. (intransitive)
Who decided to *sit* Madeleine next to her ex-husband? (transitive – object *Madeleine*)

▶ Lie and lay

The transitive/intransitive problem lies behind one of the most common errors in English: the confusion of the verbs *to lie* and *to lay*. It does not help that the past tense of *to lie* is *lay*, the same as the present tense of *to lay*. *To lay* is **transitive**, so it is correct to write or speak about 'laying eggs', 'laying cards on the table', 'laying your hand on someone' or 'laying a ghost'. It is not correct to refer to 'laying down for an hour'. That is **intransitive** and requires the use of *to lie:* 'lying down for an hour'.

Intransitive	Transitive
He is lying down.	He is laying the table.
She lay hidden by the rock.	She laid her head on his shoulder.
The dog has lain there for an hour.	The dog has laid its bone at my feet.

VERBS OF BEING

Verbs of the third basic category, **verbs of being**, are much fewer in number. *To be* (with all its strange forms such as *am*, *is*, *was* and *were*) is the main one and the other verbs of being fulfil a similar function. For instance, we might take the sentence:

Mrs Bradshaw was very well informed about the novels of Dickens.

This states what is so. If you wish to state that, as far as you can tell, she is well informed, but you are not sure, you might write:

Mrs Bradshaw seemed (or appeared) well informed about the novels of Dickens.

If she used not to be well informed, but developed her knowledge gradually, you would probably express it as:

Mrs Bradshaw became very well informed about the novels of Dickens.

Clearly *seemed*, *appeared* and *became* are fulfilling the same function as '*was*' and are therefore verbs of being.

Verbs of being require something to complete their meaning, just as do transitive verbs. However, following a verb of being, clearly nothing or nobody has suffered the action (there is no action), so these are not objects, but **complements**, also known as **intensive complements**. A complement is something which completes and the intensive complement completes the meaning of the verb of being.

▶ Nouns and pronouns as intensive complements

One of the most common forms of complement occurs when the complement echoes the subject in the form of a noun:

That man is Mr Patel.

That man (subject) and *Mr Patel* (complement) are equivalents, referring to the same man. Even in more complicated sentence structures, the same form can often be detected:

The result of the financial state of the new theatre trust is likely to be the resignation of the treasurer and half the committee.

Despite the many phrases and the longer sentence it is possible to pick out the equation: *result* (subject) = *resignation* (complement).

At the other extreme, a sentence as simple as 'This is it' provides another example of the same sentence structure, in this case with pronouns as subject and complement.

Insight

The use of pronouns as complements provides a thorny problem, only to be solved by common sense. Unlike nouns, some pronouns have different forms for subjective and objective use: *I/me, he/him, she/ her, we/us, they/them*. If used as complements, they should take the subjective form: after all, they are echoing the subject, but who feels natural saying 'It is I' or 'It is she'? In conversation 'It's me' or 'It's her' is perfectly acceptable; in informal conversation one would even regard 'It's I' as unsuitable. It is, however, wiser in formal writing to use the subjective form of the pronoun for the complement: 'It is I/he/she/we/ they who must take responsibility for this disaster.'

▶ Adjectives as intensive complements

If the purpose of the sentence is to describe the subject, rather than just identify him/her, the verb of being can be followed by an adjective or adjectival phrase. The structure is identical to that described above:

> The current MP seems *the best candidate.* (complement noun)
> The current MP seems *very efficient.* (complement adjective)
> The Mansion House is *a fine 18th-century building.* (complement noun)
> The Mansion House is *most impressive.* (complement adjective)

Insight

A potentially confusing, but amusing, novelty is the existence of words that are both verbs of being and verbs of doing. *Appear, look* and *grow* are probably the most frequently used. If you say, 'He *appeared* as Widow Twankey in the pantomime', that is clearly a verb of doing: he has to *do* many things, from learning lines to putting on masses of make-up. But what about 'He *appeared* flustered'? Here the meaning is much the same as *seemed* and 'flustered' is the complement. As for *look* and *grow*, decide for yourself which are the verbs of being and which the verbs of doing:

> The doctor *looked* closely at her patient.
> He *looked* ill.
> She *grew* vegetables.
> He *grew* extremely fat.

▶ Adverbial complements

The final main form of the intensive complement involves using an adverbial phrase to complete the statement. In these cases the relationship with the subject is still evident, but the complement expresses *When?* or *Where?* rather than *Who?* or *What?*:

> The clock was *on top of the cupboard.*
> Her birthday seemed *too far away.*

The same adverbial phrase can be used simply to modify the verb, but in the cases above it **completes** the meaning of the verb. Compare the two following examples:

> My new pen is *in my pocket.*
> My new pen is *safe* in my pocket.

In the first example *in my pocket* is the complement of the verb *is*.
In the second example *safe* is the adjectival complement and *in my pocket* is an adverbial phrase modifying the verb and its complement.

Finite and non-finite verbs

The major distinction in the form of verbs is between the **finite** (**tensed**) and **non-finite** (**non-tensed**) forms. A finite verb has a **tense** and takes a subject; this means that a finite form of the verb tells you *when it happened* and *who/what did/was it*. Broadly tenses can be defined as **past, present** and **future**:

> Vicky *trains* hard. (present)
> Vicky *trained* hard last year. (past)
> Vicky *will train* hard once she gets a place in the first team (future)

We are told the subject of the sentences (*Vicky*) and what time each sentence relates to. *Trains, trained* and *will train* are **finite verbs**.

The main non-finite forms are past and present participles and the infinitive (i.e. the basic form: *to work, to be*, etc.). A non-finite verb does not give information on time and cannot take a subject without the use of an auxiliary verb. *Training* is the present participle, but it does not indicate that the action takes place in the present. The auxiliary verb dictates the tense and allows the use of a subject:

> Vicky *training* hard. (present participle: this does not make sense as a sentence, though it could be a caption to a picture)
> Vicky *is training* hard. (present participle used with auxiliary (*is*) referring to the present.)
> Vicky *was training* hard. (Present participle with different auxiliary (*was*) now refers to past)

We will examine tenses and participles in more detail, but you need to be clear about the distinction between finite and non-finite verbs: **every full sentence must contain at least one finite verb.**

Tenses

It is important to understand the relationship between tenses in verbs for two main reasons. It is very easy (and wrong) to slide between tenses in a narrative. While it is correct (and, sometimes, very effective) to recount past events in the present tense to gain immediacy, it is clumsy, confusing and generally undesirable to alter tense for no reason:

I *ran* down the hillside towards the cottage, shouting a greeting to Joan as she *takes* the dog for his walk.

Secondly you need to maintain the correct relationship between tenses. If you use the **present** and **future** tenses in the same sentence, but then change the present to the **past,** you must use the tense quaintly termed **future in the past:**

If I *receive* the cheque in time, I *will give* you your share on Friday.
James said that, if he *received* the cheque in time, he *would give* me my share on Friday.

There are two major difficulties in learning about tense. One is the massively complicated tenses which you can create: do we really need to find a name to apply to the tenses in 'Mrs Baines *would have been running* the factory if it *had not have been* for the Board's sexist policies'? The second is the variety of names for the various tenses. If you are familiar with the names of tenses from other languages or from old textbooks, you may find the terminology different and confusing. The intention in this section is to go beyond the simple present/past/future division, but avoid obscure and seldom-used tenses, and, wherever possible, to give alternative names for tenses.

TENSES FORMED WITHOUT AUXILIARY VERBS

Tenses can be formed by:

▶ alterations to the stem of the verb;

▶ use of an auxiliary (helping) verb: *have, will, to be,* etc. The auxiliary is used with a non-finite part of the verb to create the desired tense: infinitive (*will find*), present participle (*are finding*), past participle (*have found*).

The two tenses formed by changes to the verb itself are the **present** and the **simple past** (often referred to as the **preterite**).

▶ The present tense

This is very straightforward, often the same as the infinitive, with -*s* added for the 3rd person singular, with an inevitable extra *e* when pronunciation requires it following a sibilant last consonant or multiple consonants like -*sh*, -*ch* and -*tch*:

The dog bark*s*.   Time pass*es*.   She catch*es* the bus.

Irregular forms are not a problem, though, of course, *to be* pursues an eccentric course, mainly using *are*, but including *I am* and *he/she/it is*.

The present tense in English is used:

▶ to indicate events happening now;

▶ to refer to events that happen regularly, even if they are not occurring at this moment.

For instance, in the middle of the week, you are quite likely to say:

> Jenny *goes* into town on Saturday mornings. I *saw* her in the market last week.

Jenny is not going into town at present (it is, after all, Wednesday, not Saturday); you know she went there in the past (hence the verb *saw*); you expect her to go there in the future. However, the present tense is correct as referring to an action that, as things are, happens regularly.

▶ **Continuous tenses**

Any tense in English can have its continuous form and, as the **present continuous** is much used, this is a good place to consider them, but these comments apply equally to **past continuous, future continuous,** etc. A continuous tense (which uses the present participle) represents, naturally enough, an action that is continuing; in other words, you do not see it end:

> Pat *prepares* the final draft. (present)
> Pat *is preparing* the final draft now. (present continuous)

The first sentence tells of a decision or a regular practice; the second indicates what is going on now. The present continuous does not indicate a successful (or unsuccessful) outcome. Pat may open the door in a minute's time with the work complete or with an apology that she is having problems with her computer.

This is best revealed by the use of the **past continuous.** Compare the following:

> Jo *planted* her new shrubs yesterday. (past)
> Jo *was planting* her new shrubs. (past continuous)

In the second sentence, at some time in the past, when you passed Jo's house or rang her up or heard the news from her sister, she was engaged in planting the shrubs. Unlike the first example, there is no guarantee that she completed it successfully.

The next phone call will begin, 'Did you get your shrubs in all right?' Though the action is past, we do not know if it has been completed: it is continuous.

▶ **Simple past tense (preterite)**

What we will define as **weak verbs** and **strong verbs** form their past tenses in different ways. The **weak verb** (which we can also call **regular**) simply adds -*ed* (or -*d* for verbs ending in *e*) to the basic form of the infinitive. In some, very few cases -*t* can replace -*ed* (*burn/burned* or *burnt*). Final consonants are doubled when it is necessary to keep a short vowel sound in the preceding syllable:

help/helped	*talk/talked*
trip/tripped	*fire/fired*
reminisce/reminisced	*pad/padded*

With weak (regular) verbs the past tense and past participle are usually identical.

The **strong verbs** form the past tense by altering the central vowel of the basic form, sometimes making other changes as well: *buy*, for instance, becomes *bought* and *leave* turns into *left*. More often it is simply the vowel sound that changes:

shoot/shot	*strive/strove*
fight/fought	*give/gave*
find/found	*blow/blew*
grow/grew	*bind/bound*

In those cases where the past tense ends with *d* or *t*, the consonants which also end the regular past tense, the past participle is unchanged. In other cases the past participle takes an -*(e)n* ending:

strive/strove/striven	*give/gave/given*
blow/blew/blown	*grow/grew/grown*

This needs care in writing. Avoid statements like 'He's *blew* for time' and 'She's *gave* it me': past participles are needed.

Especial care is needed with *write*. Though the past tense *wrote* ends with a *t* sound, the past participle is *written*. So the correct usage is:

My sister *wrote* to me.

but

My sister *has written* to me.

The strongest and most irregular of verbs in forming the past tense are *to be* (inevitably) and *to go*. Each of these assumes a totally different identity in the past tense (*was/were* and *went*) before reverting to a comparatively conventional infinitive + *(e)n* for the past participle: *been/gone*. Be sure to avoid constructions like *He's went* in writing, though in some areas it is common practice in speech.

The fact that the verb *to be*, unlike other verbs, distinguishes between singular and plural in the past tense also needs care. *We was* is quite a common usage and *I* (or *he/she/it*) *were* is normal speech across much of the north of England. However, neither is acceptable in formal speech or written English.

TENSES FORMED USING AUXILIARY VERBS: PERFECT TENSES

The main tenses formed with auxiliary verbs can be split into two pairs:

1 the (**present**) **perfect** and **past perfect**, and

2 the **future** and **future in the past**.

The two perfect tenses use the auxiliary verb *to have* with the past participle and the only real difficulty with the form of the tense concerns the past participle of strong verbs (dealt with above). Its usage is somewhat more complex. The **perfect** or **present perfect** implies an action in the past which may be complete (perfect), but which continues to the present (hence present perfect). For instance, we might take these examples:

Fiona *finished* her lunch. (simple past or preterite)
Fiona *has finished* her lunch. (present perfect)

In each case the action is complete, but the first could refer to any time (it might even refer to a visit Fiona made at lunchtime a week ago) whereas the second implies a recent completion. If we say 'Mrs Ross *has left* the building', we are implying that this is the latest information. If we know she left two hours ago, we would say: 'Mrs Ross *left* the building two hours ago/at 3 o'clock/when she had completed the survey.'

An interesting comparison is between the sentences:

Every time *we went* on holiday in Scotland, *it rained*.
Every time *we have gone* on holiday in Scotland, *it has rained*.

In each case the holidays might have been years ago, so how can we say that the present perfect deals with events in the past leading up to the present? In this case, the simple past (*went/rained*) implies that holidaying in Scotland is a thing of the past; the perfect (*have gone/has rained*) indicates the likelihood of repeating the experience.

The **past perfect** (sometimes called the **pluperfect**) is in relation to the past as the perfect is to the present; it is one stage further back in time. So, taking the previous example, we have:

We decided (simple past) to take a holiday in Wales next year as *it had rained* (past perfect) every time *we had been* (past perfect) to Scotland.

There is always a natural tendency towards simplification of grammar in English and many people would replace the second past perfect with *went*.

Insight

The sequence of tenses requires the sort of shifts in time we are considering: present reference to past use of the perfect brings in the past perfect, present reference to past use of the future requires the future in the past, etc. Sometimes it all becomes too complicated: 'I said that she *would have been living* a life of luxury' is creating a tense that might be called future in the past perfect continuous. Note the simplification of tense if we add a conditional clause, 'I said that she would have been living a life of luxury *if she* had won *the Lottery*'.

TENSES FORMED USING AUXILIARY VERBS: FUTURE TENSES
The **future tense** as such is formed by adding the auxiliary *will* or *shall* to the basic form of the infinitive (minus *to*). Apart from

the distinction between *shall* and *will* (see below) this is very straightforward and refreshingly exception-free:

> Our coach will leave at 5 o'clock. There will be three stops after Doncaster. The coach will arrive in Newcastle at approximately 10.30.

You will be aware, however, that there are other ways of referring to the future than by using the future tense. You could as naturally and correctly say, 'Our coach *is going to leave* at 5 o'clock' or 'Our coach *leaves* at 5 o'clock.' These are largely interchangeable, but there are slight differences in the way they might be used:

▶ *is going to leave* is the least formal;

▶ *will leave* may have a suggestion of intent: if you want to imply that latecomers will be left behind, *will* is the right word;

▶ *leaves* would definitely be used if you were referring to a regular service, every day or every week.

Future in the past bears the same relationship to the future as past perfect does to perfect and its form is like the future, but using *would* and *should* with the basic infinitive:

> Daniel *told* (past) Natalie that she *would get* (future in the past) the job.

What Daniel actually said was, 'You *will get* the job', a statement in the future tense made in the past.

Insight

For the 1st person singular and plural (never for the 2nd or 3rd person) *shall* and *should* are frequently used instead of *will* and *would*. This is a difficult area of advice, especially because of other auxiliary uses of *should* and *would*, as dealt with later (**Auxiliary verbs**). To be strictly correct, you should write:

> *I shall* be at the meeting next week. (future)
> We never thought *we should* see our home again. (future in the past)

This is, however, a rule that is often broken: *I will* and *I would* are normal in speech and informal writing. Furthermore it is preferable to use *will* when there is a suggestion of intent. So, if there is a hint that you might be voted off the committee or might stay at home to nurse a cold, it is normal to scotch the rumours with, 'I *will* be at the meeting.'

Active and passive voice

The form of the verb is dictated by the **voice** as well as the tense. So far we have considered the **active voice** only; each of these tenses has an equivalent in the **passive voice**. It is not advisable in the interests of good style to make excessive use of the passive voice: it can be cumbersome and lack sharpness and precision. However, there are times when it is an essential means of expression.

Fortunately the names of the two voices are clear indicators of their meanings. In general use *active* means 'working' or 'energetic'; *passive* means 'suffering the action'. These are exactly their grammatical meanings. Normally the subject of a sentence is the person or thing doing an action or being described or identified. Sometimes, when using a transitive verb, we wish to feature the person or thing suffering the action – and this is when we employ the **passive voice**:

> The left-winger *scored* the second goal. (active)
> The second goal *was scored* by the left-winger. (passive)
> The news *shocked* everyone in the village. (active)
> Everyone in the village *was shocked* by the news. (passive)

Sometimes the doer of the action (identified by *by* in the above examples) is not identified at all, and sometimes not even known:

> When I left my car at the station, the radio *was stolen*.
> I found that all the mess *had been cleared away*.

The form of the passive voice consists of the auxiliary verb *to be* (in whatever tense is required), plus the past participle of the verb. Remember that the past participle is also used in the perfect tense, but with the auxiliary *to have*:

> The window cleaner *has broken* his wrist. (perfect tense active)
> It was when he fell off the ladder that his wrist *was broken* (simple past tense passive)

Auxiliary verbs

We have already seen that auxiliary verbs can be used to help form tenses when linked with a non-finite form of the main verb:

> *to be* + present participle: all continuous tenses
> *to have* + past participle: the perfect tenses
> *to be* + past participle: all tenses of the passive voice
> *will/would/shall/should* + infinitive: the future tenses

There is one other auxiliary that helps to form tenses, but in a somewhat specialized way. The question form often involves dividing the verb in two on each side of the subject:

> The guest speaker *has arrived*. (statement)
> *Has* the guest speaker *arrived*? (question)
> The floods *will subside* soon. (statement)
> *Will* the floods *subside* in time for the fête? (question)

But what if the verb consists only of one word, as in the simple present and past tenses? How can it divide? That is the specialist task of the auxiliary verb *to do*:

> Manoj *found* his way to the cinema. (statement)
> *Did* Manoj *find* his way to the cinema? (question)
> Mr McCann *attends* the Presbyterian church. (statement)
> *Does* Mr McCann *attend* the Presbyterian church? (question)

In questions the simple present and past tenses are replaced by the relevant tenses of *to do* + the basic form of the infinitive. The same also applies to the simple tenses in conjunction with the negative *not*:

> Manoj *did not find* his way to the cinema.
> Mr McCann *does not attend* the Presbyterian church.

This construction can, of course, be used in ordinary positive statements, but is employed much less often than in questions. The specialized uses in statements include:

▶ **Insistence:** 'I do love you!' would mean exactly the same minus *do*, but would seem slightly less urgent.

▶ **Contradiction:** 'But I did return the files!' might be your response to an accusation based on the opposite assumption.

▶ **Doubt:** 'If she did catch the school bus, where is she now?' expresses an idea half-believed.

▶ **Realization:** 'The boss does have a heart after all' conveys surprise at a new idea.

▶ In all these cases the intention is to draw attention to the statement: all could be classified under the heading **emphasis**.

Modal verbs

The majority of auxiliary verbs do not operate purely to establish tense (**primary auxiliaries**), but serve to create mood as well or instead (**modal verbs**). Though they serve a primary function in establishing the future tenses, *will/would/shall/should* are modal verbs. Other important modal verbs include:

    can/could   *may/might*   *must*   *ought (to)*

All of these are followed by the basic infinitive and are themselves unchangeable. There is no past tense *musted*, for instance: you have to use *must have*. It is true that *could* and *might* operate as the past tenses of *can* and *may*, but they also have meanings and fixed usages in their own right:

Paula *can run* the 400 metres faster than Jo. (She is able in the present to do this.)
Paula *could run* the 400 metres faster than Jo. (Two possible meanings: in the past she was able to do this or it would be possible in certain circumstances for her to do it now.)
I may be able to get time off work next week. (a possibility in the present – *might* would also be correct)
I hoped I might get time off. (*might* as the past tense of *may*)
If I had asked politely, *I might have got* time off. (referring to a possibility that no longer exists – *may* is incorrect in this case)

Thus words like *could*, *might*, *should* and *would* are equally likely to establish a sense of past (to *can*, *may*, *shall* and *will*) and to fulfil their own modal function, usually to do with possibility.

Insight

'Can I go out and play now?' or 'Can I bring my friends round?' used always to provoke the maternal reply, '*May*, not *can*' before permission was refused or granted. Traditionally *may* and *can* have been thought to refer to things you are able to do, *can* because you are clever/strong/rich/lucky enough, *may* because you have been given permission. In fact it is acceptable to use *can* in both senses:

I *can* recite the 7 times table.
I *can* stay up late tonight.

May, however, remains the more formal and polite way of asking or receiving permission.

SHOULD, WOULD *AND* OUGHT

Should and *would* can be seen as having three functions which overlap at times. We have already examined their role in building the future in the past tense. Another tense-creating role, but more obviously modal, concerns what we may call the **conditional** which refers to events that have not happened and possibly never will, unless certain conditions apply. Here again it is normal to use *should* with the 1st person and *would* with the others:

> If we can avoid traffic in the town centre, *we should* be in time.
> *Jamie would* be an excellent worker if only he could concentrate.

The third function is purely modal and the mood in question is one of moral advice and preferences expressed:

> *I would* take the bypass, then cut across to the A43.
> *You would* go on strike if you had been let down like this.

Now *should* and *would* separate on grounds of meaning, rather than which person is involved. *Would* certainly deals with choices and the right course of action, but *should* more often gives peremptory moral instruction or postulates the 'correct' situation:

> *You shouldn't* have taken that corner so fast.
> *He should* take more care of his children.
> The train *should* have been here ten minutes ago.

Subjunctive mood

The normal form of finite verbs is the **indicative** mood, dealing mainly with things that were, are or will be, though in conditional tenses there is movement towards the possible and the predictive. The **subjunctive** mood never deals with matters whose occurrence is definite, solely those that are ordered, doubtful or wished for.

If you have studied another language, it is quite possible that you have encountered a full set of subjunctive tenses equivalent to the indicative. It is, however, debatable whether English ever embraced the subjunctive to that extent and what remains is both slight in quantity and sometimes optional in use.

THE PRESENT SUBJUNCTIVE
The form of the present subjunctive is identical with the basic infinitive form which means that, in most cases, it can be distinguished from the indicative only in the 3rd person singular.

infinitive/present subjunctive	present indicative	
leave	I/you/we/they leave	He/she/it leaves
try	I/you/we/they try	He/she/it tries
But be	I **am**/you/we/they **are**	He/she/it is

All the uses of the present subjunctive suggest **a possibility, an intention** or **a wish**. Probably the most common is the construction based on words like *insist*, *request* and *demand*:

> I *insist* that he *leave* the meeting.
> Mr Ahmed *requested* that the committee *examine* his difficulty.
> You have ignored *my demand* that he *be* severely reprimanded.

Note that this form (the present) is also used in the past, as in the last two examples.

The subjunctive also provides an alternative to the conditional tense (*would* and *should*):

> Even if the manager *fire* the entire workforce, we cannot back down.
> Even if the manager *should fire* the entire workforce, we cannot back down.

Each is perfectly correct, but which of the two alternatives do you prefer?

There is also a range of cases in which the subjunctive expresses a wish in a set exclamation, very often reduced to a formula. 'God save the Queen!' is the best example, but 'God forbid!' and 'Heaven preserve us!' represent the same usage. This begins to overlap with the **imperative** (see below): there is a clear resemblance to orders given at the scene of a fire or a ship sinking. However, we may presume we are not giving God orders! Perhaps the best way of understanding the use of the subjunctive here is to imagine the word *may* expressing a wish: 'May God save the Queen!'

Insight

The slightly archaic use of the subjunctive is often to be found in set phrases of various sorts. Two interesting ones concern the word *need*, one as noun, one as verb. We all commonly use 'if need be', using the present subjunctive of *to be*. If, however, we rephrased it, we might well not use the subjunctive, though the grammatical situation is the same. *If the need arise* is less likely than *If the need should arise* or even the indicative *arises*. Stranger still is *he/she/it need not*, as in 'He *need not worry* where his next meal is coming from.' One would think that *he does not need to worry* would be more logical. In this case it is debatable whether *need* is the subjunctive or whether it is being used as a modal auxiliary. In either case it is more elegant phrasing than the longer version.

THE PAST SUBJUNCTIVE

This has almost totally disappeared, existing solely in the use of the word *were*. Since this is the plural (and 2nd person singular) of the simple past indicative, it means that the past subjunctive exists as a separate form only in the 1st and 3rd person singular of the verb *to be*. Increasingly this tends to be replaced by *was*, especially in informal English, but the distinction between the two is useful. The subjunctive can be used in such cases as:

> Suppose I *were* to offer you an increase...
> If only he *were* happier at school...
> I would rather she *were* left at home.

Let us examine the difference in usage between *were* and *was*:

> If I *were* Prime Minister, I would improve the transport system.
> If I *was* in the area last night, it was only for a few minutes.
> Though he *were* twice my size, I couldn't let him get away with it.
> Though she *was* an excellent student, she found the examination difficult.

The two examples of *were* (subjunctive) deal with things which not only have not happened, but never will. Even when *if* is used, the examples of *was* (indicative) deal with actual events. In the first example the speaker obviously cannot remember and admits the possibility of having briefly been in the area; in the second example her excellence is confirmed.

Or we can take the clause *If he were/was hungry* and discover the different ways in which the verbs are used. The indicative refers to a definite time and event in the past:

> If he *was* hungry, he went to the chip shop in his lunch break.

The subjunctive refers to a potential situation:

> If he *were* hungry, he could always ring through on the intercom.

Imperative mood

The final type of finite verb need not detain us long, but should be noted. The imperative is used for commands and is the same in form as the indicative (and therefore, incidentally, the present subjunctive):

> *Stand* up straight! *Leave* the building immediately!

The imperative can, of course, be more polite:

Please *stack* the plates over here.
Bring me your report if you have time.

A sort of imperative can even spread to the 1st person:

Let's drive down to visit Sinead.

You will note that the imperative is the only form of finite verb that operates without a subject. Normally a noun or pronoun expresses the doer of an action or the person/thing involved in the situation. With the imperative the subject is implied: it is *you*, the person or animal being addressed. 'Sit down!' effectively means '(You) sit down!'

SOME MATTERS OF NUMBER

Before we leave finite (tensed) verbs, it is worthwhile considering a few matters of number. Normally it is very easy to distinguish **singular** and **plural**. However, there are some deceptive situations:

▶ Collective nouns are singular

Remember that a collective noun refers to one group, though it may be made up of 11 cricketers or 600-plus MPs:

The programmers *have* all got a week's holiday because the department *is* closing down for Christmas.

▶ *There is/are* plus complement

The use of *is* or *are* after *there* or *here* is decided by the number of the complement: *there* is not the subject, so the complement is the all-important element. So:

There *is* my father.

but

There *are* my parents.

and

There *are* my father and uncle John.

▶ Several singulars make a plural

Remember that a subject of two or three singular nouns takes a plural verb: 'In the pantomime Buttons *was* the funniest character', but 'Buttons and the Baron *were* the funniest characters.' An exception can be made for those pairs of words so closely linked as to seem one unit. *Fish and chips* can be followed by *is* or *are* ('Fish and chips are all we serve' or 'Fish and chips is all we serve') and anyone asking 'How much are a gin and tonic?' might provoke a bemused response.

▶ Singular for distributive pronouns and adjectives

As detailed in Chapter 4, words like *each*, *every* and *either* are singular:

> All answers *are* right.

but

> Every answer *is* right.

Insight

What is the difference between these two sentences?

> The Prime Minister, Foreign Secretary and the Chancellor of the Exchequer were present at the conference.

> The Prime Minister, with the Foreign Secretary and the Chancellor of the Exchequer, was present at the conference.

In the first case the subject is made up of three people (plural) and the verb *were* rightly follows. In the second sentence the subject is the Prime Minister (singular) and the other two ministers have been relegated to a phrase explaining who were accompanying him. So, despite the reference to the presence of three people, *was* is indeed correct.

Non-finite (non-tensed) verbs: the infinitive

A non-finite verb has no firm link to a period of time, cannot take a subject and therefore cannot be the main verb of a sentence or clause. The **infinitive** is the basic form of the verb, existing as a single word or following *to*. It is the form by which you identify the verb (*to be*, *to have*, etc.); you would never give the 'name' of a verb as 'being' or 'had'. Also the infinitive, as explained above, is frequently used with auxiliary and modal verbs.

In its own right the infinitive is used to form phrases which can be used as noun or adjectival phrases. Let us analyse four examples using the phrase *to pass the examination*:

To pass the examination *is very easy.*
I wanted to pass the examination.
To pass the examination, *you must revise very thoroughly.*
I do not know how to pass the examination.

The first two sentences are **noun phrases** – the first the subject of the sentence, the second the object of the verb *wanted*. If you find it difficult to envisage these as noun phrases, just consider nouns that might replace the infinitive phrase: '*English* is very easy' or 'I wanted *my certificate*'. The third and fourth examples show the infinitive phrase with an adverbial function, in the second case dependent on the preposition *how.*

An infinitive can also be used in a common construction relating to the action that the *object* of the sentence is performing or might perform. This sounds contradictory as the object is the 'done-to' part of the sentence, but all becomes clear with the following examples:

The children watched *the birds* (object) *fly* (infinitive) overhead.
I saw *three ships* (object) *come* (infinitive) sailing in.

With verbs like *want, ask, advise, persuade* and *allow*, the *to* form of the infinitive is used:

She wanted *me* (object) *to go* (infinitive) to the party.
The Prime Minister persuaded *the Cabinet* (object) *to accept* (infinitive) the cuts.

PAST INFINITIVES
Just as participles have past and present forms which do not in themselves determine the tense, there exists a **past** (or **perfect**) **infinitive** using the auxiliary *to have* + past participle:

to find/to gather/to avoid (present infinitive)
to have found/to have gathered/to have avoided (past infinitive).

The choice of which infinitive to use depends on the time relationships within the sentence, not on the time of the main event of the sentence. Compare the following examples:

To write my autobiography is a long job.
To have written my autobiography makes me very proud.
To write my autobiography required the assistance of a ghost writer.
To have written my autobiography seemed a major achievement at the time.

The first example is set totally in the present, the last one is set totally in the past: at some time in the past the writer had completed his/her autobiography and felt it was a major achievement. The most interesting examples are the second and third, both a mixture of present and past. The second sentence is in the present tense, but the past infinitive shows that now he/she has completed the task. The third sentence is in the simple past tense, but, as it refers to an event which was happening at that time, not one that had been completed, we use a present infinitive.

Participles and gerunds

Much more complex in their use are **past and present participles**. The form of the present participle causes no difficulty, consisting of *-ing* added to the infinitive, with the usual doubling of consonants after short vowels and removal of final silent *e*: *feel/ feeling, pin/pinning, remove/removing*. The form of the past participle can give some problems: see the previous section on the past tense, dealing with possible confusion between past tense and past participle.

The problem with participles is that the same form can fulfil the functions of several parts of speech. We have already looked at one of the participle's verbal functions, creating tenses with the aid of auxiliary verbs: *are chasing, have eaten*, etc. Participles can also be used purely adjectivally. To add to the difficulty, the **gerund** (or verbal noun) has exactly the same form as the present participle. So the same form of the verb (the *-ing* form) can be used:

▶ in forming continuous tenses;

▶ in creating phrases where, like a verb, it attracts objects, complements and adverbial phrases;

▶ as an adjective;

▶ as a noun (gerund).

Let us examine some of these functions, bearing in mind that one thing a participle cannot do on its own is join with a subject and take on a tense to form a sentence: in other words, **a participle** can do many things, but it **cannot become finite**.

VERBAL USES OF PARTICIPLES AND GERUNDS

Participles are frequently found in **participial phrases**, for example:

skating on the lake
defeated by a better opponent

revising for examinations
debating the future of transport
shocked by his apparent callousness

These can function as various types of phrase:

Skating on the lake, the minister made a splendid sight.
(adjectival phrase with participle)
Skating on the lake has been banned because of thin ice. (noun
phrase with gerund)
Josie is *revising for her examinations*. (adjectival phrase – with
participle – as complement – or present continuous tense)
Revising for her examinations makes Josie irritable. (noun phrase
with gerund)
Defeated by a better opponent, I conceded the frame. (adjectival
phrase with participle)

In adjectival phrases care needs to be taken with the **dangling
participle** (otherwise termed 'hanging', 'misrelated' or 'unattached').
Place the participial phrase next to the noun being qualified:
'*Walking to the buffet car*, the train suddenly lurched and I fell over.'
The meaning is clear, but what this actually says is that the train was
walking to the buffet car. The correct version would be something
like: '*Walking to the buffet car*, I fell over when the train gave a
sudden lurch.'

PARTICIPIAL CLAUSES

These participial phrases can often seem like shortened versions of
clauses – that is, statements containing finite verbs. What, you may
ask, is the essential difference between the following sentences?

When he was working for the government, Mr Smirke was
required to sign the Official Secrets Act.
When working for the government, Mr Smirke was required to
sign the Official Secrets Act.

In each *Mr Smirke was required to sign...* is the main clause. In
the first case the first part contains a finite verb (*was working* –
past continuous tense), so forming an adjectival **clause,** whereas
there is no finite verb in the second example. Traditionally this has
been regarded as an adjectival **phrase,** but more recently the term
participial clause has become common in such cases:

Dismayed by the huge crowds, the children decided to go home.
The rival fans became violent, *throwing bottles and glasses
around the pub.*

PARTICIPLES AS ADJECTIVES

The distinction between a participle, a participle used adjectivally and an adjective derived from a verb is often a subtle and perplexing one (also considered in Chapter 6). How would you describe the following participles?

> I've just seen a *terrifying* film.
> After the earthquake struck, the villagers tried to avoid *falling* masonry.
> *Visiting* friends in Scotland, we were struck by the beauty of the scenery.
> *Retreating*, the army soon ran short of food.

Each of these is a participle, each modifies a noun or pronoun (*film, masonry, we, army*). Each could therefore be called a participle used adjectivally. However, we tend to see *terrifying* as an adjective and *falling* as a participle used adjectivally simply because we are so accustomed to use *terrifying* (like *charming, interesting* or *amazing*) on its own with a noun. Perhaps a test of whether a participle has become an adjective in its own right is whether we regularly modify it with an adverb of degree:

> *quite* terrifying   *absolutely* charming   *very* interesting
> *totally* amazing

In the final two examples we are more aware of the participle's verbal function. In the last case *The retreating army* would stress the adjectival function more than *Retreating, the army...*

Insight

What is one to do with a word like *fleeting*? *Fleet* has many meanings, the noun (number of ships) the most common and the adjective (swift) also familiar, if rather poetic and archaic. But whoever now encounters the verb, meaning 'to pass rapidly away'? Few, if any, of us, except in references to *fleeting pleasures* or *fleeting joys*. Is *fleeting*, then, an adjective or present participle? Strictly speaking, it is a present participle until *fleet* as a verb is officially pensioned off. Few grammarians, though, would raise an eyebrow at its being described as an adjective.

GERUNDS AS NOUNS

The same situation applies as with participles. The gerund can be used to form a **noun phrase**: '*Eating people* (subject) is wrong' or 'I enjoy *cycling round the Lake District* (object)'. You might like to note that, as the first example proves, gerunds can take objects: *Eating* is the gerund, *people* the object of the gerund and *Eating people* the subject of the sentence.

However, these same verbal nouns can also be used on their own with the function of nouns:

Eating is forbidden in the library.
Cycling improves your health.

Let us look at the word *speaking*. It can be used in constructions as participle and gerund that emphasize its origin as a part of a verb:

Speaking before a large audience terrifies most people. (gerund)
Speaking before a large audience, the Leader of the Opposition called for reduced taxes. (participle)

But it is so established as a noun in its own right that, when the National Curriculum was introduced, one area in English was entitled *Speaking and listening*. And it is so well established as an adjective that it has one meaning at a metaphorical distance from its verb (*a speaking likeness*) and is also enshrined in such compounds as *speaking-clock*.

In these complexities two things are important:

1 Separate form and function: a gerund is a verb form with a noun function, a participle is a verb form with an adjective function;

2 Use common sense and keep a sense of proportion.

Insight

The verb, as this section should have made clear, is the essential word of all words. Hence it is not surprising that it derives from *verbum*, the Latin word meaning 'word'. What, then, does the adjective 'verbal' mean? Confusingly, it can mean both 'to do with verbs' and 'to do with words'. You will find it used in both senses in this book and the only solution is to use the context (the surrounding words) to indicate the meaning:

He is weak at figures, but has excellent *verbal* ability. – 'with words'

The gerund is a *verbal* noun. – 'derived from the verb'

I shall not be writing to the manager, but please note this *verbal* complaint. – words, but here used to distinguish speech from writing.

Commas, subjects and participles

Look at the way in which commas are used in the following examples:

> The journey, being long and difficult, seemed to last for ever.
> The journey being long and difficult, we were highly relieved to arrive safely.

In the first case *journey* is the subject and *seemed* the verb. The participial phrase, *being long and difficult*, modifies the noun *journey* and is, as usual, placed next to the noun and separated from the rest of the sentence by commas.

However, something different is happening in the second example: with the first comma removed, *the journey* is part of the participial phrase. In a case like this, which is referred to as an **absolute phrase**, the participle retains its verbal function, with *journey* being the subject of the phrase, not the sentence. *We* is now the subject of the sentence. Read the following examples and note the use of the commas:

> Mrs Dunphy, having won the Lottery, never bought another ticket.
> Mrs Dunphy having won the Lottery, her neighbours organized a party for her.
> The stolen van, turning right at the lights, sped off down Richmond Street.
> The stolen van turning right at the lights, the police car followed close behind.

Note that the participle is still not a finite verb, although in the second and fourth sentences it has a subject. The **tense** is decided by the main verb of the sentence: in the case of the police chase, the tense is past, but a simple alteration to *follows* or *had followed* changes the tense of *turning* as well as the main verb.

Commas are used to separate one part of a sentence from another. Subjects and objects are part of the main line of a sentence which so often runs **subject–verb–object**. So you should note that phrases using the gerund as subject or object require no commas. Compare the following with the earlier examples:

> Turning right at the lights is not allowed under the new road system.
> I always try to avoid turning right at the lights.

Test yourself

5.1 Identify the finite verbs in the following sentences (possibly more than one in the same sentence) and decide whether each is a transitive verb of doing, an intransitive verb of doing or a verb of being:

a The body lay hidden behind the bushes.

b It was 10 o'clock before the secretary brought the message.

c Did he appear in time for the meeting?

d The inspector questioned the youth for several hours.

e He appeared confused by the questions.

f Mrs Jenkins laid her bags down and sighed with relief.

g Did I tell you that Sue became the area supervisor last year?

h We have found that older workers are more reliable.

i An all-inclusive holiday seems the best idea.

j All through the meeting they whispered to each other.

k I never said that.

l If she has applied as well, then I have no chance of the job.

m While we were on holiday, the whole family went on a trip to the old city.

n This is the best day we have had all summer.

o I can tell he is growing impatient.

p Kick the door down!

5.2 In the following sentences change the finite verb (in italics) into the tense indicated in brackets:

a Each of the brothers *had* a job with the Post Office. (present)

b I *am* sure that he *has taken* the key. (simple past/past perfect)

c The goods *arrived* on Tuesday. (future in the past)

d I *think* that she *goes* to her night class on Mondays. (both simple past)

e The machine *works* perfectly. (past continuous)

f Britain *opts* out of the treaty. (present perfect)

g The band *had* a gig in Warrington. (present)

h Your father *will speak* to you about it. (present perfect)

i Someone *smashed* the window last night. (simple past – passive voice)

j No one *has broken* the 100 metres record. (future – passive)

5.3 Form the simple past and past participle of the following verbs:

a define

b try

c run

d treat

e   swim

f   saw

g   lead

h   scan

i   pay

j   hang

k   smite

l   go

m   sow

n   choose

o   found

p   bend

5.4 Identify the auxiliary verbs (including modal verbs) in the following sentences some of which contain more than one. Explain the functions the auxiliaries serve:

  a The boat has run aground.

  b The supermarket chain is run by an international company.

  c The bonus should be paid next month.

  d I would collect the children if I thought it would help.

  e The council is voting on the proposal.

  f Do you often go to the theatre?

  g We have finished the briefing and you can leave whenever you want.

  h I had hoped to move in next week.

  i Ms Frazer does not know that the firm has gone into liquidation.

  j I do know where India is.

  k Political dissenters have frequently been imprisoned.

  l I am attacked on all sides.

  m We shall call you when you are needed.

  n She said she would write soon.

  o My brother might call round tomorrow.

  p Parents ought to be more strict about what their children are allowed to do.

5.5 The following sentences refer to possible uses of the subjunctive. Choose the correct alternative from the two words in brackets:

  a If there (was, were) a chance of promotion, it has disappeared now.

  b If I (was, were) England manager, I would bring in younger players.

  c Though I (was, were) to inherit a million pounds, I don't think she would be interested in me.

d Though he (was, were) at school at the same time, his experiences were quite different from mine.

e The assistant insisted that Mrs Jones (sees, see) the manager.

f Mrs Jones insisted that she (was, were) in a hurry.

g When it (is, be) 9 o'clock, we open the shop.

h I request that the official opening time (is, be) 9 o'clock.

i Just suppose she (was, were) to miss the ceremony.

j If she (was, were) late, I'm sure there was a good reason.

k The developer bought the old cinema as it (was, were) without any improvements.

l By developing it as a theatre, he hoped to create a new Stratford, as it (was, were).

5.6 The following sentences all contain at least one, often more, non-finite (non-tensed) verb: infinitive, participle or gerund. In each case identify the type of non-finite verb and describe its function in the sentence:

a To find an ancient site is every archaeologist's dream.

b Dr Jamieson, hoping to give an interesting lecture, chose the Ancient Sumerians as his subject.

c Driving on the wrong side of the road is a sure way to get arrested.

d I don't like receiving bills.

e Snoring is a very irritating habit.

f I am not snoring.

g Elated by her triumph in her final examinations, Amy was depressed when she failed to find a job.

h Have you fixed the broken window?

i The battered yacht was towed into harbour.

j Climbing in the Alps, we encountered a party from Japan.

k Climbing in the Alps is dangerous.

l I never enjoyed climbing in the Alps.

m My neighbours have been climbing in the Alps.

n To err is human.

o To forget her name again is shocking.

5.7 Each of the following sentences contains an error relating to some aspect of English covered in this chapter. See how many you can correct:

a The Ambassador coming to meet the Prime Minister, nearly tripped over.

b Each of the answers are right.

c The Bishop, with acolytes, servers and members of the choir, are due to enter at any moment.

d Here is the Bishop and the choir.

e The choir have joined the Bishop.

f If we had got up earlier, we may have caught the train.

g Haven't you ate your tea yet?

h If I had been notified in time, I would prepare the room.

i There is two reasons for leaving early.

j I was dreading, meeting the Lord Mayor.

Modifiers: adjectives and adverbs

In this chapter you will learn:

▶ *the similarities and differences between adjectives and adverbs*

▶ *the varied functions of both within a sentence and the role of adjectival and adverbial clauses*

▶ *how to form comparatives and superlatives.*

Describing words?

When schoolchildren are first introduced to the basics of grammar, those reassuring terms 'naming words' (nouns), 'doing words' (verbs), 'joining words' (conjunctions), etc., are used. For **adjectives** the phrase 'describing words' is common, but this is rather more misleading than the others. What both **adjectives** and **adverbs** do is to 'modify' or 'qualify', to apply some sort of limitation to the generalized noun or verb. This may be done by description, but very often it is done by demonstration or a simple statement of fact.

Let us take the example *train*, a noun. A passenger at Birmingham New Street enquiring how to reach Euston is not helped by the reply, 'You'll have to get the train.' The word 'train' needs to be qualified, but how? A statement of fact is probable – 'The *next* train' – or, in an **adjectival phrase**, 'The train *at platform 3*'. A simple demonstration is also likely: '*That* train.' It is possible, but not too likely, that the answer will involve description: 'The *blue* train *with red stripes on the side.*'

Descriptive or not, *next* and *that* are just as much adjectives as are *blue* and *red*.

TYPES OF ADJECTIVE

It is not necessary to know all the terms for different types of adjective; indeed, you will often find inconsistency over the correct terms to use. It is, however, helpful to be reminded of some of the various kinds of adjective:

▶ **Descriptive**

This is the obvious type of adjective: *red, tall, violent, obsequious*, as long a list as you care to make. The only point to remember is that not all adjectives are describing words.

▶ **Demonstrative**

Adjectives can simply demonstrate or point out which one you are referring to: *that* book, *this* summer, *those* flowers. These same words are **demonstrative pronouns** and current practice is always to refer to them as such, but traditional grammar makes a valid distinction. Used with a noun they are adjectives; used on their own, they are pronouns. 'Do you stock *this* (demonstrative adjective) magazine?' 'No, but *these* (demonstrative pronoun) might interest you.'

▶ Possessive

According to traditional grammar, such examples as '*my* friend', '*your* ticket' and '*their* luggage' are possessive adjectives. Like demonstrative adjectives, they are now often considered as **pronouns** (see Chapter 4).

▶ Numerical

The **cardinal** numbers (*one, two, three*, etc.) can be nouns ('the score was 3–1' or 'Flight Number 5034') or adjectives ('She had a choice of two cars' or 'a majority of 507 votes'). The **ordinal** numbers (*first, second, third*, etc.) tend to be adjectives. In addition to the actual numbers, there are other adjectives of **quantity** such as *few, many* and *several*.

▶ Interrogative/exclamatory

There are several words that can be used with many different functions, two of which are to join nouns in asking questions (**interrogative**) or making exclamations. You do not need to know these terms, but should be able to identity *which* and *what* as adjectives in the following: *Which* bus goes to the town centre?/*What* time is it?/*What* stupidity to expect me to believe that!/*What* sharp eyes you have!

▶ Definite and indefinite articles

The definite (*the*) and indefinite articles (*a/an*) are a category of their own, usually classed nowadays as belonging to **determiners** (see Chapter 4), but in older grammar books they will be found under **adjectives**.

▶ Factual

Some adjectives simply identify the noun without actually describing it: the *last* bus, *new* regulations, the *top* floor. These are not necessarily a separate category, but you need at least to remember to give the word 'descriptive' a wide definition.

THE ROLE OF ADJECTIVES

The function of adjectives is to **modify or qualify a noun or pronoun**. A common placing for an adjective or adjectives is before the noun:

a *sunny* day	*three new* players	the *last* bus
red herrings	*this bold new* initiative.	

They can be placed after the noun: this can sound old-fashioned and/or poetic, but can work well when you have a list of adjectives or an adjective phrase:

The tourist, *confused, penniless* and *demoralized*, asked for help.

There are limits to the situations in which an adjective can qualify a pronoun. In most of the examples above, if we replace the noun with a pronoun, the use of an adjective becomes impossible. References to *the last it* or *three new they* simply sound absurd. Following a pronoun with an adjective phrase, however, is possible, if frequently a little awkward:

I, *too short to see the procession*, could hear the cheering.

The most natural use of an adjective to modify a pronoun occurs when the words are separated from each other:

She realized the bus had gone and, *cold*, *wet* and *miserable*, prepared for a long wait.

ADJECTIVES AS COMPLEMENTS

The major use of adjectives at a distance from the nouns and pronouns they modify is as **complements** (now known as **intensive complements**). Like many of the terms in grammar ('modifier', for instance), a complement is more easily understood if you think of its original meaning. A complement is something that **completes.** When you use **verbs of doing**, they sometimes complete the sense in themselves: *The car stopped*, *We laughed*, etc. This is not the case with **verbs of being**. They need something to complete the meaning. *They seem* does not make sense and *She is* only exists as a reply to a question, with *first in the queue* or *the new accountant* as an implied complement.

A complement is the word or phrase that completes the sense after a verb of being. It can take the form of a noun, a pronoun or an adjective (or a noun, adjectival or adverbial phrase). An adjective in this situation is modifying its noun/pronoun (the **subject** of the sentence or clause) at a distance as part of a free-standing statement:

This *violent* crime needs to be punished. (adjective as modifier in front of noun)
This crime is *violent*. (adjective as complement at the end of the statement)

In the following examples of adjectives as complement, note:

▶ in some cases they are modifying pronouns, not nouns;

complements can complete questions, exclamations and commands as well as statements:

The approach to the castle was *steep* and *circuitous*.
Despite the counsellor's help, I felt very *depressed*. (modifying pronoun)
Are you *lonesome* tonight? (modifying pronoun in a question)
They appeared *cheerful* after their ordeal. (modifying pronoun)
How *conceited* he is! (modifying pronoun in an exclamation)
At least try to appear *intelligent*. (command)
The English examination was surprisingly *easy*.

Insight

Many adjectives are created by adding suffixes to other words. Two of the most common endings are the opposites *-ful* and *-less*: *hopeful/ hopeless*, *cheerful/cheerless*, *helpful/helpless*, *fearful/fearless*, *tasteful/ tasteless*, etc. Because the word *full* exists with similar meaning, the tendency to double the *l* on *-ful* words is understandable, but wrong. In this case there is a clear spelling rule. Sadly, this is not the case with *-ible* and *-able*. Both mean 'able to do' or 'able to suffer', but all spellings need to be learned separately. To take only one column of the dictionary, there is no logic behind the difference between:

irreparable/irreplaceable/irreproachable

and

irresistible/irresponsible/irrepressible.

COMPARISONS OF ADJECTIVES

Many adjectives can be graded by degree. This means that they exist in three forms:

1 the **simple** (*great*);

2 the **comparative** for comparisons between two nouns (*greater*), and

3 the **superlative** for comparisons between the noun and everything else (*greatest*).

Some adjectives, however, by reason of their meaning, can only exist in their basic positive form. Consider these few examples:

▶ *Only* specifies one single person or thing. There is no possibility of being more only than you were or the most only person in the room. On the other hand, *lonely*, with a not dissimilar meaning, expresses a feeling and there are degrees of feeling. Everyone in the club might be lonely, but A could well be lonelier than B.

▶ *Unique* famously cannot be qualified, whether by *more* or *most* or by words like *fairly*. If something is unique, it is unique, no more or less, but, if you choose to use *unusual*, you can find that something is *more unusual* than something else: perhaps it has three or four odd features, not one or two.

▶ *Right* and *wrong* describe a single positive state, and degrees of correctness are better served by using a different adjective: *more* (*or less*) *accurate*, for instance.

▶ The ordinal numbers (the *third* man, the *tenth* wicket) cannot be graded by degree.

▶ If a runner in a race increases her lead, she is still simply *ahead* as she was before. There is no such thing as *aheader* or *more ahead* and a different modifier has to be found: *further ahead*.

Insight

Next and *last* are derived from the Old English superlatives for *near* and *late*. As the centuries have passed, both words have taken on a separate identity and *near* and *late* have had to find new superlatives: *nearest* and *latest*. It is interesting to reflect on the subtle differences between *last* and *latest*. Actors on chat shows plug 'my *latest* film', the current or most recent one, whereas 'my *last* film' is either the one before that or the final one of a career: 'My *latest* film, but certainly not my *last*!' Needless to say, there are no comparatives or superlatives for *next* or *last*.

THE FORMS OF COMPARISON

As in much of English grammar the form of the comparative and superlative depends largely on common sense, with just a few bizarre exceptions. The basic rule is that the comparative is formed by adding *-er* or using the word *more* and the superlative is formed by adding *-est* or using the word *most*. In most cases the choice of using the ending or the auxiliary word is made on the grounds of what sounds best. If you were to use the word *beautifullest*, you would be understood, but the word would sound ugly and be difficult to pronounce; if you used *more big*, it would sound rather childish, though making perfect sense. As a generalization short words use *-er* and *-est*, longer words *more* and *most*, though it is impossible to apply mathematical rules: the six-letter *humble* giving us *humbler* and *humblest*, the five-letter *rapid* becoming *more rapid* and *most rapid*. (Of course, *humbler* is only two syllables, whereas *rapider* would be three, and speech is the key factor here, not appearance on the page.)

▶ Most and most

Some confusion may be caused by the fact that *most* has two very similar, but not identical, uses when linked to adjectives. *Most* is the form of the superlative, but is also an alternative to *very*. So *most satisfactory* can mean *very satisfactory* as well as more satisfactory than anything else. In practice you would usually place *the* before the superlative. 'This is most satisfactory' means that you are very satisfied with it. 'This is *the* most satisfactory' means that you have compared several and this is best. If a noun follows, the difference is marked by definite or indefinite article: '*the* most satisfactory solution' (superlative: you have made the comparison); '*a* most satisfactory solution' (one that pleases you very much: no comparison made).

In adding *-er* and *-est*, you follow rules that are familiar from other cases of added endings:

- ▶ *y* at the end changes to *i*: *friendly/friendlier/friendliest*;

- ▶ this does not apply when *y* follows a vowel: *grey/greyer/greyest*;

- ▶ a final *e* is absorbed into the ending: *noble/nobler/noblest*;

- ▶ single final consonants are usually doubled: *grim/grimmer/ grimmest*.

The exceptions are, as usual in English, with some of the most common words, notably *good* and *bad* which have *better/best* and *worse/worst* as their comparatives and superlatives. As well as helping to form other comparatives and superlatives, *more* and *most* stand on their own as the comparative and superlative of *much* or *many*. *Little* has two forms of comparison. If you are referring to the size of something or someone individual (cases where you could use *small* instead) you use the normal form: *The Littlest Hobo*, for example. When referring to a quantity rather than an individual, there is an alternative form:

> I found *little* difficulty with the examination.
> You will find *less* difficulty if you revise properly.
> Of all the exams I had *least* difficulty with English.

Note, by the way, that *less* and *least* always refer to quantity, not number. It has become common to use phrases like *less than twenty* which should be *fewer than twenty*. The distinction between the two can be summed up in the sentences:

> I prepared *less* food as we expected *fewer* guests.
> The stall sold *fewer* hotdogs as the crowd became *less*.

The use of *less* instead of *fewer* is now widely accepted and may well soon become the norm, but it is worth preserving a useful distinction between the two.

Insight

A common error, forgivable enough in informal speech, but not in formal situations or in writing, is to use the superlative to compare **two** things. The superlative is used to make comparisons between everything in the same category; for comparisons of two things, use the comparative. You will be familiar with such statements as 'May the *best* team win'. Assuming that there are only two teams playing, it should be *better*. Referring to two parents/children/friends/colleagues, many people would say, 'I find X the *most* difficult to deal with' – this would be correct with three or more, but with two you should use '*more* difficult'.

ADJECTIVAL USE OF OTHER PARTS OF SPEECH

You will sometimes find that other parts of speech are used adjectivally, in particular, nouns and the participle form of verbs. How, then, should you refer to these: as nouns/verbs or as adjectives? Again it is a matter of common sense. Look at the following examples:

fish shop   *street* corner   *cricket* ball   *nature* reserve

All the words in italics are clearly nouns, but they are being used to modify other nouns, the normal role of an adjective. In the first example, for instance, given the noun *shop*, we need more information: *large*, *new*, *prosperous* and *empty* (all adjectives) could give us information, but so could the nouns *fish*, *antiques*, *clothes* and *sports*. In these cases it is better to refer to these as 'nouns used adjectivally' rather than try to redefine them as adjectives.

A participle is the form of the verb lacking specific reference to subject and time. Words like *lying* and *running* (present participles) and *written* and *fallen* (past participles) attach themselves to nouns or other verbs to achieve their meaning. (Remember, though, that many verbs end in -*ed* both in the past tense and as past participles, so *attacked* or *laughed*, for instance, can be either.) Phrases like 'the *running* man' and 'the *fallen* tree' show participles being used in an adjectival role. Again it is sensible to refer to them in that way, not as adjectives. On the other hand, most people would accept words like *fascinating*, *charming*, *scared* and *delighted* as adjectives simply because of the frequency of their use as such. And, though dictionaries may list the verb *deject* as meaning *depress*, in reality *dejected* now exists only as an adjective.

Insight

In the first part of the 21st century, when under too much pressure, we describe ourselves as *stressed* or *stressed out*. *Stressed* is still recognizable as the past participle of a verb, though its adjectival use is increasingly common. So it is worth considering the history of *fraught*, a slightly less up-to-date term for the same sad state. In Middle English *fraught* was the past participle of a verb meaning to *load* or to *burden* (still found in the word *freight* for the cargo that is loaded). *Fraught* therefore is an adjective that once was a past participle and still retains pretty much the same meaning of (over-) *burdened*.

ADJECTIVAL PHRASES AND CLAUSES

Participles are often used within adjectival phrases:

> *Shaken* by the result of the vote, the Chairman resigned.
> *Trembling* with fear and cold, the walkers were finally found on the moors.

However, an **adjectival phrase** does not need to contain either an adjective or a participle used adjectivally. An adjectival phrase is **a group of words which carries out the function of an adjective** – that is, modifying a noun. If we take the second example above, there are many different ways in which we can be given further information about the walkers:

> *miserable* (adjective)
> *frightened* (past participle)
> *trembling* (present participle)
> *in a state of exhaustion* (adjectival phrase)
> *from the Yorkshire Boy Scout association* (adjectival phrase)
> *without protection against the cold* (adjectival phrase)

Note that the three adjectival phrases given above do not contain adjectives, but do serve to tell the reader more about the walkers. As *walkers* is a noun, the phrase fulfils the function of an adjective. In terms of function, it is the same to write 'the *elegant* (adjective) man' and 'the man *in a Saville Row suit* (adjectival phrase)'.

Equally **adjectival clauses** fulfil the function of an adjective: for a full explanation of the differences between phrases and clauses, see Chapter 8. In traditional grammar a clause contains a **finite verb** and a phrase does not. So *organizing the raffle* is an adjectival phrase, *who organized the raffle* is an adjectival clause. This is the definition used here: Chapter 8 will consider the current terms **non-finite clause** and **participial clause**, but the correct usage is unaffected by the terms used.

THE PLACING OF ADJECTIVAL PHRASES

A phrase should be placed next to the noun it is modifying. There is no indication of who or what is performing or suffering the act, so a phrase will attach itself to the nearest noun. For example, let us imagine that you wish to write that Marie stepped into the road and a car nearly hit her and you have decided to use the adjectival phrase *Stepping into the road*. Sentences like the three following are often to be seen, but only one is correct:

> *Stepping into the road*, Marie just managed to avoid the car.
> *Stepping into the road*, there was nearly a collision between Marie and a car.
> *Stepping into the road*, a car nearly hit Marie.

The first is correct. The second is meaningless as there is no noun or pronoun for *stepping* to relate to. The third is nonsensical since it states that a car stepped into the road.

Avoid sentences such as '*Arriving in the office*, the manager was waiting for me' or '*On the way to a swimming lesson*, the bus left Jason standing at the stop.' These mean that the manager was the one who arrived and the bus was taking to the water! You can do this by turning round the main clause: 'Arriving in the office, *I found* the manager waiting for me.' Or you can replace the **adjectival phrase** with an **adverbial clause** which tells us who did what: '*When Jason was on his way to his swimming lesson*, the bus left him standing at the stop.'

Insight

The situation described here is often caused by so-called 'dangling participles', past or present participles left in the air by having no noun to attach themselves to and no auxiliary verb (like 'have' or 'was') to place them with the subject. You can have fun thinking of examples:

> *Severely damaged by fire*, the orchestra played the first concert at the restored hall.
> *Climbing wearily up the hill*, the observatory came into view.

However, though the prospect of fire-damaged musicians or exhausted observatories can raise a smile, this needs to be avoided in non-comic writing.

HOW TO USE ADJECTIVES

Adjectives are more functional than the term 'describing words' suggests: they have important roles in identifying, questioning and defining. However, it must be admitted that adjectives have more of a decorative role than, say, pronouns or prepositions, even nouns and verbs (though these can be decorative as well as functional). So it is appropriate to conclude the section on adjectives with a reminder that two weaknesses of English style can be over-exaggeration and lack of precision.

We are too ready to describe something as 'a *remarkable* achievement' (or, in rather looser English, 'a *fantastic* achievement') when really it could fairly be described as *impressive* or, even further down the scale, *sound*. What terms are then left to you to describe achievements that really are remarkable? If a *tragic* accident puts a footballer out of the game for six months, what word is left for some horrific incident with multiple deaths? This tendency is not confined to the use of adjectives, but, in their describing function, they frequently fall victim to it.

Lack of precision leads to boring repetition. Try to avoid using general terms like *bad*, *good* and *nice* all the time when there are more exact alternatives. Remember the old joke:

> 'Are you coming to see United on Saturday?'
> 'No, why should I? They never came to see me when I was bad.'

There the pun depends on the sloppy use of *bad*: to mean incompetent or useless as well as sick or ill, when after all what it really means is evil.

The difference between adjectives and adverbs

The functions and form of adjectives and adverbs are very similar. In most cases the adverb consists of the adjective with *-ly* added (*beautiful/beautifully*); this will be considered in more detail later. Their roles in the sentence are to act as modifiers, adapting or intensifying the meaning of other words. Adjectives qualify nouns and pronouns; **adverbs** primarily qualify **verbs** (and this similarity in names makes the difference between adjectives and adverbs easy to remember).

Intelligent and *foolish* are words of opposite meaning, but there is no guarantee that intelligent people will not act foolishly. Similarly someone whom we could not describe as intelligent will display surprising acuteness of mind on some occasions. Thus there is a considerable difference between the word we might use to describe someone (an adjective describing a noun) and the word we might use for what he/she did on one occasion (an adverb describing a verb):

> Mr Barwell proved an *intelligent* Managing Director over a ten-year period.
> Mr Barwell acted *foolishly* in not foreseeing the slump in sales.

These sentences are not contradictory. The adjective, *intelligent*, accurately describes Mr Barwell; the adverb, *foolishly*, accurately describes what he did or failed to do on one occasion. If we add, 'His Deputy responded more *intelligently* to the situation', we are not necessarily implying the Deputy's general intellectual superiority.

Some cars are fast; some are not. However, even the fast cars go slowly at some times: a Formula One car in the pits or a sports car in a traffic jam on the M25. So, when you write, 'The car was moving *slowly* (adverb)', that is not the same as referring to a '*slow* (adjective) car'. This is the essential difference between adjectives and adverbs.

A COMMON ERROR

In spoken English the use of the adjective form for the adverb is very common. Football managers are famed for saying, 'The boy *done good*' (instead of 'The boy *did well*') which uses past participle for past tense as well as adjective for adverb. References to people having *played brilliant*, *acted stupid* or *behaved bad* are not hard to find. Though these are to be avoided, there are two factors which complicate the issue and make the error very understandable:

▶ **1 Informal spoken English**

Informal speech generates many different words for high approval and high disapproval, some of which come and go with fashion. Some are obviously slang (*ace* or *mega*), others are more confusing because they are distortions of the meaning of existing words. *Fabulous* and *fantastic* are two of the longer-lasting examples of this category. Their original meanings, from *fable* and *fantasy*, both to do with the worlds of magic and imagination, are often forgotten. *Great* and *fine* are two simpler words used to express general approval. Often the approval is so generalized that 'He *did* fantastic' or 'She *did* great' becomes almost equivalent to the correct 'He *was* fantastic' or 'She *was* great'. We are much less likely to make this error when using the words in their original sense. Most of us would have to admit to 'She did *fine* for her first driving lesson' when we would always refer to 'fine*ly* chiselled features' or 'writing fine*ly* with a calligraphy pen'.

▶ **2 In some cases the same phrase can be correct with an adverb or adjective**

The second problem concerns the fact that the same phrase or clause may be correct with either adverb or adjective, but with a very small adjustment of meaning. Let us look at the statements 'Tom acted *violent*' and 'Tom acted *violently*'. Both are correct, although the first is sometimes used instead of the second incorrectly. *Violently* qualifies the verb *acted* and this means that Tom committed violent acts: physical attacks, smashing glasses, producing a weapon, that sort of thing. That is the most common usage and you would normally expect the word 'violent*ly*' in this sentence. However, 'He acted *violent*' can be correct. It asks us to assume words such as 'as if he were'. *Acted* here becomes a verb of being; *violent* becomes the adjectival complement describing Tom. In this case Tom may or may not have committed violent acts (*acted* suggests the possibility of 'putting it on').

THE FORM OF ADVERBS

When formed from adjectives, adverbs nearly always add *-ly*. However, matters are not totally simple. You must remember that *well* is the adverb from *good*, for instance, and make sense of those adjectives that end in *-ly*: e.g. *lovely, ugly, gingerly*. When turned into adverbs, *lovely* becomes *lovelily* while *gingerly* stays the same and *ugly* lives up to its name with the logical, but odd-looking, *uglily*.

Insight

Well is one of the odder words in the English language. It has multiple meanings: a source of water or an indeterminate expression, for example. What is confusing is that it is not only the adverb from *good* ('The first day of the holidays went *well*'), but an adjective in its own right with a similar, but slightly different, meaning, 'in good health' or 'satisfactory': *The Well Woman Clinic* or *All is well*.

The rules governing the addition of *-ly* are mostly fairly straightforward, though subject to exceptions:

▶ Adjectives ending in *ll* simply add *-y* so that the adverbs are equivalent to those formed from adjectives ending in single *l*: *full* and *frightful* become *fully* and *frightfully*.

▶ As is common practice in English, a final *y* following a consonant is transformed into *i* before the addition of the ending: *dry/drily*, *gloomy/gloomily*, etc. The most common exceptions are *shyly* and *slyly*. Oddly there is at least one case where a final *y* following a vowel is changed in the same way: *gay/gaily* is, however, an exception.

▶ Adjectives ending in *-e* are subject to change. Words ending in *-le* after a consonant usually just change the final *e* to *y*: *subtle/subtly*, *agreeable/agreeably*, etc. In cases where a final *e* follows a vowel it is usually omitted: *eerie/eerily*, *true/truly*, etc. There are exceptions to both these rules, with, for instance, *whole* dropping the e (*wholly*) without being in either of these categories. In the case of words like *sole* and *vile* the adverb form is normal: *solely/vilely*.

▶ Perhaps the most confusing change is that most adjectives ending in *-ic* form the adverb by *-ally*: *basic/basically*, *characteristic/characteristically*, etc. In cases where the adjective can have either an *-ic* or an *-ical* ending, the adverb always ends *-ically*: *comic(al)/comically*, *geographic(al)/geographically*. Beware of *public/publicly* and note that the adverb from *frantic* can be either *franticly* or *frantically*.

▶ There are, of course, very many words that exist only as adverbs, not as formations from adjectives. Many of these are extremely common words: *here*, *there*, *soon*, *very*, *quite*, *again*, *today*, *tomorrow*, *however*, *therefore*, etc. There are also words like *before* and *on* that can function as adverbs and prepositions.

▶ Finally, there is a group of adverbs which have exactly the same form as the related adjectives: e.g. *hard*, *full*, *fast*, *only* and *long*. Compare:

  ▶ 'His *hard* (adjective) work paid off' and 'He worked *hard* (adverb)'.

  ▶ 'A *full* (adjective) theatre is always welcome' and 'He hit me *full* (adverb) on the nose'.

  ▶ 'I caught the *fast* (adjective) train' and 'She drove too *fast* (adverb)'.

  ▶ 'She remains my *only* (adjective) rival' and 'It is *only* (adverb) right to obey'.

  ▶ 'It's been a *long* (adjective) time' and 'I'd *long* (adverb) expected it'.

THE USES OF ADVERBS

The most widely used function of the adverb is modifying the verb, but adverbs have many other uses:

▶ **Modifying adjectives**

Though adjectives themselves are modifying or qualifying nouns, we frequently add an adverb to intensify or describe the adjective. For instance, the original phrase might refer to an '*efficient* (adjective) manager', but not all efficient managers hit the same level of efficiency or do it with the same style, so we might wish to add extra details:

Ms Thompson is an *extremely* efficient manager.
The manager is *fairly* efficient.
The manager is *usually* efficient.
Mr Briggs is a *briskly* efficient manager.
Mrs Green's management style is *calmly* efficient.

The first two statements show the degree of efficiency (there are many words we could have used, notably *very*). The next statement suggests some slight lack of consistency and the last two describe his/her manner (we could have chosen *relentlessly*, *gently*, *aggressively*, etc.). All the words in italics are adverbs.

▶ **Modifying other adverbs**

This is essentially a similar function to modifying adjectives and the same 'specialist' adverbs are much used, especially those expressing degree: *very*, *quite*, *fairly*, *less*, etc. In the case of the sentence 'The actors performed *very well*', *well* is an adverb modifying the verb *performed*, *very* is also an adverb, but modifying *well*. There is no sense in which *very* can be seen as modifying the verb. You could easily replace *very* with *fairly* or *extremely* or a more descriptive adverb (not one of degree) such as *surprisingly, extraordinarily* or even *untypically*.

The position of the adverb in the sentence can make a difference (see the subsequent section on 'The placing of adverbs'). Let us examine two very similar sentences:

> She *usually* drove her car *quickly*.
> She drove her car *unusually quickly*.

In the first sentence both adverbs (*usually* and *quickly*) modify the verb (*drove*). *Quickly* is an adverbial complement and *usually* is placed before the verb and is telling us something about both that verb and its complement. In the second sentence *quickly* has the same function as before, but *unusually* has been placed in front of the adverb *quickly* which it is modifying: it is the speed, not the driving, that is unusual.

▶ **Modifying whole sentences or clauses**

Sometimes adverbs relate to the whole sentence or clause. It is impossible to see them as relating to the verb only which is where they would have been placed in traditional analysis. Many of these 'whole-clause' usages have become rather meaningless: words like *actually*, *really* and *seriously* are often used as little more than punctuation, protestations of truth or appeals for attention:

> *Seriously*, I'm going to the pictures.
> *Actually* he's my next door neighbour.

In these cases the adverbs are simply insisting that the speaker is telling truth.

Insight

The favourite cliché of the last years of the 20th century sums up the meaningless use of adverbs to modify a whole sentence very well. It is in fact an adverbial phrase, not an adverb, but the function (or lack of one) is the same: *at the end of the day*. What does it mean to say, 'At the end of the day it's a long way to travel to work'? *After all* or even *When all is said and done* come rather nearer to the intended meaning of 'When you've taken everything into consideration'.

There are many adverbs that serve a much clearer function when modifying the whole sentence:

> *Incredibly* England gained a first innings lead. (suggesting that the whole statement is highly unlikely)
> *Therefore* we have decided to cut short your contract. (suggesting that the reasons have been given in previous sentences)
> *Indeed* I was hoping to see her myself. (suggesting a contradiction of previous implications or intensifying previous arguments)

An interesting use of adverb-to-modify-clause is the current meaning attached (very usefully) to the adverb *hopefully*. This has always meant 'with hope' applied to some action (modifying the verb); recently it has also come to mean, 'It is to be hoped', suggesting that the whole clause or sentence is something to be desired. It would be perfectly correct now, though somewhat graceless, to write:

> *Hopefully* our daughter will approach her examinations *hopefully*.

Both are adverbs. The first modifies the whole sentence, telling the reader that this is what you, the writer, want to happen. The second modifies the verb *approach*, indicating the spirit in which you hope your daughter will take her examinations.

OTHER FUNCTIONS OF ADVERBS

Adverbs tend to be the maids of all work among parts of speech, so you will find all kinds of function being carried out by adverbs. There are the **interrogative adverbs** that express questions, mostly beginning with *wh* (*where*, *why*, *when* – not *who* and *which*), but also including *how*. Then *well* can fulfil many functions, even modifying prepositions: '*well into* the night'. Even some nouns and pronouns can be modified by adverbs, not adjectives: '*almost* everyone', '*nearly* all'.

THE PLACING OF ADVERBS

The fact that an adverb can modify different parts of the sentence means that it is necessary to take care where you place it. There are no specific rules about where an adverb modifying the verb should go, so that, in an uncomplicated statement with only one adverb, you could write:

> *Quickly* the secretary made a note of his name.
> *or* The secretary *quickly* made a note of his name.
> *or* The secretary made a note *quickly* of his name.
> *or* The secretary made a note of his name *quickly*.

Which sounds best? That is the only guide. However, there are cases where ambiguity can set in, with the adverb *only* a particular nuisance. What do these sentences mean?

> He *only* wounded two of his victims.
> He wounded *only* two victims.

In the first sentence *only* is connected to the verb *wounded* which it modifies: he only wounded them, he did not kill them, perhaps he killed some other victims. In the second sentence *only* has been linked to *two*, the adverb is modifying an adjective and the meaning is that the number wounded is low, not that they escaped something worse.

Or consider these sentences:

> *Clearly* she gave evidence today.
> She gave evidence *clearly* today.

In the first case the adverb modifies the whole statement. From something you have heard, it is certain that she gave evidence today: how clearly she gave evidence is not stated. In the second sentence the adverb modifies the verb *gave* and describes the quality of her performance in the witness box.

The placing of adverbs needs care, particularly since there is no single rule to observe. In many cases the adverb needs to be placed before the word it is modifying (for example, the examples with *only*), but this is far from being a universal rule, as the secretary example shows. The key question to ask yourself is, 'Is there any ambiguity of meaning?'

Insight

Let us remind ourselves of the vexed question of the split infinitive, since it is usually an adverb or adverbial phrase or clause that is doing the splitting. The infinitive is the basic form of the verb: *to go, to write, to listen, to prevaricate*. There is absolutely no grammatical reason not to split *to* from *go* or *listen*. There may, however, be a reason of style. We can easily imagine a preposterous example: 'He decided to quickly in case the police found him hide in the cellar' – the infinitive split by seven words, the result a quite appalling sentence. But do you object to 'He decided to quickly hide in the cellar'? Most people now would think it quite normal. So split infinitives are not incorrect, but avoid them if you feel that they spoil the sound of the sentence – for most of us, that means a split of any more than a word or two.

ADVERBIAL PHRASES AND CLAUSES

As with adjectives, groups of words that may well not even contain an adverb can perform the function of adverbs: these are **adverbial phrases** and **adverbial clauses**, clauses containing a finite verb, phrases not. Traditional grammar books list something like ten or twelve different categories of adverbial clause and, while learning about adverbial clauses of concession is probably unnecessary, some awareness of these types conveys the wide range of adverbial functions.

▶ Time

A major adverbial function is to state when the action occurred/will occur. Hence:

Yesterday my brother felt ill. (adverb)
In the evening my brother felt ill. (adverbial phrase)
When he arrived back from holiday, my brother felt ill. (adverbial clause)

▶ Place

As important as when the action took place is where it took place:

Our friends met us *there*. (adverb)
Our friends met us *at the station*. (adverbial phrase)
Our friends met us *where we asked them to*. (adverbial clause)

▶ Manner

This is the *How?* to go with the *Where?* and *When?*:

The meeting went *smoothly*. (adverb)
The meeting went *like clockwork*. (adverbial phrase)
The meeting went *just as we planned*. (adverbial clause)

▶ Reason

The final question is, of course, *Why?*:

Inevitably the customers complained. (adverb)
The customers complained *in protest at the high prices*. (adverbial phrase)
The customers complained *because the store increased prices*. (adverbial clause)

Among other types of adverbial phrase or clause that you might wish to take note of are ones dealing with **comparison** (The

Millennium Dome cost more *than had been planned*), **purpose/result** (often using *so that* or *in order to/that*), **contrast** or **concession** (usually with *though* or *although*) and **possibility** or **condition** (using words like *if* and *unless*).

COMPARISON OF ADVERBS

Essentially the comparison of adverbs is the same as adjectives, except that the use of the *more ...* and *most ...* form is almost universal. Interestingly enough, adjective endings in *-ly* often form comparatives and superlatives by the addition of *-(i)er* and *-(i)est*: *lively/livelier/liveliest, friendly/friendlier/friendliest*.

These, of course, become more cumbersome words in their adverbial form, so that we write 'The *friendliest* of the people interviewing me...', but 'The Managing Director treated me *the most friendlily*.'

The main exceptions are some of those words which retain the adjectival form as adverbs: 'He tried *harder* than ever' or 'She stayed *longest* in the house.' This probably increases the difficulties with distinguishing between adjectives and adverbs. Use of the *-er* and *-est* forms is incorrect with most adverbs, so that we have: 'a *brighter* (adjective) light', but 'The sun shone *more brightly* (adverb)'. It is very understandable (but, sadly, incorrect) to use *quicker* as an adverb on the analogy of *faster*:

> He drove *faster* in practice.
> He drove *more quickly* in practice.

Well and *badly* take the same comparative forms as *good* and *bad*: *better/best, worse/worst*.

However, with few exceptions, adverbial comparisons proceed on straightforward lines:

> Mrs Aston answered the questions *more successfully* than her husband.
> The Bradford factory was working the *most efficiently*.
> The new director coped with the problems *more ably* than his predecessor.
> When I returned, the dog greeted me *most affectionately* of all.

Test yourself

6.1 In the following sentences pick out all the words and phrases modifying nouns and divide them into four categories: **adjectives**, **participles** used as adjectives, **nouns** used as adjectives, adjectival **phrases**:

   a   The receptionist at the front desk greeted me politely.

   b   We waited in the empty theatre car park.

   c   Don't put the red shirt in with the other clothes.

   d   The new exhibition gives a fascinating glimpse of life in the 19th century.

   e   Even people at the back could see the large television on the stage.

   f   The peace-keeping force had to separate the warring factions.

   g   Separated from his parents, the small boy began to cry.

   h   Shall I meet you in the wine bar?

   i   We were looking at preliminary designs for a new advanced combat aircraft.

   j   I chose this dress in preference to that.

6.2 In the following sentences all adjectives and adjectival phrases are in italics. Can you decide which are modifying a noun in the usual way and which are intensive complements?

   a   The *big red* bus struggled up the hill in *low* gear.

   b   The house *in the valley* seemed *lonely* and *desolate*.

   c   I was *sure* that the lights were *green*.

   d   The runner seemed to be *at his last gasp*.

   e   The *bright* sun *in her eyes* caused *major* problems *with driving*.

   f   I am delighted to say that you are the *successful* applicant.

6.3 Check whether the following sentences use the comparative and superlative of adjectives correctly:

   a   The efforts of the staff ensured that the loss was *littler than last year.*

   b   Our Dalmatian received a prize for the *Best in Show.*

   c   It is difficult to say which of the two favourites will be *most comfortable* on the wet track.

   d   I feel *fitter than I did* last week.

   e   When we heard that Julie was seriously ill, I felt even *desperater* than before.

   f   Given a choice of Florida, California or New York, Ravinder chose the *latter*.

   g   Why not sit in the *most comfortable chair*?

h The *most fast run* came from the *youngest of the two teenagers* taking part.

6.4 Rewrite the following passage, with more precise replacements for *bad* and *nice:*

I was suffering from a bad knee, so it was nice that Sue should offer me a lift. There was bad traffic in the city centre and we were afraid we would be late which would have been really bad, but we hit a nice stretch of road and kept up a nice average speed until we reached Sutton. There's a bad turn just before the college where they have set up temporary traffic lights, but a nice man waved us through. At the gates we had some difficulty because the direction signs were really bad, but we found a nice parking space and got into the lecture in nice time.

6.5 Check that you can tell the difference between adjectives and adverbs by identifying the italicized words in the following sentences. Remember that an adverb can modify many other things besides a verb:
a *Evidently* we have lost a *crucial* document again.
b I was *afraid* to confront the *violently angry* mob.
c The *new* model worked *very well.*
d *Never* have I seen such an *attractive* picture.
e When did you see such dreadfully slow service?
f Her charm is *only superficial.*
g The *chief* minister was *present.*
h The road seemed *longer* on the way back.
i I should have waited *longer* for the bus.
j The *final* stage was *dangerously fast.*

Having identified adjectives and adverbs, try to decide exactly what function each is taking in the sentence.

6.6 Form adverbs from the following adjectives:

happy	subtle	good	helpful
final	hard	basic	friendly
incorrigible	gay	shrill	definite

6.7 Pick out the adverbs, adverbial phrases and adverbial clauses in the following sentences, classify them as adverbs, phrases or clauses, and explain their functions in the examples:
a The Government withdrew support suddenly and for no good reason.

b Indeed, when the news broke, we were incredibly unprepared.

c If I take the job, I shall have to travel over 50 miles each day.

d We did not agree to start work tomorrow.

e Regularly, on the 15th, you will receive your monthly salary.

f In the event of fire, gather immediately in the car park.

g Slowly I returned home.

h Where the M1 meets the M25, there is often a hold-up.

i The result was desperately close.

j From the balcony there is a much better view of the cathedral.

6.8 Many (not all) of the following sentences contain errors relating to adverbs or adverbial phrases or clauses. Can you detect and correct them?

a We need to finally put an end to the rumours.

b The group played bad at its first gig.

c The group was bad at its first gig.

d At the end of the day the journey yesterday morning took twice the normal time.

e I hoped to despite the opposition win the election.

f Hopefully we will make the rest of the deliveries tomorrow.

g When questioned by police, she acted stupid.

h I only found the handbag and umbrella.

Function words: prepositions and conjunctions

In this chapter you will learn:

▶ *how prepositions and conjunctions fill an essential role*

▶ *the meanings of different prepositions – and possible areas of confusion*

▶ *the difference between co-ordinating and subordinating conjunctions.*

What function?

Though the division is not always clear-cut, it is possible to divide words into **lexical words** and **function words**. Lexical words which are subject to more change than function words have a meaning in their own right. If we hear the word *telephone*, we have an immediate image, though we don't know what is happening with the telephone or even what type of instrument it is. Similarly with *dance* or *red*: our images are imperfect and will differ from those of other people, but they do exist.

Function words are what is termed a **closed class**, far less numerous and subject to much less change. The meaning of function words is defined by their relationship to other words: it is hard to have an image of *but, between* or *upon*. This chapter deals with **prepositions** and **conjunctions** whose job or function is to join together words or parts of a sentence.

As so often, the meaning of these words is best approached via their Latin origins. **Preposition** means 'placed in front of': the prefix *pre-* meaning 'before' added to *position* – where something is placed. So a preposition goes in front of a noun, pronoun or noun phrase to establish its relationship with all or part of the rest of the sentence. **Conjunction means** 'joined together': think of *junction* as in 'road junction' and add the prefix *con-* meaning 'with' or 'together'. The role of a conjunction is to join together clauses, though *and* in particular also joins together single words and phrases.

Prepositions

A preliminary warning that prepositions can also serve as other parts of speech is in order. Think of the words *down* or *on*:

> I am waiting for the *down* train. (adjective modifying noun *train*)
> The elm tree has blown *down*. (adverb modifying verb *blown*)
> Sandra came running *down* the lane. (preposition linking *lane* to the sentence)
> Can you find the *on* switch? (adjective modifying noun *switch*)
> The Blackpool Illuminations will be turned *on* next week.
> (adverb modifying verb *turned*)
> Tom kept treading *on* his partner's toes. (preposition connecting *his partner's toes* to the main statement)

TYPES OF PREPOSITION

Prepositions can be divided into three categories:

1 **Simple prepositions:** The basic form of the preposition, a single morpheme, is usually a short word, often of one syllable, sometimes of two: *in, on, by, through, against, between.*

2 **Compound prepositions:** These are made up of two simple prepositions, sometimes joined into one word (*into, onto*), sometimes still two words (*out of* almost merges into one word, but there are also more cumbersome examples like *in between*).

3 **Complex prepositions:** A preposition with a single meaning may be made up of two or three words: *as well as, except for, in favour of.*

Insight

Prepositions, it is said, cannot end a sentence. Winston Churchill was moved to indignation at this petty-fogging rule: 'This is the sort of nonsense up with which I will not put!' Of course prepositions usually do not finish a sentence, simply because they go in front of something – which means, obviously, that there is something after them. However, sentences are often turned round with the form of questions or subordinate clauses. 'I am going *to* Scotland' has the preposition before the noun, but use a subordinate clause or a question and everything changes:

I have no idea where he is going *to*.

Where are you going *to*?

Unless you fancy the old-fashioned *whither* (I have no idea whither he is going), what else can you use? Admittedly more formal reporting is helped by the use of preposition + *which*:

The Minister made a speech *in which* she considered the main advantages of her policy.

PREPOSITIONS WITH PRONOUNS

The noun or pronoun following a preposition is technically the object of the preposition and is therefore in the objective case, but nouns, of course, remain unchanged. It is, however, important to remember that any pronoun so used must be in the objective case:

I sold my car to *him* yesterday.
She walked past *me* without speaking.
I've brought the children's presents for *them*.

This becomes less straightforward when there are two objects to a preposition, but the rule still applies:

> *Between you and me* I don't know what I'm going to do.
> Some old friends are here *with my husband and me*.

The grammatical construction remains the same whether or not there is an extra noun or pronoun. This error most often occurs with using *I* instead of *me*, perhaps because of a lingering sense that it is more polite, but simply remember that, because you would write or say 'for *me*' and 'to *me*' you must also use 'for *my wife and me*' and 'to *my friends and me*'.

The same applies to *who/whom*, which you might use in questions or subordinate clauses. In more formal style, you should write:

> Nick was the guest *with whom* we had the greatest difficulty.
> *At whom* exactly is this attack directed?

In informal English the pronoun can disappear (Nick was the guest we had the greatest difficulty with), but, if a pronoun is used, *whom* is, strictly speaking, correct. You will have to judge the context and your audience for yourself: you may feel that '*Whom* is this attack directed at?' sounds pompously formal in some settings.

PREPOSITIONS IN DIALECT AND SLANG

Prepositions are often affected by regional variations, though it must be said that some variant usages are very difficult to attribute to a specific region and may be more effectively seen as general colloquial forms. Look at the following examples:

> Have you seen the new shop *up* the village?
> I'm just going *down* the supermarket.
> It's more difficult nowadays for children to play out *on/of* a night.
> Becky's *out* the back making up the deliveries.

Some of these can be more economical usages than the 'correct' preposition. *Up* and *down* are used in place of *at*, *in* or *to*, but can also convey a sense of direction, though this is sometimes metaphorical, *up* being applied to a more important place. *Out* replaces a compound preposition, probably *out at*.

Of and *on* (which here are used instead of *at*) are sometimes interchangeable in colloquial English. Probably the form *some on 'em* for *some of them* is based around easier pronunciation; it is not normally heard with the full word *them*. On the other hand *of* can replace *on* in phrases like *of a Sunday*. You will notice a tendency in informal speech to add the indefinite article to prepositional phrases of time: *on a night* for *at night, of a Sunday* for *on Sunday.*

Though not necessarily completely national, all the above can be heard in many different areas. Other prepositional usages are more narrowly regional: *while* for *until* in parts of Yorkshire and Lancashire, *off of* in London and a whole series of localized variants on *to, at* or *in.* All these examples are normal and understandable in speech, but to be avoided in formal writing. Furthermore the variations demonstrate how difficult it can be to attribute a precise and fixed meaning to a preposition.

Insight

British and American English are often separated by prepositional use. Let us examine three cases. The British say, 'talk to', the Americans 'talk *with*'. Pleasingly people are realizing that the use of one or the other can mark a subtle difference in the conversation, *with* being more two-sided. Another recent development is the use in Britain of *through to* in terms of time or place ('I'm going *through to* Hereford' or 'We're staying open *through to* 9 o'clock') which combines the British *to* and the American *through* in the same situation. If you wish to change something, in Britain you appeal or protest *against* it. In the United States these verbs are transitive: you *appeal a verdict* or *protest the tax* – is this spreading into Britain and, if not yet, when will it do so?

SOME MEANINGS OF PREPOSITIONS

A preposition serves to establish the relationship between a noun/ pronoun/noun clause or phrase and the rest of the sentence. So, despite some blurring of margins of meaning, it is useful to examine some of these relationships:

▶ **Place and time**

Oddly enough the same prepositions can serve for both:

   I'll meet you *in* the evening *at* the restaurant.
   I'll meet you *in* town *at* 8 o'clock.

In the first case *in* refers to time, *at* to place. In the second case the opposite is true. A few examples of other prepositions in this category are *outside, near, beyond* and *across* (place), *before, after* and *during* (time) and *by* (both – *by the door, by next week*). Prepositions of place are perhaps the best examples of the power of the preposition in dictating meaning. Take the sentence, 'I put the parcel (*preposition*) the table' and think of the differences between using *by, on, under, next to, behind*, etc.

▶ Possession

Among the most commonly used prepositions is *of*, but the idea of possession or belonging covers a wide field. Think of the differences in meaning between 'the first act *of* the play', 'built *of* brick', 'the symphonies *of* Beethoven', 'a picture *of* happiness' and '*of* dubious origins'.

▶ Cause, reason, etc.

Obviously the compounds *because of* and *owing to* bulk large here, but there is also *through*, yet another preposition with widely diverse meanings: 'I lost the job *through* no fault of my own' (reason), 'Have you been *through* the Channel Tunnel?' (place), 'I stayed awake all *through* the night' (time).

▶ Instrument of action

The prepositions *by* and *with* can indicate who or what did an action, particularly valuable with the passive voice (The Arts Centre was opened *by* the Mayor), but also in sentences such as 'I cut myself *with* a knife.'

Insight

In addition to their variety of basic usages (for example, *by* as time, place and instrument) prepositions can present the same meaning personally and externally – or literally and metaphorically. Who or what did you leave the party with: your husband, a headache or a sense of relief? What were you in last evening: your car, doubt or a foul temper? This can be exploited to humorous effect by what is called zeugma: 'The Chairman left the meeting in a Rolls-Royce and a state of panic.' If you are being serious, avoid this, either by repeating *in* instead of using *and* or, where possible, finding another preposition.

PREPOSITIONS IN REGULAR CONSTRUCTIONS

Many nouns, verbs and adjectives regularly take set prepositions. You have an *aversion to* guilt which is *preferable to* being *ashamed of* your actions and you are to be *congratulated on* your *tendency to* retain *confidence in* yourself, *opposite to* many people today.

Inevitably there are some complications here. Many people say *different to* when the 'correct' form is *different from*. However, it is difficult to disapprove when *different to* was the accepted form in Victorian times and when the American *different than* is making inroads into English usage. For the moment, however, *different from* is safest.

Then there are words which take different prepositions depending on the connection being established. A number of *to/for* usages relate *to* a person, principle or institution *for* a particular reason or act: we might apologize *to* somebody *for* what we have done or be responsible *to* the management *for* one area of production.

Other interesting examples include:

▶ **inform of/on:** *Of* relates to the information given ('I have informed the police *of* the break-in'); *on* refers to incriminating someone ('Fortunately a member of the public informed *on* the criminal') or a general area of knowledge ('Keep me informed *on* the case').

▶ **sympathy for/with:** *With* is used for a sharing of opinions and feelings ('We have sympathy *with* the view that a new transport policy is essential'); *for* most often relates to a person and expresses sorrow rather than agreement ('Of course we feel sympathy *for* the victims').

▶ **free(dom) from/of/with:** *From* and *of* overlap somewhat, but *free from* is most often used of escaping an actual unpleasant situation (*free from* prison/poverty/pursuit) and *of* most often suggests the area in which the freedom operates (*freedom of* choice/conscience/religion). *Free with*, however, suggests unwarranted liberty: 'He made *free with* my hospitality.'

▶ **agree to/with:** Traditionally we are said to agree *to* a thing or *with* a person. This is not strictly true. If we agree *with* a person or principle or action, we think that it is a good thing. If we agree *to* a proposal, we accept that it will be put into practice, not quite the same: 'Although I *agree with* your plans for redevelopment, I cannot *agree to* the proposal to include them on next year's budget.'

▶ **authority on/over:** This relates to two different meanings of authority. It can mean someone very well informed ('Professor Butt is an *authority on* ancient Indian manuscripts') and a position of power ('In the colonial period European nations claimed *authority over* most of Africa').

Conjunctions

The function of conjunctions is to join together clauses into **compound** or **complex** sentences and you will probably need to turn to Chapter 9 for details of how they fulfil this function. The actual form of conjunctions is relatively simple. Two forms of conjunction exist: **co-ordinating conjunctions** and **subordinating conjunctions.** Co-ordinating conjunctions *conjoin* clauses which are equal or *co-ordinate*, most obviously in the case of the conjunction *and*:

> I drove into town *and* met Mrs Ross.

Each half is equal; no attention is focused on one part at the expense of the other. When there is a different subject in the second half, some writers prefer to add a comma:

> I drove into town, *and* the traffic was dreadful.

There are few co-ordinating conjunctions, each providing a very basic guide to the relationship between the two halves: *and* tells us nothing more than both halves took place, *but* implies that the second clause is a contrast, *so* suggests that it is predictable and *or* expresses alternatives:

> The weather improved, *but* the game was called off.
> The weather deteriorated, *so* the game was called off.
> The weather must improve *or* the game will be called off.

Insight

A common feature of style, colloquially acceptable, but to be avoided formally, is the misuse of *try and*.... This is correct in '*try and* try again' and when *try* (with the meaning *make an effort*) needs no qualification and the sense moves on to another verb: 'At least with Jane you can be sure that she will *try* and not give up at the first problem.' Where *try and*... is not correct is when you hope to achieve what is expressed in the following verb. In that case *try to* (using the infinitive) is correct: 'I'm going to *try to* fix the guttering', 'We all should *try to* do everything we can for the homeless.'

TWO FINAL NOTES ON CO-ORDINATING CONJUNCTIONS

This section deals particularly with conjunctions in their function of joining together clauses. However, *and*, *or* and *but* (as in 'slow, *but* sure') can also join together words or phrases. This is still regarded as a conjunctional usage. *So*, as in *so near and yet* (a less used conjunction) *so far*, can also be used as an adverb.

Over-use of *and* can be a weakness of style. *And* tells us nothing about the relationship between the units on each side of it, with resulting sloppiness of expression. Generally you should avoid more than one *and* (in its function of joining clauses) in a sentence without some deliberate reason. On the other hand, lists of clauses can be effectively dramatic or humorous, usually saving *and* for the final junction, just as in lists of words:

The saucepan was boiling over, the cat had a half-eaten chicken leg on the floor, the children's castle had collapsed all over the hallway, the milkman stood on the doorstep still waiting to be paid, *and* Mrs Merrick sat at the kitchen table engrossed in her latest Mills and Boon romance.

SUBORDINATING CONJUNCTIONS

Subordinating conjunctions not only link parts of a sentence, but have meanings, sometimes very precise meanings, of their own, in introducing subordinate clauses, usually **subordinate adverbial clauses**:

> Time: *after, before, since, when, as, whenever*, etc.
> Place: *where*
> Manner: *as*
> Reason: *because, as, since*.
> Possibility: *if* (positive), *unless* (negative)
> Contrast/concession: *though, although*.
> Purpose/result: *(in order)(so) that* (positive), *lest* (negative)

That is also commonly used to introduce subordinate noun clauses: 'She told me that I must work harder.'

Insight

You will notice that many subordinating conjunctions can operate as adverbs or prepositions as well: 'You should have told me that before (adverb)'/'You should have told me that before (conjunction) I bought the car.' Also there is an overlap of function in the cases of *as* and *since* which can refer to both time and reason: 'As we parked the car in the forecourt, we might as well wait here' (reason)/'As we parked the car in the forecourt, the landlord started shouting at us' (time).

THE FUNCTION OF SUBORDINATING CONJUNCTIONS

These meanings make the function of subordinating conjunctions different from that of co-ordinating conjunctions.

The subordinating conjunction:

▶ connects together two clauses;

▶ dictates which one is the main focus of our attention;

▶ specifies the relationship of the other clause to that main clause.

If you take the two statements, *Judith finished reading her book* and *Judith came over for a coffee*, you can join them in many different ways, the most obvious and least interesting being by placing *and* in the middle. But what is the difference between the two following sentences?

> When Judith finished reading her book, she came over for a coffee.
> Before Judith came over for a coffee, she finished reading her book.

In terms of meaning, there is no difference, but the first example makes coming for a coffee the main statement and the second makes reading the book the centre of attention: *when* and *before* are subordinating conjunctions introducing the less important part (a **subordinate adverbial clause**). The choice of which is the most important clause helps indicate what is the theme of your narration. You might therefore expect the first example to continue '...She stayed for an hour and told me about her problems at work', whereas the second might go on to tell us about what the book was and how much she enjoyed it.

As well as directing our attention to one part of the sentence, the subordinating conjunction establishes a relationship between the clauses which may alter the whole meaning of the sentence. What does it tell us if we insert different conjunctions between *I won't go to the cinema*, and *There is a horror film showing?*

	unless	
	although	
I won't go to the cinema	*when*	there is a horror film showing.
	because	
	until	

Because and *although* suggest that you are referring to this week only: *because* means that you avoid horror films; *although* means that you would like to see the horror film, but don't wish to go for some other reason. The other three refer to your regular policy: *when* means that you refuse to watch horror films; *unless* that you watch nothing else; and *until* that you watch nothing else, but the cinema never shows them! By employing different subordinating conjunctions, you are thus able to comment on the characters and situation as well as effecting a grammatical junction.

Test yourself

7.1 All of the words in italics in the following passage can be used as prepositions. Decide which ones are actually prepositions and see if you can identify which parts of speech the others are:

> Travelling *to* London, Jamie and Rebecca decided *to* use the train. They enquired *about* the availability of tickets, *but* were told that, *during* the Christmas period, many trains were full. This was a possibility which they had not thought *about* and, *after* he had put *down* the telephone, Jamie moaned, 'Why didn't we think *of* this *before*?'. Rebecca looked *at* him *in* despair and said, 'You're not giving *up* so easily, are you? Look: the bus terminus is right *by* the railway station. *In* a minute or two, when I've put my lenses *in*, I'll go *across* and check the trains and coaches *at* the same time. Don't look so *down*.' Jamie cheered *up* and agreed *to* her suggestion. He even offered *to* keep an eye *on* the dinner and take it *out of* the oven *at* one o'clock.

7.2 Insert the correct prepositions in the following sentences. Most of them will not have been considered in the preceding pages:

 a We must protect children ... injury.
 b This book is similar ... the last one I read.
 c Mrs Arthurs had a grudge ... her neighbour.
 d My brother is an authority ... non-league football.
 e Many of us are not averse ... occasional over-indulgence.
 f I congratulate you ... your academic achievements during the last year.
 g Young people like to feel that they are independent ... their parents.
 h The local operatic society is dependent ... its patrons for success.
 i My views are opposite ... yours.
 j It is all too easy to digress ... the subject.
 k The Prince of Wales is heir ... the throne.
 l The name of the firm should be synonymous ... quality.
 m The library encourages a thirst ... knowledge.
 n I cannot agree ... the closure of the Library every Thursday.
 o Such a proposal is typical ... the present council.
 p Temporary closure is preferable ... huge losses.
 q Brothers and sisters often vie ... each other for attention.
 r The management is not conscious ... any failings in customer service.
 s She has a taste ... poetry.
 t This sponge has a taste ... ginger.

7.3 Decide whether each of the following sentences has an error involving a preposition:

a Her sister looked quite different to her.

b This is the artist who we were telling you about.

c His paintings really appeal to Sue and I.

d Are you coming down the playing fields?

e The herd is guaranteed free of infection.

7.4 Identify the subordinating conjunctions in the following sentences and decide what function they have:

a When the flowers are in bloom, the garden looks wonderful.

b I told him that I would come round after.

c Unless I am much mistaken, there will be an election next year.

d If governments take no action, the consequences of global warming will be disastrous.

e The police have found out where he is.

f Where the council offices used to be, they are building a car park.

g Our family has lived here since the 18th century.

h Since the management announced the closure next month, audiences have doubled.

i We might as well leave since you are not interested in our proposals.

j Mr Morrison refused to invest in the stock market lest he should lose his money.

k If Yasmin is your personal assistant, she should be able to deal with it.

l He gets up when it suits him.

m The traffic lights always change to red as I approach.

n My contract runs until the end of next year.

o Until I am confident that you are up to the job, I cannot give you a permanent contract.

7.5 Insert as many different subordinating conjunctions as you can into the following sentences to give different meanings. Place the conjunctions at the beginning or in the middle and alter the order of the clauses if you wish:

a Ms Christophers received a rise...She planned to look for a new job.

b The police started interviewing a new suspect...A new series of break-ins occurred.

c The aeroplane was due for take-off...the cabin crew went through safety procedure.

d Don't open up a new till...There are more than five in the queue.

e Mandy decided to go to the party...Craig was supposed to be there.

Phrases and clauses

In this chapter you will learn:

- ▶ *the essential difference between a phrase and a clause*
- ▶ *how to identify phrases (and some clauses) with individual parts of speech*
- ▶ *the form of a main clause and the functions of subordinate clauses.*

The difference between phrases and clauses

A phrase in normal parlance is any group of words combined together. Its meaning in grammatical terms is very similar, but with one exception: any group of words containing a finite verb, with subject either real or implied, is defined as a **clause**. (The question of non-finite clauses can be left until later in the chapter.) A clause can be an entire sentence in itself or the main element of a longer sentence or an equal element in a sentence or a minor (**subordinate**) part of a sentence. Phrases and subordinate clauses function as a specific part of speech and are identified as such. All of this will be examined in more detail later in the chapter and Chapter 9, but a few examples may help at this stage:

> *The builders start work tomorrow.* (a sentence of one single clause)
> *Tomorrow the builders start work* and I have to catch the early train to the office. (two equal clauses joined by *and*)
> *When the builders start work*, I'll have to set the alarm for 7.00. (a subordinate clause functioning as an adverb)
> *Having the builders in* is a nuisance. (a phrase functioning as a noun – subject)
> A lorry *with a load of bricks* has arrived. (a phrase functioning as an adjective – modifying *lorry*), etc.

HOW BIG IS A PHRASE?

This is an unanswerable question. Although a clause contains a key element lacking in a phrase (a finite verb), a phrase can be much longer than a clause, as long as you like and your reader/listener will tolerate:

> *When summer comes...* (clause)
> *In the months of July and August, with extended holidays from work, excursions to the seaside, foreign travel, long sunny days, Test matches and Wimbledon...* (phrase)

At the other extreme there is a tendency among modern grammarians to classify everything, no matter how short, as a phrase: some contemporary grammars designate a group of words or a single word as a phrase. This does not seem particularly helpful: a noun phrase is so called as it fulfils the function of a noun, so to call a single noun a noun phrase seems to be taking us for a second lap on the same circuit. No matter: the important thing is to identify the functions of phrases. In the following sentences the italicized phrases form the subject of the sentence; all are therefore **nouns**:

> *The shop* is open today. (noun or, in contemporary terminology, noun phrase)
> *Hudson's fine new shop* is opening today. (noun phrase)
> *The new shop* <u>in the High Street</u> is opening today. (noun phrase: the underlined section can also be defined as an adjective phrase modifying *shop*, just as the adjective *new* does)

NOUN PHRASES

All phrases assume the functions of the part of speech they are identified with, so for noun phrases key functions include subject, object and complement of a sentence. A noun phrase will customarily include a noun or noun equivalent (pronoun or gerund). The most useful definition of the possible elements in a noun phrase comes in contemporary terminology, though one might take issue with the inclusion of **head word** or **head word plus determiner** as sufficient to form a phrase.

The development of a phrase is as follows:

▶ **head word:** the basic noun/noun equivalent which in the case of plurals, pronouns, gerunds and proper nouns can be used on its own: *women, he, reading* or *Manchester.*

▶ **determiners:** other nouns usually need a determiner which is likely to be the definite or indefinite article or a demonstrative adjective: *the road, a car, that coat.*

▶ **modifiers:** you may need to add one or more modifiers (adjectives/nouns or verbs used adjectivally): *the ring road, a new car, that heavy coat.*

▶ **qualifiers:** a phrase added after the noun to modify or qualify it further, also fulfilling an adjectival function: *the ring road under construction, a new car with power steering, that heavy coat in the window.*

▶ **pre-determiners:** it is possible to modify the determiner: '*Half the size*' is very different from '*twice the size*'.

A noun phrase with all five elements in place might read:

> *All* (pre-determiner) *the* (determiner) *tall* (modifier) *men* (head) *in the team* (qualifier)

But compare the two following sentences and you will see that the function is exactly the same as a single noun:

> The photographer asked *all the tall men in the team* to stand at the back.
> The photographer asked *Mark* to stand at the back.

Each is fulfilling the function of direct object of the verb *asked*.

Remember that, in traditional terminology, noun phrases can be formed with **gerunds** (the *-ing* form of the verb used as a noun), although these are alternatively known as **non-finite clauses:**

> *Reading private correspondence* is wrong. (subject)
> I really enjoyed *experimenting with a new recipe*. (direct object)

Insight

You will find references in this section which suggest that one phrase may be included within a different sort of phrase. Don't worry: this is perfectly true – and normal. Let us take the example of noun and adjectival phrases: a noun is often accompanied by a modifying adjective and together they make up the full noun phrase (*the red bus*). It is exactly the same with adjective phrases as with adjectives. The noun phrase *dozens of people in fancy dress* includes the noun *people* which is then modified by the adjective phrase *in fancy dress*. If we take the noun phrase, *the court of the Emperor of China*, a studious survey could reveal as many as three other noun and adjective phrases contained within it: *of China* (adjective), *the Emperor of China* (noun), *of the Emperor of China* (adjective).

VERB PHRASES

Quite simply those verbs consisting of more than one word because of the use of **auxiliary** and/or **modal verbs,** are referred to as **verb phrases**. The verbs are italicized in the following examples:

> The big bay horse *led* the field.
> The big bay horse *was leading* the field.

The second example may be referred to as a verb phrase – very straightforward, though it is as well to remember that verb phrases can be surprisingly long:

> We had all thought that the coastguard *would have been trying to rescue* the crew since Monday.

Insight

You might think that both the terms *verb phrase* and *phrasal verb* would mean a group of words fulfilling the function of a verb – and you would be right. However, this does not mean that they are the same! A phrasal verb is one which consists of a verb and an adverb, with a regular set meaning. If you write 'The horses had to jump off against the clock', *jump off* is a phrasal verb, with an exact meaning that you do not find in a sentence such as 'I was afraid to jump off the diving board'. Other examples are *lay off* (workers), *turn out* (to support), *turn over* (sums of money), etc. These are always two separate words, but, if there is a noun equivalent, it is often hyphenated or a single word.

ADJECTIVAL PHRASES

These can be divided into three categories (plus single adjectives which some contemporary grammars regard as adjective phrases):

1 **adjective phrases proper** which all grammar systems acknowledge as such. These usually use adjectives with extra modifiers (a *joyfully triumphant* expression, the *carefully restored* brickwork) or intensifiers (*very fine* lace, an *extremely dry* summer).

2 **participial phrases** which are now sometimes regarded as clauses, but according to traditional grammar are phrases. Remember that a participial (adjective) phrase and a gerund-based noun phrase may look identical; only the function makes a difference. '*Whistling a happy tune* (gerund – noun phrase) can cheer you up'/'A nun *whistling a happy tune* (participle – adjective phrase) comes as a surprise.'

3 **prepositional phrases** which can be so termed because they are introduced by a preposition, but which can also be named according to the part of speech they replace. *In a bad mood* or *outside the gate* are prepositional phrases, but in the following examples they are used adjectivally: 'Mr Stevens *in a bad mood* was someone to avoid', 'The postman *outside the gate* refused to come in while the dog was loose'.

ADVERBIAL PHRASES

A group of words which refers to such things as the time, manner, place and cause of the events in the sentence is an **adverbial phrase**. Of course many of these can be categorized as **prepositional phrases**, but if you look at the following examples you will see that they perform an adverbial function:

The painters came back from their dinner *fairly quickly.*
(adverbial phrase of time consisting of two adverbs)
The painters came back from their dinner *in about half an hour.*
(adverbial phrase of time/prepositional phrase)
Pirates were supposed to hide their treasure *extremely carefully.*
(adverbial phrase of manner consisting of adverbs)
Pirates were supposed to hide their treasure *with extreme secrecy
and cunning.* (adverbial phrase of manner/ prepositional phrase)

Main clauses

Though we tend to use the term **grammar** for the form of
interconnections between words, sentence construction, etc., the
correct term for the organization of a sentence is **syntax**. The most
important syntactical unit is the **main (or principal) clause.** All
sentences have at least one, some sentences have a main clause
and nothing else and it constitutes the smallest unit that makes
syntactical sense on its own.

In defining the form of a main clause, traditional and contemporary
terminology are in agreement to an unusual degree. Traditionally it
consists of (parts in parentheses not always present):

subject	+	predicate
noun or noun equivalent	+	**verb (direct object or complement)**
		(indirect object) (adverbial
		qualification)

Contemporary grammars are more likely to phrase it thus:

subject + predicator: i.e. verb + (complement) + (adverbials)

The **predicat(e)(or)** is what is said about the subject: the definitions
vary in so far as this refers to the verb only or the full gamut of
his/her/its action/condition. The more modern description defines
the **complement** as being in three forms: **intensive complement**
(the traditional complement), **objective complement** (object) and
adverbial complement (adverbs and adverb phrases). Logically
enough the word complement is applied to anything that is
necessary to complete the meaning of the clause. More examination
of direct objects and complements can be found in Chapter 5.

SUBJECT AND PREDICATE

The **subject** is the doer of the action, the sufferer of the action in
a passive sentence or the person/thing whose condition is being
stated. Remember that, as the above section and the later section

on **noun clauses** show, the subject can be extended through many words.

The **verb** similarly can be more than one word, with the use of auxiliaries and modals. The only qualification necessary is that it must be a **finite (tensed)** verb. Interestingly the only case where the part of speech and part of the sentence/clause share an identical name, it is not difficult to recognize.

If the verb is **intransitive**, the predicate can stop there. If it is **transitive**, we need to follow it with a **direct object (objective complement)**, the person/thing who suffers the action. If it is a **verb of being**, we need to follow it with a **complement (intensive complement)** to complete the meaning. Thus the simplest forms of main clauses may be exemplified as follows:

> *The river* (subject) *flows* (predicate – verb only).
> *Mrs Beeton* (subject) *wrote a famous book* (predicate – verb + direct object).
> *Charles Dickens* (subject) *was a distinguished author* (predicate – verb + complement).

THE INDIRECT OBJECT

Though any of the nouns in a sentence may be accompanied with adjectives/adjective phrases, there are only two more parts (both optional) of the main clause: the **indirect object** and the **adverbial qualification**, both of which can be defined in terms of complements.

Some actions can have two different forms of object. If you give a pound to a charity collector, whom or what is your action done to: the pound or the collector? Both, of course, one experiencing it directly, the other experiencing it indirectly by receiving it. So, in the following sentence, *a pound* is the direct object and *the collector* the indirect object:

> I gave the collector a pound.

Look at the following examples to reinforce your awareness of the difference between **direct** and **indirect** objects:

> The RSPCA awarded *Susan* (indirect) *a medal* (direct).
> My wife sent *me* (indirect) *a message* (direct).
> He accidentally struck *his friend* (indirect) *a blow on the face* (direct).

The last example shows that the use of the word 'indirect' can be misleading. If the sentence had read 'He struck his friend', *friend* would have been the direct object.

ADVERBIAL QUALIFICATIONS

These may take the form of single adverbs or adverbial phrases, but the main distinction is between those that are necessary to complete the sense of the verb (**adverbial complements**) and those that simply add information to a verb whose sense is complete. This information may possibly be essential to the understanding of the sentence, but not to the completion of the verb. Look at the slightly different functions of *in the corner* (in all cases adverbial) in the following sentences:

> The table is *in the corner.*
> We placed the sideboard *in the corner.*
> He is quite happy *in the corner.*

In all the sentences the phrase is important, but only in the first is it used as a complement. In the second it is an adverbial qualification in a sentence where a transitive verb takes a direct object (*sideboard*). In the third, the other example of a verb of being, the adjectival *quite happy* serves as an intensive complement. So perhaps we should look at two examples (the first a verb of doing, the second a verb of being) of a main clause presenting all the features possible:

> *Late every afternoon* (adverbial qualification) *the delivery man from the bakery* (subject, including adjectival modification) *brought* (verb) *the corner shop* (indirect object) *a supply of cakes* (direct object).
> *Councillor Pilkington* (subject) *will become* (verb) *Chairman of the Ways and Means Committee* (intensive complement) *next year* (adverbial qualification).

MAIN CLAUSES AS QUESTIONS

All the above comments have been based on the **main clause as statement**. The essential structure remains unchanged for **questions**. Three very straightforward changes occur for questions:

1 If the verb is a single word, it must divide into two: *likes* into *does like*, *drive* into *do drive*, *found* into *did find*, etc.

2 The word order is then changed to place the subject after the first part of the verb. These two rules apply both when an interrogative word (*how, why, where*, etc.) is used and when the question is a simple one requiring a *Yes/No* answer.

3 The sentence ends with a question mark. Therefore '*I found* the tickets in the sideboard drawer' becomes:

Where *did you find* the tickets?

or

Did you find the tickets in the sideboard drawer?

COMMANDS AND EXCLAMATIONS

In the case of a **command** the subject of the main verb customarily disappears; the doer is the person addressed:

The staff (subject) always locked the shop door at 6 o'clock. (statement)
Lock the shop door at 6 o'clock. (command with *you* implied as subject)

Sometimes names may be used, but these are not really the subject of the sentence:

Jane, lock the shop door at 6 o'clock.
Jane is the person addressed (what in Latin is called the **vocative** case), not the subject: note the comma.

Exclamations are of no real grammatical importance. They fall into two categories:

1 Some phrases (*Heavens above! Goodness gracious me!* etc.) or even single words (*Jiminy! Crivvens!*) exist as 'set' exclamations, some with no life of their own outside this. These operate outside the general syntax of the piece. All you need to remember is that, from a punctuation point of view, they are normally regarded as full sentences and the exclamation mark is followed by a capital letter. (Some authors, understandably, go their own way on this.)

2 Anything (except a question) can become an exclamation and the punctuation mark simply tells us the tone of voice or emphasizes the drama/surprise/comedy of the situation. *Bring me my brief case at once!* suggests an angry boss or a dilatory employee, while *Aunt Louisa walked into the room!* makes sense if the assembled company thought she was stuck in a snowdrift in the Cairngorms or had just been slandering her character.

Subordinate clauses

Traditionally subordinate clauses, like phrases, bear the name of the parts of speech whose function they fulfil. The essential functions of a noun are to act as subject, object (direct or indirect) or intensive complement. So **a noun clause** is any group of words containing a finite verb that fulfils one of these functions. In just the same way a group of words containing a finite verb and modifying a noun can be seen as an **adjective clause**. Superficially they can look very similar:

> The umbrella *that I left at the airport* was never found. (adjective clause modifying *umbrella*)
> *That I left in a hurry* shows how boring the meeting was. (noun clause – subject)
> Didn't you know *that I left my umbrella behind*? (noun clause – direct object of *did know*)
> The reason I got out of the car park so easily was *that I left early*. (noun clause – intensive complement relating to subject 'reason').

Insight

Apart from the differences in method and terminology between traditional and contemporary grammarians, you will notice slight differences in terminology between people in basic agreement and even within the same book: it may well be that you will do so within this book. Reassuringly there is no difference between an **adverbial** and an **adverb** phrase or **adjective** and **adjectival** clause. Be warned, however, that the adjective from **noun** is **nominal**: if elsewhere you find references to a **nominal clause**, for instance, it simply means a **noun clause**.

RELATIVE CLAUSES

A different method of categorizing these subordinate clauses refers to the means by which they are linked to the rest of the sentence. Those clauses introduced by a **relative pronoun** (*who, which, that,* etc.) or a phrase including one (*by whom, for which*, etc.) are commonly called **relative clauses**.

Adnominal relative clauses modify a noun and are thus what are traditionally termed adjectival clauses:

The book *which I ordered* is out of stock.
The share offer *in which the company was interested* has now lapsed.

Nominal relative clauses take the role of nouns and can be distinguished from other relative clauses by the absence of any **antecedent** to the relative pronoun: that is, no word or phrase to which *that, which*, etc., can refer back (*The book* and *The share offer* are antecedents in the previous examples):

What interests me is how we can get our customers to remain loyal.

Sentential relative clauses refer, like adnominal clauses, to an antecedent, not merely to a noun or noun phrase, but to a larger block of words, often a whole sentence, possibly a whole paragraph:

Then Greenow ordered that the expedition should proceed up the Orinoco River without a support convoy, *which proved to be a fatal decision.*

Here the relative clause refers back not to *Greenow, the expedition, the support convoy* or even *the Orinoco River*, but to a statement recounting the action in no fewer than 16 words.

I was confined to bed with flu for four days, then found that the car battery was flat and the garage didn't open until the New Year, *as a result of which I missed all the celebrations.*

This time the antecedent is not much below 30 words and you will have noticed that the relative clause is introduced, not by a single relative pronoun, but by a phrase containing one: *as a result of which*.

NON-RESTRICTIVE RELATIVE CLAUSES

An interesting subdivision of adnominal relative clauses is into **restrictive** (or **defining**) and **non-restrictive clauses**. In practical terms it is mainly useful as a guide to punctuation. A restrictive clause gives key information which helps to define the noun it is modifying. For instance:

The youngsters *who play the Munchkins* will have to attend rehearsal every Tuesday.

Only those youngsters cast as Munchkins need attend: the relative clause defines which people the statement refers to. A non-restrictive relative clause adds interesting or useful information, but does not define the noun:

> Alex, *who is playing the Cowardly Lion*, says the show should be good.

The information is relevant, but we know who Alex is without the relative clause. Note that non-restrictive relative clauses are usually separated from the rest of the sentence by commas at each end – rather like a parenthesis.

A final pair of examples may clarify further:

> This is the young man *who has been offered the job*. (restrictive/defining)
> My cousin Hilary, *who has been offered a new job*, is coming to visit me next week. (non-restrictive)

Hilary is coming to visit you because she is your cousin, not because she has been offered a new job. The information about the job is not part of your **definition** of your visitor, simply an interesting and relevant piece of information about her.

NON-RELATIVE NOUN AND ADJECTIVE CLAUSES
However, though a majority of noun and adjective clauses are introduced by relative pronouns, many are introduced by **subordinating conjunctions** and may take exactly the same form as **adverbial clauses,** though functioning as nouns or adjectives.

Let us take, for example, the clause, *Where I spent my holidays*. Beginning with the subordinating conjunction *where*, it looks like an adverbial clause of place – and so it can be. Now let us examine three entirely different usages of the clause:

> *Where I spent my holiday*, there is a wide bay with hotels and casinos surrounding it.
> How do you know *where I spent my holiday?*
> The village *where I spent my holiday* is in the foothills of the Alpujarras.

The first is the predicted adverbial clause of place, but what of the other two? The second is the object of *know* and thus a **noun clause**. The third modifies the noun *village* and is an **adjective clause**. Examine the following examples referring to time:

> *When the fog lifts*, we shall be able to see the mountains. (adverbial)

When the fog lifts is the best time to cross. (noun)
The time *when the fog lifts* is a matter of guesswork. (adjective)

APPOSITIVE NOUN CLAUSES

The form of appositive clauses is very like that of relative clauses, but rather than relating to or modifying the noun, an appositive clause stands **in apposition to** it; in other words, it is equivalent in grammatical function and, to an extent, in meaning, referring to the same person or thing. Examples of nouns and phrases in apposition are:

Mr Bromilow, the Town Clerk
George Eliot, the famous Victorian novelist
the first supersonic airliner, Concorde.

In the each case the name and the phrase refer to the same person or thing. Two phrases can work in the same way:

The first speaker, the local secretary of the Townswomen's Guild.

Appositive clauses maintain this balance of equivalents:

I've just heard *the news* (1) *that the supermarket is closing down.* (2 – appositive clause).
My parents always gave me *strict instructions* (1) *that I should be careful crossing the road* (2 – appositive clause).

In each case 1 and 2 are equivalent; in the first example the sentence would read smoothly with either the noun or the appositive clause omitted. Compare that with the relative clause:

I've just heard the news *that Chris shouted up to me.*

The relative clause is an adjectival clause modifying the noun *news* which is essential to the meaning of the sentence.

ADVERBIAL CLAUSES

Earlier in this chapter the account of main clauses referred to adverbial qualifications. If these consist of single adverbs or adverbial phrases, they are part of the main clause. On the other hand the same function can be taken on by a clause which then becomes a **subordinate adverbial clause**. In traditional grammars the list of possible types of adverbial clause can be alarming and unnecessary, but the following list (which could be applied also to adverbial phrases) is probably helpful and sufficient:

time, place, manner, reason, purpose/result, possibility/condition, contrast/concession.

▶ Time, place and manner

These answer the big questions *When? Where? How?*. Adverbial clauses of **place** are usually introduced by the subordinating conjunction *where* (*wherever* can also be used, as can the almost archaic *whither* and *whence*, meaning *to where* and *from where*). Adverbial clauses of **time** may well use *when*, but there is a much greater range of possibilities: not only *whenever*, but also *after, before, as, since, whil(e)(st)*, etc:

> *Where the children used to play*, you can still see the swing.
> I will put the box *wherever you want it*.
> *As the ship lurched from side to side*, we all held on tightly.
> Mrs Jordan used to shudder *whenever she passed the scene of the crime*.
> *Before Sarfraz let the building to us*, he used it as a workshop.

Adverbial clauses of **manner** differ in that the key question word (*How?*) is not used as an introductory subordinating conjunction. Usually such clauses are introduced by *as* or some phrase using *as*:

> Jeremy climbed into the racing car *as if he had been doing it all his life*.
> The results came out *as I expected*.

Of course, the versatile *as* can also convey time or reason. You may also be puzzled by the statement that *how* is not used to introduce adverbial clauses: surely *how* can be a subordinating conjunction. True, but the clauses it introduces are *noun clauses*:

> *How it got here* is a mystery. (subject)
> The police inquiry established *how the weapon was concealed*. (direct object)

Insight

In the example given above, 'The results came out *as* I expected', many would say or write, 'The results came out *like* I expected.' Is this, then, not correct? Strictly speaking, *like* in this sense (it has many meanings) is a preposition and therefore precedes a noun or noun equivalent: 'The results were *like last year's*.' Again strictly speaking, you should write, 'Joe gets his books from the Library *like me*' or 'Joe gets his books from the Library *as I do*.' However, *like* is increasingly used instead of *as*, even in fairly formal situations, but *as* is still to be preferred in writing and very formal speech.

▶ Reason, purpose and result

These answer the questions *Why?* and *To what effect?* For **reason** you use the subordinating conjunctions *because* and (again) *as* and *since*. Clauses of **purpose** and **result** it is hardly necessary to separate: both deal with consequences and both use *so that* (*purpose* also uses *in order that*). Clauses of **purpose** imply more intent, but the distinction is not one to worry about. Both clauses of reason and clauses of purpose/result deal with Event B happening because of Event A. A subordinate clause of **reason** deals with Event A and accompanies a main clause telling of Event B. A clause of **purpose/result** deals with Event B and accompanies a main clause telling of Event A. Let us take the example of a river flooding (Event A) and a village being cut off (Event B). There are two opposite ways of expressing the same idea:

The village was cut off *because the river flooded*. (reason)
The river flooded *so that the village was cut off*. (purpose/ result)

The following example implies more intent (**purpose**):

Christina worked hard *so that she could pass her examinations*. (purpose/result)
Because Christina worked so hard, she passed her examinations. (reason)

There is a negative subordinating conjunction expressing purpose or result: *lest*. This sounds very formal and we often prefer the normal *so that* with an added negative, though it is a longer construction. The two following examples mean exactly the same thing:

We need to maintain the sea wall *lest there should be* (or *is*) *widespread flooding*.
We need to maintain the sea wall *so that there will not be widespread flooding*.

▶ Possibilities and contrasts

The other main forms of adverbial clause (traditionally known as clauses of **condition** and **concession**) are used in sentences dealing with things that might happen and things that contrast with each other. If you find the terms **possibility** and **contrast** more easily memorable, there is no reason why you should not use those instead. The subordinating conjunctions *if* and *unless* introduce **clauses of condition**, providing the positive and negative forms of what might happen:

If the Government calls an election (a possibility expressed in positive terms), the result is hard to predict.

Unless the Government calls an election (a possibility expressed negatively), the new Public Order Bill will be passed this year.

The subordinating conjunctions *though* and *although* introduce clauses (of **concession**) which are in contrast to the main clause. The co-ordinating conjunction *but* can perform the same function, but *though* and *although* focus attention on what is important in the sentence while *but* links equal halves. Let us imagine that we have two pieces of information about an employee: she has worked for the company for only a year and she is a senior manager. The short service and the senior position are in contrast, but the relationship can be expressed in at least two different ways:

Though she is a senior manager, she has only a year's experience.
Though she has only a year's experience, she is a senior manager.

Each uses the same information to give a different insight. The main statement in the first is that she is junior in time: in other words, although she is your boss, do not expect her to remember the supply problems you had three years ago or that scandal with the Managing Director and his last-but-two secretary. The second concentrates on her senior position: it is simple admiration or envy or a warning to the listener to be respectful even though he has more years' service.

▶ **Other adverbial clauses**

There are limits to how many terms it is productive to learn and the categories dealt with here cover most adverbial clauses, but you should be aware that some clauses do not fit into any of these groups, but are nonetheless adverbial clauses. You may wish to make a comparison, for instance:

Jackie filled her box with strawberries more quickly *than Helen did*.
I can sing better *than I can play the piano*.

The extra interest of this lies in the fact that we tend to omit the final verb if it refers to the same act as the main verb: 'Jackie filled her box with strawberries more quickly *than Helen*'. This presents no problem since, although grammatically it could mean that Jackie filled her box more quickly than she filled Helen with strawberries, this is evident nonsense.

However, what does it mean when you say, 'You kissed Tom more often *than Helen*?' Has the person spoken to kissed Tom more often than he/she has kissed Helen or more often than Helen has kissed Tom?

SUBORDINATE NON-FINITE CLAUSES

To the traditional grammarian the term 'non-finite clause' is a contradiction in terms: what makes a clause a clause is the presence of a finite verb. In a contemporary grammar, however, you are likely to encounter the terms **non-finite clauses** and **participial clauses**. The justification for this is that these 'clauses' often fulfil the same function as finite clauses, though in an abbreviated form.

For instance, 'The remote village *coming into view over the hill*' can be seen as a shortened version of the adjectival relative clause *which was coming into view over the hill*. With or without a conjunction, participial clauses can have the same effect as finite clauses:

> *Attempting to break the world record*, he overstepped the take-off board.
> *When making tea*, you should always warm the pot.

Generally speaking, it is a matter of no importance whether these are designated as clauses or phrases. What is important is that you recognize the difference between subordinate finite clauses and non-finite/participial 'clauses'. A subordinate finite clause has the essential features of a main clause (subject/predicate including finite verb); a non-finite clause lacks the finite verb and subject. Therefore it borrows both tense and subject from the rest of the sentence – and this can result in error:

> *When performing in pantomime*, actors like to gauge the mood of the audience.

In this case, the participial clause borrows subject (*actors*) and tense (present) from the main clause:

> *When performing in pantomime*, the audience mood is important to the actors.
> *When performing in pantomime*, there is sometimes a problem finding the right level of humour.

Participial clauses can so easily lead to the **dangling, hanging** or **misattached participle**. In the first case the clause has borrowed the wrong subject (*audience mood*); in the second there is no subject at all to borrow and the likeliest noun is the complement *problem*. With a finite clause (*When actors are performing in pantomime*), such problems do not occur.

HOW DO YOU USE A SUBORDINATE CLAUSE?

A subordinate clause is 'subordinate' or minor not because of what it lacks, but because of what it contains. Let us start with a main clause which could be a sentence in its own right:

Henry bought a new car three weeks ago.

As it is, that is a complete statement, but, if you add a subordinating conjunction, it becomes incomplete:

If/when/because/although Henry bought a new car three weeks ago...

All these leave the reader/listener saying, 'Then what?' All these make it clear that the main statement is elsewhere, though connected with Henry buying his new car:

Although Henry bought a new car three weeks ago, his business is in financial difficulties.
When Henry bought a new car three weeks ago, the garage offered him 0 per cent finance.

Similarly we might wish to concentrate on something else that Henry is doing, so we create a relative clause with the pronoun *who*:

Henry, *who bought a new car three weeks ago*, is now thinking about moving house.

These subordinate clauses are not complete sentences because words like *when, where, until, who* and *which* link them to the main statement. These words form bridges and, without the main clause on the other bank, they end midstream. Chapter 9 examines their part in **complex sentences**.

8.1 In each of the following sentences a group of words is italicized. Decide whether those words make up a phrase, a main clause or a subordinate clause. In the case of phrases and subordinate clauses, you could try to identify what type of phrase/clause each one is:

a The car *standing outside the house* belongs to our neighbours.

b *When Mrs Eustace rises to speak*, everyone listens.

c There is a wonderful collection of wildlife *in the woods below the castle*.

d *The fishing boat put to sea* and was soon surrounded by gulls.

e The coastguard always knew *what to do in an emergency*.

f *While collecting the rent money*, he narrowly avoided being attacked.

g *While collecting the rent money*, there is a constant danger of attack.

h Jenny put in extra hours during the week *so that she could leave early on Friday*.

i I can't say I like *having to lie to our customers*.

j Wherever she goes, *she upsets someone*.

k Mrs Ramshaw made an announcement *that the next meeting had been cancelled*.

l *Unless he gets an improved contract*, the captain is likely to leave.

m *It's a lovely day today*.

n *If it's such a lovely day*, why don't you go for a walk?

o They had arranged to meet *after the party*.

p The main attraction was a *hugely expensive, but very enjoyable, firework display*.

q The firework display *in the park* was even better.

r *Because Heidi was a champion skier*, she attracted all the attention.

s The reason for the acclaim was *that Heidi was a champion skier*.

t We all hoped *to meet such a famous skier*.

8.2 In each of the following main clauses:
  ▶ identify the subject and verb;
  ▶ turn the statement into a question;
  ▶ turn the statement into a command;
  ▶ name the parts of the sentence in italics: direct or indirect object (objective complement), (intensive) complement, adverbial qualification.

a I put *the cat* out *for the night.*
b Jeff showed *me his new book.*
c *In the winter months* we close *the outdoor pool.*
d The town is *very quiet.* (no command possible)
e You must stand *for the Royal party.*

8.3 Decide which of the following italicized clauses are relative clauses and which are appositive. If possible, also decide what the clauses relate to or are in apposition to:

a The Nawaz family found themselves at the airport just as the air traffic control strike started, *which made a terrible start to their holiday.*

b Later they could laugh about the hold-up *which made a terrible start to their holiday.*

c It was Abid who gave me the news *that they had made a terrible start to their holiday.*

d It was Abid who gave me the news *which he had received from his parents.*

e *That they made such a terrible start to their holidays* was really disappointing.

f The film *which I wanted to see* finished last week.

g My favourite film was on last week and I missed it, *which was a bit silly.*

h The works manager made clear their policy *that no overtime would be available.*

i The claim *that I needed the money* made no difference.

j *What I need* is a rest.

8.4 Each of the following is a short main clause. See how many types of adverb clause (time, place, manner, reason, purpose or result, possibility and contrast) you can add to each one. Do not think of more than one of each type, so that your total clauses for each sentence will not be more than seven – or nine if you wish to separate purpose and result and think of positive and negative possibilities. Make small changes to the original if you wish:

a He sat calmly in his chair.
b A terrifying storm arose.
c Mrs Thewlis enquired diligently.
d The factory remained closed.
e I usually fall asleep.

Kinds of sentence

In this chapter you will learn:

▶ *the difference between simple, compound and complex sentences*

▶ *how to relate all parts of a sentence to each other and identify parentheses*

▶ *how to analyse a complex sentence.*

Simple sentences

A simple sentence is exactly what it says: simple in that it is a single item as well as being an easy concept to understand. A simple sentence consists of **one clause only,** the main clause as defined in Chapter 8. It can be a statement, question or command and is always terminated by a full stop, question mark or exclamation mark.

Though a single item, a simple sentence is by no means always short. The subject may be modified by an adjective **phrase** (*the man in the iron mask*) or can consist of multiple subjects (*Athos, Porthos, Aramis and D'Artagnan*). The verb can quite easily become a verb phrase (*may be about to start*). If the verb is transitive, there is scope for direct and indirect object, both capable of as much development as the subject. There is no reason why adverbial qualifications should not multiply, covering time, place, etc. This complicated sentence is a **simple sentence:**

> In the 19th century the Count of Monte Cristo and the Three Musketeers presented images of romantic heroism to the eager novel reader via the fictions of Alexandre Dumas.

The sentence begins with one adverbial phrase (time – *In the 19th century*) and ends with another (manner – *via the fictions of Alexandre Dumas*). If the verb (*presented*) is one word only, the multiple subject preceding it consists of nine words. Fairly lengthy objects follow: *images of romantic heroism* (direct) and *to the eager novel reader* (indirect). Why, then, do we call the sentence simple? There is only one finite verb, all the other additions are merely phrases and a simple structure underlies the verbiage:

> subject – verb – direct object – indirect object – adverbial qualification

Insight

There is little point in considering exclamations as they may well be structurally statements or commands, the exclamation mark merely signifying emphasis. If you take the sentence 'X will play in Europe next year', where X is a football team, you might want to add an exclamation mark if X = Port Vale, but the sentence remains the same. Then many exclamations are not sentences at all: *Blimey!, What!* But don't forget that the shortest sentences are exclamations, commands with the subject implied: *Help!* is a four-letter sentence!

Compound sentences

If you put together two or more main clauses (**co-ordinate clauses**) in one sentence, that is known as a **compound sentence.** Alternatively two co-ordinate clauses can be said to make a **double sentence,** more than two a **multiple sentence**. The normal way of forming a compound sentence is to place a **co-ordinating conjunction** between the clauses:

> The doctor suspected flu, *but* it was only a bad cold.
> The waiter will bring your soup *or* you can collect it from the buffet.
> The public address system began paging Walter, *and* he soon came into sight.
> The *Three Musketeers* books sold well *and* made Alexandre Dumas very famous.

You will, incidentally, note differences of practice in terms of whether or not to include a comma before the conjunction. A comma is usually required before *but*, but not *or*. *And* is subject to more variation: the wisest policy is never to include a comma when the second clause uses the same subject (usually not repeated) as the first, as in the final example where *The Three Musketeers books* is the subject of both clauses. If the subject changes, it is sometimes preferable to include a comma.

Compound sentences can be more than two clauses long, but normally it is clumsy to have more than one *and*. Although separating two clauses by a comma with no conjunction is usually to be avoided, a series of co-ordinate main clauses can be treated like a list:

> The electricity came back on, the fire began to warm up *and* the kettle started boiling.

This is a perfectly acceptable sentence, although 'The electricity came back on, the fire began to warm up' would have required *and* or a different punctuation mark.

It is, of course, quite usual to have compound sentences using more than two co-ordinate clauses and a variety of conjunctions:

> The kitchen was well equipped *and* the cook took pride in her work, *but* Mr Jephcoat usually ate a sandwich *or* asked them to prepare a small salad.

COMPOUND SENTENCES WITHOUT CO-ORDINATING CONJUNCTIONS

As already stated, a comma is not sufficient to separate two co-ordinate main clauses without the use of a conjunction. However, using a **colon** or **semicolon** can create compound sentences without a conjunction.

A **semicolon** is used for those situations where a comma seems too slight and a full stop too complete a pause. In terms of compound sentences, this is of assistance when you are faced with two separate statements which are so closely linked that you do not wish to start a new sentence:

> Helen searched upstairs; her sister decided to examine the cellar.

A full stop would also be correct; you may well prefer a semicolon.

The **colon** has a more specific function. When the second main clause explains or enlarges on the first, the colon is the necessary punctuation:

> We struggled up the hill: the surface was slippery after the rain. The supermarket was running low after the holiday: it had run out of milk, bread and some fruit.

Chapter 14 will examine more fully the functions of colons and semicolons. For now it is enough to note their function in creating compound sentences.

HOW DO YOU MERGE TWO STATEMENTS?

Let us examine these two statements, two separate sentences, and decide how to make them one:

> The vicar was ill last Christmas.
> The special family service was cancelled.

You could, of course, use a co-ordinating conjunction (*and*, *so*) to form a compound sentence and, as the next section will show, a rather more interesting method is to choose a subordinating conjunction (*because*, *when*, etc.) to form a **complex sentence**.

There are ways, however, of merging the two into **one simple sentence**:

▶ Refine one of the sentences into a noun/noun phrase:

   ▷ The vicar's illness last Christmas caused the special family service to be cancelled.

▶ Create an adverbial phrase (of reason or time):

   ▷ Owing to/because of/after the vicar's illness last Christmas the special family service had to be cancelled.

▶ Create a non-finite/participial clause:

▷ With falling ill last Christmas, the vicar had to cancel the special family service.

Note that it is essential to place *the vicar* next to the participial clause.

Complex sentences: choosing the main clause

A complex sentence is defined as one containing a main clause and one or more subordinate clauses. What these subordinate clauses might be is detailed in Chapter 8. We are here concerned with how they are assembled. The first stage is to decide what constitutes the main clause. What differences can you find in the following pairs of sentences? In each the main clause is italicized:

A Though I thought Emily was a suitable candidate, *Mrs Tankard disagreed.*
Though Mrs Tankard disagreed, *I thought Emily was a suitable candidate.*

B Where the old Fire Station used to be, *the Khans have opened a nursery.*
The old Fire Station used to be where the Khans have opened a nursery.

C When the town centre has a bit more life, *new shops will open.*
The town centre will have a bit more life when some new shops open.

In every pair each sentence contains the same information, but the emphasis is quite different. In A we receive a lower opinion of Emily in the first sentence because Mrs Tankard's opinion is the point of focus, whereas the second sentence pays more heed to the speaker/writer's more favourable opinion. In B the listener knows the whereabouts of a different place (the Khans' nursery or the old Fire Station) in each sentence and is being told about the other place. In C it is a question of whether new shops will enliven the town centre or a lively town centre attract new shops – the sequence of improvement varies from sentence to sentence. A choice between main and subordinate clauses is a choice of focus for your complex sentence.

SUBORDINATE ADVERBIAL CLAUSES

The different types of subordinate adverbial clause have been detailed in Chapter 8. An adverbial clause is any statement containing a finite verb and relating to the action or state of the main clause. As such there is no rule about the placing of an adverbial clause in the sentence:

After I have been shopping, I might find time for some gardening.
I might find time for some gardening *after I have been shopping.*

There is absolutely no difference between the meaning of these sentences. Furthermore adverbial clauses frequently multiply in a complex sentence, placed at various stages of the main clause; for instance:

When Mrs Johnson visited the hospital (1), she always drove to Car Park D *unless the space was already full* (2), *as she could easily walk to the ward from there* (3).

Adverb clause 1 (time), 2 (negative possibility) and 3 (reason) all tell us something about the main statement: where Mrs Johnson parked. In theory the order of these clauses could change, although the order employed here is the most logical. Sometimes there may be more pressing factors in deciding word order: if, for instance, a possibility applies only to one person in the main clause:

As we are short of trainees, I have offered posts to Chris, *if he passes his finals,* and Karen, *before our competitors step in.*

Here you will notice that the main clause is split up because of the placing of the adverbial clause.

The placing of an adverbial clause may also be affected by the presence of a word like *only* which should, whenever possible, immediately precede the word/phrase/clause it relates to. Check the difference in meaning between the two following sentences:

1 Only *if he smartens up* would I give Chris a job *after he completes his training period.*

2 *Even if he smartens up* I would give Chris a job only *after he completes his training period.*

Apart from very small changes the words are the same, the meaning is very similar, but the main obstacle for Chris has shifted from smartness in sentence 1 to training in sentence 2.

SUBORDINATE NOUN CLAUSES

The integration of noun clauses into a complex sentence differs from that of adverbial clauses. An adverbial clause has many functions relative to the entire sentence (commenting on the time, place, possibility, etc.) or the action. A noun clause takes the place of a key unit of the sentence, the **subject** or some form of **complement**: direct object, indirect object or intensive complement.

The first difference that you may notice is one of punctuation. The noun clause becomes an integral part of the flow of the main clause: the essential movement from subject to verb and (usually) on to some form of completion of the verb. Therefore a noun clause is seldom separated from the rest of the sentence by a comma. Think of a complex sentence of a mere 12 letters that is familiar to all as the motto of the SAS and the title of various books, films and articles:

Who dares wins.

Who dares is a noun clause meaning a daring person or someone who takes risks and is the subject of the sentence which has as its main verb *wins*. The noun clause is more fully integrated into the main clause than the adverbial clause would be:

If someone is daring, he will win.

Also, being defined entirely by its function in the complex sentence, a noun clause has no predictable range of subordinating conjunctions. You would expect *if the work is finished* to be an adverb clause of possibility, but look at the following sentence:

I don't know if the work is finished.

The clause is the direct object of *don't know* and, thus, a noun clause.

ADJECTIVE CLAUSES

The integration of an adjective clause (or adnominal relative clause) into a complex sentence is again different from either adverb or noun clauses. This modifies a noun and therefore it can occupy two different places in the sentence:

1 next to the noun/noun phrase it modifies;

2 after a verb of being as the intensive complement.

Misplaced adjectival clauses can cause confusion:

> The Northern Manager decided to pay a call on the branch *which coincided with his visit to Northumberland.*

On the other hand, a lengthy adjectival clause mid-sentence can be ugly and equally confusing:

> The Northern Manager decided to pay a call *which coincided with his visit to Northumberland* on the branch.

A little tinkering with word order can often bring results:

> The Northern Manager decided to pay the branch a call *which coincided with his visit to Northumberland.*

The use of an adjective clause as an unaccompanied complement is less frequent, but does occur. Its use is much more common with *whoever* or *whichever* than with *who* or *which*:

> The most popular candidate is *whoever makes the most promises.*
> My choice of video recorder is *whichever is easiest to operate.*

More usual is to precede it with a noun/pronoun which echoes the subject, especially the relevant personal pronoun or *one* used as a sort of auxiliary noun:

> The Independent candidate is the one *who seems the most popular.*
> Rumpole's wife is she *who must be obeyed.*

Strictly speaking, the noun clause (including *the one* or *she*) is the complement, and adjective clauses can, of course, be part of an orthodox noun complement:

> Ms Brady is *the board member <u>who has made the strongest impression</u>.*

In that case the italicized section is the noun clause complement and the underlined section within it the adjectival clause.

COMPLETING THE COMPLEX SENTENCE

The subordinate clauses in a complex sentence can relate either to the main clause or to another subordinate clause. It is important that you should be able to trace back the connection of anything you write to the main stem of the sentence. It is equally important that you should remember that complicated is not necessarily impressive: a constant sequence of simple sentences is very boring (unless there is a special reason), but sprawling, difficult-to-follow long sentences can be equally ineffective. The following examples are both correctly formed sentences (with an explanation of how they are joined together in the next section 'Analysing a complex sentence'), but you can decide for yourself whether they are examples of well-written English:

Example A

As the celebration this year falls on July 15th (1), which coincidentally is also the founder's birthday (2), the Board of Governors, which is constituted to deal with such situations (3), felt it advisable, before the sub-committee reported back (4), to discover what festivities which might emanate from other sources (6) are planned (5).

Example B

After the King who had been at Whitehall (2) called a new Parliament (1) which might prove when it assembled (4) to be as difficult as the one of the previous year (3), His Majesty's advisers, who were well informed as to the nation's opinions (5), recommended him to reconsider his actions if it were not too late (6).

ANALYSING A COMPLEX SENTENCE

English teaching of the early and middle 20th century set **great** store by **sentence analysis** and **clause analysis**. By this was meant working out the elements in a sentence or the relationship between clauses in a sentence by using patterns, charts and diagrams, with set terminology. This could be counter-productive, the system emerging as more important that the actual understanding. As such it has no place in this book, but analysing a complex sentence certainly has, in the sense of identifying how the elements fit together. Let us consider the above two examples which represent correct English of the sort that few of us admire, but many of us have to understand.

Example A

The main clause is: *The Board of Governors felt it advisable to discover* **(Clause 5 – object:** *what festivities are planned*) – **straightforward and sensible, even if buried by subordinate clauses**.
The subordinate clauses relating directly to the main clause are:
1 (*As the celebration this year falls on July 15th* – **adverb of reason**),
3 (*which is constituted to deal with such situations* – **adjective modifying** *Board of Governors*), **4** (*before the sub-committee reported back* – **adverb of time**) and **5/6** (*what festivities are planned* – **noun as direct object**).
The subordinate clauses relating to another subordinate clause are: 2 (*which coincidentally is also the founder's birthday*) **and 6** (*which might emanate from other sources*), **both adjectival clauses modifying** *July 15th* **and** *festivities* **respectively**.

RELATING THE SUBORDINATE CLAUSE

With its subject and finite verb the subordinate clause has a fair amount of freedom to act on its own: we cannot be confused about who did the act or when. However, the clause remains subordinate. The subordinating conjunction or relative pronoun means that it exists only in inferior relationship to something else: the main clause or another subordinate clause or some element like a noun within another clause.

You need to be absolutely clear what your subordinate clause relates to. Examine the following examples in which the subordinate clauses are italicized:

> I decided to trust Kerrigan with the message *although he was rather forgetful* I thought at least he would be tactful.
> The fireworks went off *when midnight struck* the crowd burst into shouts, cheers and the occasional song.
> It was difficult to find our way on the mountain, scrambling down the rocky slopes *as darkness fell swiftly and no lights could be seen*, we found ourselves beneath a crag we had never seen before.

These are three examples of a common error. The subordinate clause in the middle could relate to the main clause either before it or after it. You must choose which one you want:

either

> I decided to trust Kerrigan with the message although he was rather forgetful. I thought at least he would be tactful.

or

> I decided to trust Kerrigan with the message. Although he was rather forgetful, I thought at least he would be tactful.

No connection has been made between the two main clauses by means of a co-ordinating conjunction or even a suitable punctuation mark (colon/semicolon). Therefore they remain separate sentences, not the halves of a compound sentence. The third example has been deliberately chosen as a longer sentence with more clauses because this sort of situation makes the error more likely. However, the difficulty coming down the mountain and the sight of the crag are not joined syntactically, no matter how much you write about the coming of darkness.

Insight

Speech does not always reflect sentence punctuation: a **semicolon** sounds much like a full stop. Even so, connecting the right subordinate with the right main clause matters in speech: think of unprepared newsreaders confronted by a piece of late news. In *A Midsummer Night's Dream* Peter Quince is trying to introduce the play he and his fellow workers have prepared.

See how many phrases and subordinating clauses you can find placed in the wrong sentence:

*Consider, then, we come but in *despite.*	*scorn
*We do not come as *minding to content you, Our true intent is. All for your delight*	*intending
*We are not here. That you should here *repent you*	*regret your decision to hear us
The actors are at hand; and by their show	
You shall know all that you are like to know.	

Compound-complex sentences

For ease of analysis we have been treating compound and complex sentences as though they are completely different from each other. This is necessary to establish the connections between different elements in a sentence, but it oversimplifies sentence structure. Read the following sentence and decide how it has been put together:

> When the January sales start, the larger stores experience huge crowds and usually stay open late so that they can satisfy the demand.

At the centre of the sentence are two **co-ordinate main clauses** (with the verbs *experience* and *stay*). The first of these main clauses has a subordinate adverbial clause of time (*When the January sales start*) attached to it; the second main clause leads on to an adverbial clause of purpose (*so that they can satisfy the demand*). So what is this perfectly normal sentence to be called? Predictably it is known as a **compound-complex sentence.**

Compound-complex sentences combine all the characteristics of both forms of sentence. A co-ordinating conjunction or a suitable punctuation mark joins the main clauses and each main clause accumulates subordinate clauses on the basis described earlier in the chapter. As with any complex sentence, the writer needs to be clear about exactly what any subordinate clause relates to. Two further examples (the second using a colon rather than a conjunction) may clarify further:

▶ **Examples of compound-complex sentences:**

A If we can get a cheap fare to Malaga (1), I would like to go for Christmas (2), but, if it means paying too much (3), I would be quite happy to stay here (4) and visit the relations (5) when our Welsh cousins come over on Boxing Day (6).

B The group has decided to put on *Bedroom Farce* (1): it is a very popular play (2) which will build on the good audiences (3) we got (4) when we last did an Ayckbourn (5).

Sentence A has three co-ordinate main clauses (2, 4 and 5) joined by co-ordinating conjunctions: I *would like to go for Christmas*, but … I *would be quite happy to stay here* and *visit the relations*. Each of these has an adverbial clause attached to it: 1 and 3 of possibility (using *if*), 6 of time (using *when*).

Sentence B is a quite different structure: the two co-ordinate main clauses (1 and 2) begin the sentence separated by a colon as 2 is an explanation of 1. Clause 2 then sets up a family tree of subordinate clauses: two relative adjective/adnominal clauses: 3 modifying *play* in the co-ordinate main clause 2, then 4 modifying *audiences* in subordinate clause 3. The omission of relative pronoun *which* in front of *we got* is common. Finally an adverbial clause of time (5) modifies clause 4.

The analysis of these sentences makes them sound complicated, but they do not seem such on reading or hearing. The reason for this is that, while hardly elegant English, they are examples of correctly interlocking clauses relating exactly to each other.

It is worth emphasizing at this point that subordinate clauses can attract the same range of additional clauses as a main clause. Let us take the sentence:

> The wind blew fiercely *and* the thunder crashed.

That is an orthodox compound sentence, but we can very easily add the subordinating conjunction *when* to the start of the sentence and add a new main clause:

> When the wind blew fiercely and the thunder crashed, we quickly took shelter.

The first part of the sentence becomes what we might term a compound subordinate clause.

VISITORS IN THE COMPLEX OR COMPOUND SENTENCE: PARENTHESES

All the above make the English language sound precisely structured. Those who read, write and (especially) speak or listen to it know this not to be the case. Informal speech, of course, need not abide by the rules of sentence construction, though many a formal speech maker plants his or her pauses carefully to place subordinate clauses with the correct statements.

Even in formal written English it is possible to include inserts which have no grammatical connection to the surrounding sentence. Such inserts are known as **parentheses** and can be marked by brackets, dashes or commas. It is important to include the punctuation mark at each end of the parenthesis unless it runs up to the end of the sentence and a terminal point (full stop, etc.). Take the following example:

> With the appearance of Inspector Bucket – Dickens was, incidentally, the first major English novelist to feature a detective and his methods – the sins and sufferings of the Dedlock family are woven into the main stream of human crime and misery.

The point being made about Dickens and the detective is a suitable case for parenthesis as its connection with the main point of the sentence is oblique, not direct. In the following sentence a straightforward relative clause is more suitable:

> With the character of Inspector Bucket, whose mixture of underground contacts, tenacity and eccentricity must have been striking to the original readers, Dickens paves the way for the many sleuths and investigators who followed later in the 19th century.

However, the use of parenthesis is very much a matter of taste and over-indulgence can seem mannered as well as spreading confusion among readers.

Insight

For Charles Dickens the parenthesis had a fatal attraction. Not only did he love developing long sentences, but the conversational flow that suggested he was talking to an audience encouraged parentheses. From *The Pickwick Papers* we take part of the second half of a sentence:

> ...away he walked, up one street and down another – we were going to say, up one hill and down another, only it's all uphill at Clifton – without meeting with anything or anybody.

Sometimes the Dickensian sentence imploded in a mass of parentheses:

> I was humiliated, hurt, spurned, offended, angry, sorry – I cannot hit upon the right name for the smart – God knows what its name is – that tears started to my eyes. (*Great Expectations*)

9.1 Decide what sort of sentences the following are and arrange them under headings: *simple sentences*, *compound sentences*, *complex sentences*, *compound-complex sentences*, *non-sentences* (for those which are not sentences at all). There is no need to separate double and multiple sentences:

a   I know what's what.

b   The Maharajah of Jaipur lived in an ornate palace.

c   When we get home from work.

d   When my mother goes into town, she always meets an old friend and disappears into a café.

e   If you go to bed early and set the alarm for half past five.

f   Mrs Fellows wanted to resign, but we persuaded her otherwise.

g   When the red red robin comes bob bob bobbing along.

h   When the birds migrate, I always think of winter drawing near.

i   Life used to be so much simpler.

j   When we finally saw the manager, we gave him an ultimatum: replace the three-piece suite or we would take him to court.

k   It was a matter of standing up for our rights or losing out.

l   What's done is done.

m   Who took the wine from the fridge.

n   Who took the wine from the fridge?

o   It is time that George set about finding a job.

p   The weather, which had been cold and wet, brightened up at the weekend.

q   I never said that I was going.

r   Whenever prices rise, we blame the government.

s   Whenever prices rise, we blame the government and the suppliers.

t   Whenever prices rise, we blame the government and make a great fuss about nothing.

9.2 Find at least two ways of joining together each of the following pairs or groups of sentences. Make small changes in the wording if needed:

a   The French farmers blockaded the Channel ports last year. Lorry drivers in France and Britain had severe problems.

b   Nancy Astor took her seat in Parliament in 1919. She was the first woman to do so.

c   There are very few black bears left in the wild. A protection order has been placed on them.

d Snow fell on New Year's Day.
My niece raced out of the house.
She slipped on the drive.

e It was a fine sunny day.
The market was crowded.
I only stayed for a few minutes.

9.3 Identify the main clauses in the following sentences:

a After profits fell to an all-time low in a year from which so much had been expected, the Managing Director resigned when the shareholders called for an emergency general meeting.

b Go to Prague before it gets completely commercialized.

c If I get on this bus, will it go all through the estate before it ends up in town?

d If at first you don't succeed, try, try again.

e John, who met us at the football match, and Eric are brothers.

f John met us at the football match and told us all about Eric.

g After his party was defeated at the election, the Prime Minister resigned the leadership and became active in industry which resulted in several well-paid directorships.

h Mr Chitty, who was notoriously short-sighted, eventually saw what his son was pointing at.

i What the world needs now is love.

j Mary and Martha, who were the sisters of Lazarus, lived in Bethany where they were visited by Jesus and witnessed several of the miracles which so impressed His followers.

9.4 Each of the following groups of clauses can be assembled into one long sentence. Decide how you would fit them together. Remember that a clause may be divided by the insertion of another clause:

a it seemed that (it) had been forgotten
who had played a considerable part
when the treaty was agreed
until their ambitions brought further conflict
what the smaller nations wanted
which was drawn up in Paris
while the interests of the Powers were safeguarded

b but we still remember
who had relied upon it for employment
when the pit had to close
which help the economy of an area
and how much hardship there was among men
there are plenty of new industries

which is showing signs of reviving
c   is it best to stand still
which might tire you out
if you lose your way on the moors
but which could lead to safety
and hope for rescue
or go looking for assistance
if you approach it sensibly

10

Direct and indirect speech

In this chapter you will learn:

▶ *the different ways of writing down speech*
▶ *how to set out and punctuate direct speech*
▶ *what changes need to be made when using indirect speech.*

Speech and writing

It is generally accepted that speech and writing operate by different sets of rules, though these overlap at certain points. Each is a medium for conveying language, but the fact that one deals with permanent graphic shapes and the other with impermanent (unless a recorder is nearby) personal sounds brings inevitable differences.

'Correctness' refers to a different set of standards. Obviously the finest speakers may be dreadful spellers, but equally it is possible to use *epitome* with great confidence in writing, but remain unaware that it is a four-syllable word.

The concepts of 'correctness' are much more certain and less controversial in writing than in speech. Does it matter that a learned speaker says *compare-able* instead of *comp-rable*? It is impossible to say: it matters to the people it matters to, whereas a spelling of 'compareable' is simply wrong. More to the point, indisputably correct pronunciations are not the same. Take the phrase *stuck fast*: inhabitants of (shall we say?) Gloucestershire, London and Lancashire will use exactly the same words in writing, but produce distinctly different vowel sounds in speech – and, though these may be 'Standard English', probably none will precisely match what used to be termed 'Received Pronunciation'.

Similarly, sentence constructions in speech are less regulated, partly through regional differences, but mainly because so much speech is spontaneous: often you don't know what you are going to say until you say it. Speech, in fact, frequently does not use sentences: the give-and-take of dialogue makes them redundant. Some modern grammars even go so far as to use the term *clause-complex* instead of *sentence* for speech because the clause patterns of speech translate awkwardly to written sentence form.

Spoken English has its own 'grammar' which cannot be reproduced in writing. The use of emphasis, pauses, direct appeals to the audience, distinctive body language, etc., conveys meaning as well as words. How can you suggest the meaning of a shrug in written English? Emphasis can be brought out by the use of bold or italic print in reports or books of this kind; the imaginative writer has to rely on well-placed words like 'actually' or 'even', single-sentence paragraphs, exclamation marks, reactions from him/herself or his/her characters, etc.

How to write speech

Frequently we have to write down what is/has been/will be spoken. Which set of rules and conventions do we abide by, those for written or spoken English? That will vary according to the situation, but we need to know which set we are employing. For instance, written preparation for a speech uses writing as symbols for a spoken end-product. Is the following an example of written English?

∴ 2021 too late – prob. urgent and action needed now – What if imports dry up in next two years?
(pause)
productivity **key issue** – shareholders **must** (!!) understand.

That makes no sense as written English. To the speaker it would make perfect sense as spoken English and furthermore gives guidance on the unique 'grammar' of spoken English: emphases, pauses, rhetorical questions, etc. This is based on the idea of speech-as-speech. Obviously many formal speeches exist in a written form first of all and are then read out, necessary in, say, a statement of government policy, rather laborious at a wedding reception. These can be judged by the rules of written English; in the case of the government statement, even spelling and punctuation matter, as copies are widely circulated.

Insight

R-E-T-H-P-E-C-T!

Such was the headline in *The Independent* in March 2001 when the newspaper featured an interview with boxer Chris Eubank, as famed for his lisp as for his destructive powers in the ring, an interview which includes such memorable sentences as 'Dougie won betht barber of the year, 1993, while I won betht-kept hair.' Is this an essential feature of Chris Eubank's persona – or just a journalistic gimmick? The problem comes inevitably when written and spoken English become entangled. A parenthesis in mid-sentence gives us 'twithted Levi's are also very stylish' (why not 'thtylith', by the way?) and at one point the interviewer adds, as herself, 'How tatheteful is that?' Not very, one fears.

Speech and drama

The main form of written English which accepts the rules and the domination of the spoken word is the play script or screenplay. The first sign of this is the absence of quotation marks/inverted commas: the spoken word is the norm and needs no indication of difference. Instead the sort of things that are part of a written narrative have their difference indicated by italics, brackets, capitals or separate lines: tone of voice, mood, movement, etc. Look at the way the following is set out (from J.M. Synge's *The Playboy of the Western World*):

CHRISTY   (*in a small voice*) God save all here!

MEN   God save you kindly.

CHRISTY   (*going to counter*) I'd trouble you for a glass of porter, woman of the house.

PEGEEN   (*serving him*) You're one of the tinkers, young fellow, is beyond camped in the glen?

CHRISTY   I am not; but I'm destroyed walking.

MICHAEL   (*patronizingly*) Let you come up then to the fire. You're looking famished with the cold.

CHRISTY   God reward you. (*He takes up his glass, and goes a little way across to the left, then stops and looks about him.*) Is it often the polis do be coming into this place, master of the house?

Even such a short extract from a play illustrates several points about the presentation of speech in drama:

▶ The language patterns are those of speech, not writing, more particularly a rather stylized version of the speech of western Ireland. Many of the sentences are not 'correctly' constructed (look, for instance, at Pegeen's speech) and there are many dialect words and phrases. With the exception of *polis* for *police*, however, Synge does not indicate pronunciation, though many playwrights do, especially in such things as the omission of an initial *h* or a terminal *g*.

▶ Actions (*He puts down coin* or *serving him*) and indications of feeling or manner of speaking (*patronizingly* or *in a small voice*) are supplied in italics and parentheses; the main information is conveyed in speech. Speech is so much the norm *that says, remarked, replies, answered*, etc., disappear along with the quotation marks.

▶ Everything is in the present tense: *takes, goes, stops*. This is guidance on how that is happening here and now, the play on stage, not a story of what happened previously, as in most prose narratives.

▶ The main narrative is conveyed in the words spoken. In a piece of narrative prose there would be sentences like, 'Christy took up his glass and moved uncertainly round the bar before stopping and looking doubtfully around him.' In this narrative the words of the speech are no longer the main factor in creating mood.

Insight

It is a matter of choice whether a playwright attempts to render a character's speech phonetically. As we see in Chapter 14, George Bernard Shaw had to abandon Eliza's accent in *Pygmalion* as an impossible task. There is, however, an honourable tradition of playwrights rendering sounds as well as speech patterns. Here is Shakespeare's attempt at the Welsh accent (Captain Fluellen in *Henry V*):

> *Captain Jamy is a marvellous falorous gentleman, that is certain ... by Cheshu, he will maintain his argument as well as any military man in the world, in the disciplines of the pristine wars of the Romans.*

and, in the same scene, the Irish of Captain Macmorris:

> *By Chrish, la! tish ill done: the work ish give over, the trompet sound the retreat. By my hand, I swear, and my father's soul, the work ish ill done; it ish give over: I would have blowed up the town, so Chrish save me, la! in an hour.*

Speech in the prose narrative

There are three main ways in which we can absorb speech into normal narrative prose. If we are interested only in the content of the speech and not the words used, we can summarize the speech, effectively making it part of our ongoing narrative:

> When the parliamentary candidate addressed the meeting, she disclaimed much of the praise heaped on her by previous speakers, but pointed out that her years in local government were remarkable for variety and quality of experience. In particular, she had been a successful chair of three of the most important Corporation sub-committees.

Here you are rendering a half-hour speech down to a few paragraphs, omitting all the detail of, 'From 2002 to 2006 as Chair of the Education Committee I was responsible for a borough-wide regeneration plan for schools...'

If, on the other hand, you wish to include speech at full length, there are two methods which you can employ to integrate it into your main narrative: **direct speech** and **indirect speech**.

Direct speech

Direct speech is, in fact, less about integration than peaceful coexistence. Within **quotation marks** or **inverted commas**, speech can operate to an extent by its own rules: colloquialisms, slang, private languages, non-sentences, etc., though obviously misspellings and odd punctuation should not occur unless for a purpose. Also, because the exact words are used, the timescale of the speech does not have to be related to the timescale of the overall narrative.

> The conductor asked me, 'Have you got a bus pass?'
> 'I'll collect the tickets next week,' said Emma.

In short simple examples like this, the **direct speech** is the direct object of the sentence (technically a noun clause or phrase), even when the main verb of the sentence follows it, as in the second example. The person spoken to, if included, is the **indirect object**. The sentence construction is easily understood if you imagine, 'He said this (direct object) to me (indirect object)' and then replace 'this' with the actual words.

However, the speech operates as a self-contained unit: if the speech starts part-way through a sentence, it is treated as a new sentence, starting again with a capital letter, though no full stop precedes it.

The fact that the speech is self-contained leads to two important issues of punctuation:

1 If the speech is interrupted (by reference to the person speaking or by any other insertion), it must be marked off from the rest of the sentence by quotation marks, both on interruption and resumption:

> 'If I am going to lend you money,' said Alexander, 'at least let me know what it's for.'

2 Note that there is no capital letter after *said Alexander*; the speech sentence simply resumes untouched by the interruption.

3 All the punctuation relating to the speech must be completed within the quotation marks. This is particularly noticeable with question marks and exclamation marks:

> We all called to Sanjay, 'Are you all right?'

4 On the other hand, if the need for punctuation is within the narration, not the speech, the mark falls outside the quotation marks:

> Did you call to Sanjay, 'We're over here!'?

5 The following, though rather inelegant, is correct:

> Did you call to Sanjay, 'Are you all right?'?

HOW TO SET OUT DIRECT SPEECH

The examples above deal with direct speech in its simplest form, brief statements, questions or exclamations inserted into a narrative. Direct speech can take a much more extended form than that, especially in reports requiring verbatim accounts of evidence, etc., and in fiction where extended dialogue creates tension, humour, character and so on.

The punctuation of an extended speech, spreading over several paragraphs, needs care. At the beginning and end quotation marks should be used in the usual way. However, at the beginning of each new paragraph from the second onwards, quotation marks should be inserted as a reminder to the reader. This is the only case where it is normal to open quotation marks without closing them. Quotation marks at the end of the paragraph would mean a change of speaker.

Large sections of dialogue between two or more characters can produce a problem of style: constant repetition of *he said* or *she said* soon becomes boring. Use of more specific terms (*answered, whispered, hinted*) helps, as does using words that refer to the mood or actions of the speaker (*glowered, smirked*) or metaphors like *exploded*. Placing the *He answered/She hinted* element at different places in the speech can relieve the monotony, but you should also consider omitting that element altogether, as in this extract from Thomas Hardy's *Far from the Madding Crowd* (incidentally, a good example of translating the dialect of speech into print):

> 'She's a very vain feymell – so 'tis said here and there.'
> 'Ah, now. If so be 'tis like that, I can't look her in the face. Lord, no: not I – heh-heh-heh! Such a shy man as I be!'
> 'Yes – she's very vain. 'Tis said that every night at going to bed she looks in the glass to put on her night-gown properly.'
> 'And not a married woman. Oh, the world!'
> 'And 'a can play the peanner, so 'tis said.'

This dialogue is between two people. Dialogue with three or more can be more difficult – it is essential that the reader knows who is speaking –, but, with the occasional 'Jo muttered' or 'The inspector insisted', it can be done, especially if the characters have distinct speech patterns. Normally it is good practice to take a new line for a new speaker; this is particularly important when you are not identifying the speaker by name.

Insight

Similar rules apply with quotations from books, plays or articles, taking a fresh line and using quotation marks. An unfortunate habit and one to be avoided is that of inserting the word *quote* before each quotation. Of course in a speech it is often necessary to identify a quotation by saying 'I quote' or something similar, but in writing the layout and punctuation do the work.

Indirect speech

It may be that you wish to give the speech in full, but not in the words of the speaker. In this case you use **indirect speech,** formerly known as **reported speech,** a useful term as it is just that: speech that the writer is reporting. It is thus taken into the main flow of the sentence and no longer self-contained. It must therefore fit in with the rules, timescale and viewpoint of the main statement. Let us take an example of the same situation in direct and indirect speech and consider what effect reporting (rather than quoting) the speech has:

> Katie said to her father, 'Do I have any chance of borrowing the car?' (direct speech)
> Katie asked (1) her father if (1) she (2) had (3) any chance of borrowing the car. (4) (indirect speech)

Said (or *shouted, exclaimed, whispered,* etc.) can only be followed by *that* – or, informally, by nothing at all: 'Katie said she was going out.' This is fine for a statement, but, with a question, indirect speech needs to be preceded by *asked* (or *enquired, wondered,* etc.) *if* (or *whether*) (1). An equivalent change happens with commands. *The policeman said, 'Sign your statement'* becomes *The policeman told me to sign my statement.*

Direct speech is self-contained. If Katie said 'I', that is what we write down. Not so with indirect speech. The sentence is not being narrated by Katie, so *she* is used (2).

The same applies to the verb. Katie uses *do have* (present), but it was in the past that she spoke. Therefore, with indirect speech, the verb shifts to become the same tense (*had* – past) as the narration (*asked*) (3).

If we end with a question mark, it means that the whole sentence is a question, but it is not: there is no doubt that Katie said these words. Therefore, unlike in direct speech, the words have to be changed into statement form to be absorbed into the sentence (4). Though normal in speech, where there is no punctuation, hybrid sentences like the following should be avoided in writing unless used for a particular reason:

> Katie asked her father could she use the car?

SEQUENCE OF TENSES

The tenses used in indirect speech reflect the sequence of tenses: *present/past tense* or *present perfect/past perfect* and *future/future in the past/future in the past perfect*. In most cases the main narrative is in the present or in the past. Clearly no change of tense is needed in the former case; if the narrative is in the past, the words spoken need to be advanced one stage on the sequence of tenses. Present becomes past:

> The desk clerk said, 'There *are* no rooms free.'
> The desk clerk said that there *were* no rooms free.

Present perfect becomes past perfect:

> The doctor said, 'Mrs Mackay, *have* you *taken* your medication?'
> The doctor asked Mrs Mackay if she *had taken* her medication.

Future becomes future in the past:

> The salesman explained, 'I *will not be* back in Bolton before June.'
> The salesman explained that he *would not be* back in Bolton before June.

The situation regarding the simple past tense (preterite) is not so clear-cut. The past tense has a less definite relationship with the present than does the present perfect, so we often feel that the situation is unchanged when events are reported at a later time. Sometimes we are reduced to writing what feels most natural:

> Susan said, '*Did* you *see* the Oscars ceremony on television?'
> Susan asked me if I *had seen* the Oscars ceremony on television.
> My cousin said, 'I *went* to college with Michael Palin.'
> My cousin said that he *went* to college with Michael Palin.

Even these examples are not absolutely clear-cut: many people would use *saw* in the first example. Where there is a definite time-relationship established, we tend to be more strict in our observation of the sequence of tenses:

Mr Potter said, 'For tea we're having the fish I *caught* this morning.'

Mr Potter said that for tea they were having the fish he *had caught* that morning.

NARRATIVES IN THE FUTURE

Though stories set in the future are common enough, it is rare to find the future used as a narrative tense. It does happen, however, usually in predictive situations. Look at the following examples and decide if the principle of the sequence of tenses holds good:

Faced with accusations of corruption, the Minister will say, 'The responsibility lies with those who deceived the Government in the first place.'

England will no doubt lose the First Test, then perhaps someone will have the courage to say, 'Our selection policy was wrong from the start.'

The librarian will no doubt claim, 'I cannot maintain adequate cover with present staffing levels.'

In none of these cases would you use the future tense. The present and past tense verbs in the speeches remain unchanged:

Faced with accusations of corruption, the Minister will say that the responsibility lies with those who deceived the Government in the first place.

England will no doubt lose the First Test, then perhaps someone will have the courage to say that our/their* selection policy was wrong from the start.

(* depending on who is reporting)

The librarian will doubtless claim that (s)he cannot maintain adequate cover with present staffing levels.

In each case the time referred to is identical, both from the present standpoint and the future statement yet to be made.

Test yourself

10.1 The following short passage is set out in play form, though it is not from an actual play. Write it out as it would be in a prose narrative, using direct speech, and then as a narrative using indirect speech, both in the past tense:

ERNEST   (*wearily*) I still don't see why it's so important. (*He slumps back in the chair.*)

AMY   How many times do I have to explain? If we can't raise some money for ourselves, the local Arts Association will refuse to help.

DIANA   Which means there's no chance of staging the concert properly.

AMY   (*wailing*) And we'll never get discovered!

ERNEST   Good thing, too, I should think.

DIANA   (*restraining Amy*) Leave him alone. He's only doing it to annoy.
   (*ERNEST gets up and goes to the window.*)

ERNEST   If you two calm down long enough, I'll tell you how to raise £1,000.

10.2 The following sentences all use direct speech. Correct any errors in the way in which it is set out:
   a   'If I can get tickets Jack said would you like to come to the club on New Year's Eve'?
   b   'The most important consideration,' insisted the superintendent. 'Is public safety.'
   c   'It is vitally important,' said the superintendent. 'The public must be protected.'
   d   Didn't you hear me say, 'The shop is shut?',
   e   One voice could be heard shouting above the turmoil, 'keep the road clear'!

10.3 Convert the following sentences from direct speech to indirect speech:
   a   Jack whispered, 'Have you got the torch?'
   b   The managing director announced, 'Job cuts are inevitable.'
   c   'As far as I can see,' argued Mrs Barnes, 'the council is just ignoring us.'
   d   Eventually the Chair of Housing announces, 'The new development can go ahead.'
   e   Margaret said, 'Can I go next?'

f 'I saw you in the supermarket on Friday,' I said to Mark.

g 'If you have finished the paper,' the invigilator stated, 'you can leave the room.'

h The holiday firm claimed, 'We will beat any other price offers.'

i 'If you are feeling better', said the captain, 'why not open the batting?'

j Kath told me, 'I met him a few years ago in Ibiza.'

Affixes: prefixes and suffixes

In this chapter you will learn:

▶ *how prefixes and suffixes are used to help create words*

▶ *the meanings of individual prefixes and suffixes*

▶ *how to deal with spelling problems caused by the use of suffixes.*

What are prefixes and suffixes?

Prefixes and suffixes are **morphemes** which have a set meaning and can be added to the beginning and end of a word respectively: the general term for both prefixes and suffixes is **affixes**. Many are of one syllable only, but this is far from being a set rule. They can, however, be safely regarded as morphemes: single units of meaning.

We need to know about affixes for two main reasons:

1 they offer an effective way of working out the meaning of unfamiliar words;

2 they are probably the most significant element in the creation and coining of new words.

Imagine that you do not know the meaning of the word *autobiographer*, though, oddly, your English vocabulary otherwise seems rather wide. It is perfectly possible to work out the meaning of the word through knowledge of the two prefixes and two suffixes which make up *autobiographer*:

▶ **auto** (prefix): you are familiar with *automatic* (works by itself), *automobile* (moves by itself), *autonomy* (self-government) and coinages such as *autocue* and *autopilot* (which work by themselves) Clearly *auto-* means *self*.

▶ **bio** (prefix): you know *biology* is the study of life and a *biopsy* is an examination of live tissue, not to mention such scientific studies as *biochemistry* and *biophysics*, the parts of these disciplines that deal with their applications to living things. So *bio-* means *life*.

▶ **graph** (suffix): words like *autograph* (self-write) and *telegraph* (write from a distance) are very common and a word such as *calligraphy* also clearly relates to writing. What about *photograph*? Literally, writing with light – creating a permanent record by means of light. Or *seismograph*? Recording (writing about) an earthquake. *Graph* therefore means *write*.

▶ **er** (suffix): indicates the agent, the doer, with a long list of examples, from *explorer* to *teacher*, from *worker* to *manager*.

Put them together and there is the meaning of the word:

Auto	*bio*	*graph*	*er*
Self	life	write	agent/doer

In other words, someone writing the story of his/her own life.

MAKING NEW WORDS

Many words involving affixes are ancient and established parts of our language, but affixes are particularly useful in helping to create new words. New words (**neologisms**) are needed not only for new inventions, but also for new theories, philosophies, ways of life, etc.

There are many ways to form new words: stealing words from other languages, for instance. When the British first needed a specialist term for the sheds to keep numbers of aircraft in, the aircraft were in France during World War One, so the French *hangar* was appropriated. Naming something after the person originally connected with it is also common: from *sandwich* (the Earl of Sandwich's favourite snack) to Biros and hoovers.

Insight

The now very common term, *paparazzi*, manages to derive both from another language and from an individual (if fictional) name. In Fellini's film *La dolce vita*, Paparazzo was the photographer relentlessly pursuing intimate shots of the rich and famous. The Italian plural, *paparazzi*, became the generic term for such people, first in Italian, then internationally, and the word now has a precise meaning in English. The singular, however, still gives trouble: you can hear a young woman being described as 'a female paparazzi' (a plural and masculine term for a single female): Italian scholars would insist on *paparazza*!

New usages can also be covered simply by extending or narrowing the meaning of existing words. A *tabloid* was 'a small flat piece of prepared substance' long before it was extended to mean a size of newspaper and, eventually (as adjective as well as noun) a style of journalism; now a sensationalist piece in a broadsheet newspaper can be described as 'typical of tabloid journalism'. There were *distributors* long before cars, *conservatives* while the party was still happy to be called Tory and *promenades* were taken when seaside resorts and Henry Wood concerts were things of the future.

Another method is to push together existing words. A new means of travel involved rails, so the British logically opted for the term *railway* and the Americans equally logically chose *railroad*. Possibly the most used word on news bulletins in recent years did not exist previously. *Brexit* pushes together Britain and exit. Presumably it will become an accepted part of English vocabulary.

However, we are mainly concerned with the use of affixes to form new words. The majority of the affixes so used are of Classical origin

(Greek or Latin) and it is usual to add them to the **root** or **stem** of the word, though examples like *autobiographer* are made up solely of affixes. Frequently cited by schoolchildren as the longest word in existence (untrue), *antidisestablishmentarianism* is a fascinating word to analyse, with its root, two prefixes and three suffixes:

▶ The root is *establish*, a verb meaning to set up officially and permanently.

▶ The suffix -**ment** is used to create an abstract noun, so *establishment* is the act or result of establishing, plus by extension the people and institutions involved: *The Establishment*.

▶ The suffix -**arian** relates to a person connected with, supporting or doing the root word. So *vegetarian, grammarian, authoritarian*, etc. (it can also form an adjective as well as a noun).

▶ The prefix **dis-** is one of many negative prefixes: to mean 'not' and variations on 'not'. We have now reached *disestablishmentarian* which means a person who wishes the establishment not to exist. The *Establishment* in question is the Established Church of England. A *disestablishmentarian* is in favour of *disestablishing* the Church: separating Church and State.

▶ The suffix -**ism** suggests a movement or theory: *Methodism, consumerism, sexism*, etc.

▶ The prefix **anti-** means 'against', so we have a final meaning: opposition to the movement consisting of people who wish to remove the connection between the established Church of England and the State.

A more sudden need to create neologisms comes with new inventions and the last century is replete with examples. The example of *car* and *automobile* is referred to in Chapter 1, but more specifically relevant to the question of affixes is the story of the christening of a new machine that enables sounds to be preserved and replayed. Clearly we want 'sound' in its name: the Greek *phon(o)* already exists in words like *phonetic* and even *phonogram* (a symbol in Pitman's shorthand!). A small imaginative leap tells us that this machine 'writes' sound, so the Greek *gram* or *graph* is added. But, if *phone* is the root, is *gra (m) (ph)* a prefix or a suffix? Have we invented the *phonograph* or the *gramophone*? Company names (like the Gramophone Company) depended on it. Later, both words were established on different sides of the Atlantic; later still, the Anglo-Saxon *record-player* took over; even later, the compact disc made the technology as archaic as the terminology; now the compact disc is in the process of being superseded and *record player* is staging a comeback.

Insight

The prefix, *tele-*, originates from the Greek for 'far' or 'at a distance'. Therefore, all the developments in long-distance communication since the late 19th century have brought a vast crop of *tele* words: *telegram* (writing at a distance), *telecommunications*, *teleprinter*, *telephone* (sound at a distance), *teleport* (carry at a distance), etc. Let us consider the words *telescope* and *television*. Both mean the same, 'seeing far-off things', but they do it in quite different ways. Possibly Logie Baird's invention would have been called the *telescope* if the earlier word had not existed. However, once a word exists, it takes on a life of its own. *Telescopic* as adjective has many different uses (some of them based on the folding properties of a telescope, not its original meaning). But *television* has spawned a much bigger vocabulary, much based only on the *tele* prefix: *telefilm*, *teleprompter*, *telecast*, *televiewer*, etc., as well as the straightforward verb and adjective, *televise* and *televisual*. In the same way, the noun *telephone* has given birth to a perfectly respectable verb, to *phone* (which, literally, means no more than 'sound').

Prefixes

NEGATIVE PREFIXES

The largest group of prefixes is those reversing the meaning of the word: *in-*, *non-*, *dis-*, *a-*, *un-*, etc. (in a stronger sense of opposition, *anti-*). Mostly these are very straightforward, but the number of warnings and explanations is greater than you might expect:

▶ *In-* is a very common negative, but sometimes the consonant has been changed, originally to make for easier pronunciation. So we have *infrequent*, but *impossible*, *ignoble*, *irreversible*, *illogical*, etc.

▶ It is possible to begin a word with two negative prefixes. *Cover* means to conceal, so *discover* means to find something out. Something that has yet to be found is thus *un-discovered*.

▶ Confusion can arise from the fact that *in-* means *in* as a prefix even more often than it acts as a negative. Words like *uninhabited* or *uninspired* are not double negatives like *undiscovered*. One of the most confusing pairs of words is *flammable* (able to be set alight) and *inflammable* (both with the same meaning, 'not flame-proof'). *Non-flammable* is used for the opposite.

▶ Many words have two different negatives. *Uncover* and *discover* are not quite the same: you would never *discover* your Christmas pudding by taking the lid off and, though you might *uncover* a crime as well as *discovering* it, you would not *uncover* your missing watch down the side of a chair. Be particularly vigilant on *uninterested* and *disinterested*. *Uninterested* means bored, finding nothing of interest ('I was uninterested in the conversation') and *disinterested* means neutral, having no personal interest or involvement ('To the disinterested spectator the argument seemed futile'). Sadly *disinterested* is taking over both meanings and a useful distinction may be lost. Now the noun *disinterest* (meaning lack of interest) is becoming established, the shift in meaning is well under way.

▶ The prefix *a-* is one we often forget in the lists of negatives and obviously most words beginning with *a-* are not using it as a prefix, but it is worth our attention here. It is often used in medical conditions, but two of the more interesting uses outside the surgery are in *apathy* and *amoral*. *Apathy* is part of a full set of words conveying different feelings (*pathos* in Greek). *Antipathy* is 'against feeling', *sympathy* is 'together or alike feeling' and *apathy* is no feeling at all. *Amoral* is similarly neutral (no moral question is raised), a useful distinction from *immoral* which implies poor morals or wickedness.

SOME OPPOSITES IN PREFIXES

Several sets of prefixes operate as opposites:

pre- or *ante-* (before)	*post-* (after)	e.g. **pre**face//**post**script
pro- (in favour of)	*anti-* (against)	e.g. **pro**tect//**anti**dote
mega- (large/great)	*micro-* (small)	e.g. **mega**lith//**micro**scope
super- (above)	*sub-* (below)	e.g. **super**natural//**sub**terranean

Well-known prefixes like these are particularly useful in that they can operate separately from roots as living prefixes and be semi-independently attached to whatever other words you want. Everyone knows what is meant by ***super**-efficient secretaries*, ***pro**-life campaigners*, ***anti**-globalization rallies*, ***pre**-Christmas treats* and *the sports of the **mega**-rich*, even though the hyphenated words are coinages. And you can coin your own. You can oppose plans to privatize hospital services by being **pro-equality** and **anti**-*privilege*; you can explain your hangover by referring to **post-**-*interview* celebrations; you can apologize for your **super**-*idiotic behaviour*.

There are, of course, problems to look out for (apart from the similarity of *anti-* and *ante-*):

▶ Do you use the word for *big* or for *small* if you are referring to making a small thing big? The answer, confusingly, is either. **Megaphone** means 'big sound' and, sure enough, a megaphone is a rather old-fashioned trumpet-like device for making the human voice louder. Much more effective at doing the same thing is a **microphone** which means 'small sound', referring to the original sound which a microphone magnifies.

▶ *Pro-* is also confusing. Operating on its own as a free agent, it always means 'in favour of'. We use it as the opposite of *anti-* (Are you pro or anti the European Union?) and we also talk of *pros and cons* as points for and against. Used strictly as a prefix, *pro-* more often means 'on behalf of' or 'instead of (*pronoun*, *proclaim*, *promoter*) and can also mean 'before' (*prologue*, *prophecy*).

Insight

The prefixes that best sum up the state of the language at the start of the 21st century are those of extremes. A generation or two ago *super* was one of the first prefixes to attain independent life as an expression of extreme approval. Now it is in the shadow of *mega*. At the same time *hyper-* (over or excessive) attaches itself to grandiose projects, medical conditions and behavioural problems and, at the other extreme, *micro-* flourishes as technology minimizes size. *Hypo-*, oddly, means under (like the *hypocaust* in Roman central heating), so **hyper**tension means unusually high blood pressure and **hypo**tension unusually low blood pressure – pronunciation and spelling are all-important!

PREFIXES OF NUMBER

In straightforward compounds the number itself is often used, especially with variants of the word '*time*': '*two-timing*', '*four-times winner*'. However, the number of Greek- and Latin-derived prefixes representing numbers is enormous, often with two prefixes for one number:

one: **uni-** (*unicycle, uniform, unison*), **mono-** (*monologue, monoplane, monopoly*) two: **bi-** (*biped, bilingual, bisexual*), **du(o)-** (*duologue, duodecimal, duplicate*)

four: **tetra-** (*tetralogy, tetrarch*), **quater-** (*quatercentenary, quaternity*)

five: **pent(a)-** (*pentathlon, pentagon, pentateuch*), **quin-** (*quintet, quintuplets*)

six: **sex-** (*sextet, sextant, sexagenarian*), **hex(a)-** (*hexagon, hexameter*)

seven: **sept-** (*septet, septuple, septuagenarian*), **hept(a)-** (*heptagon, heptarchy*)

You will be familiar with number prefixes like *tri-* (three), *oct (a) (o)-* (eight) and *dec(a)-* (ten) right up to *cent-* (hundred) and *mill(i)-* or *kilo-* (thousand), plus *multi-* (many) for less precise occasions.

Insight

What is the difference between *mill(i)* and *kilo*? Both mean a thousand, the first from Latin, the second from Greek. There is something of a difference in the ways they are used: *kilo* refers only to mathematical concepts (quantities, distances, etc. – *kilogram, kilometre*, etc.) while *mill(i)* can be used in the same way, but also as part of our general vocabulary in words like *millennium* and *millipede*. But the most interesting comparison is between words like *kilogram/kilometre* and *milligram/millimetre*. In each case *kilo-* refers to a thousand of the base unit (multiplying by 1,000) and *milli-* to a thousandth-part of it (dividing by 1,000).

HYPHENS WITH PREFIXES

The use of a hyphen to separate a prefix from the root word may occur for personal reasons: e.g. you have just coined the usage and draw attention to the fact that it is not a 'real' word. There are, however, some rules to follow:

▶ Some coinages make use of a proper noun. In these cases the capital letter is preceded by a hyphen. So the school of painters who claimed to return to the style of art before Raphael is known as the Pre-Raphaelite Brotherhood. True, the hyphen may also be used for art movements like *post-modernism*, but its occurrence before a capital letter is a rule rather than a matter of taste, drawing attention to the coinage. So, terms like *anti-Peelite* require hyphens, as would any coinages of your own: *pro-United* or *pre-OU*.

▶ Where it is clear that the prefix is operating as an independent agent to form new words, it is usually hyphenated: for instance *pro-* in the example above. *Non-* and *self-* usually work in this way. The use of *ex-* is particularly interesting. Without a hyphen *ex-* means 'out of or 'from': *exile*, *exterior*, *exhale*, etc. With a hyphen it has the specialist meaning 'former' and can be applied to whatever the writer wishes: *ex-goalkeeper*, *ex-teacher*, *ex-ambassador*, *ex-husband*, etc.

▶ Usually a hyphen is used to separate a vowel in the prefix from the same vowel in the stem: *pre-eminent*, *re-entry*, *co-operate*, though it is beginning to disappear (e.g. in *cooperate*).

Insight

What is the difference between *recreation* and *re-creation*, between *recover* and *re-cover*, *resolve* and *re-solve*, *recommend* and *re-commend* or even *resign* and *re-sign*? The first in each pair is a word that exists in its own right, the prefix *re-* (again/in return) having been absorbed long ago in words that mean 'amusement', 'regain health or possession', 'decide', 'propose or support' and 'relinquish or give up'. The second words use *re-* as a living prefix adding to an existing word to suggest repetition. So 'I needed time for rest and *recreation*', but 'We welcomed the *re-creation* of the theatre interior after years of neglect.' Or, in a single sentence, 'When the manager was forced to *resign*, we took steps to *re-sign* his predecessor.'

OTHER PREFIXES

It is clearly impossible to list all prefixes and their meanings. Exercise 11.2 in the 'Test yourself' will test your knowledge of some other common prefixes not dealt with here (and, of course, give the answers). There are, however, two more points of possible confusion to consider:

1 *en-* and *in-*: Both mean *in* as prefixes, *in-* being the more common. Oddly there are several words which exist in both *in-* and *en-* forms with similar, but slightly different, meanings The most common of these are *ensure/insure* and *enquire/inquire*. *Ensure* means to make certain; *insure* to take out insurance:

> We *insured* against rain to *ensure* that we did not make a loss on the fête.

The rule governing *enquir (e) (y)* and *inquir (e) (y)* is less clear-cut. The reputable *Oxford Guide to English Usage* insists on a distinction between asking a question (*enquire*, making an *enquiry*) and carrying out an investigation (*inquire*, undertaking an *inquiry*). Common usage and many dictionaries may simply regard the two as interchangeable, but you may possibly find the distinction helpful.

2 **for-** and **fore-**: The distinction here is perfectly clear. *Fore-* comes from the same source as *before* and often means 'front', whereas *for-* has various meanings connected with *away* or prohibition or neglect (almost a negative prefix at times). A few examples of many will suffice:

forbid	ban from doing	*forearm*	the front part of the arm
forgive	do away with guilt	*foreman*	one who has a position in front of others
forfeit	give up or the thing given up	*forecast*	predict what lies ahead

Note the problem of *forbear/forebear*. *Forbear* is to abstain from something: 'I must insist that you *forbear* from political wrangling at committee meetings.' *Forebear* is an ancestor: 'My *forebears* were responsible for founding the business.' Confusingly and inexplicably, *forbear* is accepted as an alternative spelling for *forebear*, but not vice versa. However, it surely makes more sense to preserve the distinction.

Suffixes

THE FUNCTION OF SUFFIXES

Whereas prefixes are more or less fixed units of meaning (*not*, *across*, *between*, etc.), suffixes are more likely to act as agents changing the part of speech. Of course, in establishing the new part of speech, the suffix can affect meaning as well. For instance, *-ful* and *-less* can both turn verbs or nouns into adjectives, but with opposite meanings: *help, helpful, helpless*. The suffixes *-ee* and *-er* both form personal nouns, but one represents the doer, the other the recipient of the action: the *employer* employs the *employee*. Other suffixes simply shift the part of speech: *-ly* turns an adjective into an adverb (see Chapter 6) or a noun into an adjective (*friend/friendly*), *-(i)ous* simply creates an adjective from a noun (*fury/furious*).

Let us look at what happens to the word *method* when suffixes are added. *Method* is a noun meaning 'an orderly form of procedure':

▶ A typical adjectival suffix, *-ic(al)*, creates an adjective, *methodical*, with no change of meaning.

▶ To produce the adverb, still with no change of meaning, *-ly* forms *methodically*.

▶ The verb from *method* is not much used, but it exists, again formed by a common verbal suffix, *-ise/-ize*, with alternative spellings: *methodize* or *methodise*. It means 'to arrange in an orderly manner'.

▶ The ending *-(o)logy* creates abstract nouns suggesting a branch of knowledge and *methodology* is the theory behind orderly schemes and systems.

▶ The first shift of meaning came in the 18th century when the term *methodists* was applied to a religious group which laid particular stress on order and organization: *-ist* is again a typical ending, applied to a person who is part of a group or a sharer in a belief or a follower of an idea. The abstract noun ending for the belief or group is *-ism* and, of course, *Methodism* soon gained a capital letter as a proper noun and the official name of the movement.

▶ In their turn *Methodism* and *Methodist* gave rise to *methodistic* or *methodistical* (adjective) and *methodistically* (adverb), now based on the meaning of *Methodism*, not *method*. Note that the same adjectival and adverbial suffixes are used as earlier.

Nothing very unusual happens to the word *method*, but its history is revealing in two ways:

1 The suffixes used are very common ones with specific functions in changing parts of speech. You will find many other examples of their similar use.

2 At one point (*methodist*) a shift in meaning occurred: often you will find that later derivatives seem to share no element of meaning with the original root, but a genuine family tree still exists.

SUFFIXES TO FORM ABSTRACT NOUNS

One of the most clear-cut uses of suffixes is to form abstract nouns: ones that refer to ideas, emotions and principles rather than people and objects. The addition of such suffixes as *-dom*, *-ness*, *-ship* and

-hood to a personal noun or adjective creates the equivalent abstract noun with no shift in meaning:

wise (adjective)	*wisdom* (abstract noun)
happy (adjective)	*happiness* (abstract noun)
hard (adjective)	*hardship* (abstract noun)
man (personal noun)	*manhood* (abstract noun)

Many abstract noun suffixes form pairs with adjectival suffixes or personal noun suffixes. For instance, *-acy* with *-ate, -anc (e) (y)/-enc (e) (y)* with *-ant/ent, -tion* with *-tious, -ism* with *-ist(ic)*:

accuracy (abstract noun)	*accurate* (adjective)
piracy (abstract noun)	*pirate* (personal noun)
persistence (abstract noun)	*persistent* (adjective)
ambition (abstract noun)	*ambitious* (adjective)
occupancy (abstract noun)	*occupant* (personal noun)

This account of the uses of suffixes to form different parts of speech is mostly description of common practice, not definitive rules. It does not follow that equivalent noun and adjective endings always work together with the same roots. For instance, though *ambition* and *ambitious* fit together neatly, the very similar adjective, *anxious*, is linked with the noun *anxiety*. *Artist* (personal noun) and *artistic* (adjective) might lead us to expect the abstract noun *artism* instead of *artistry*, though, of course, the original root is another abstract noun, *art*.

Other suffixes creating abstract nouns imply the existence of a certain group, belief or field of academic studies. The examples of *-(o)logy* to suggest a field of study are very numerous: *psychology* (study of the mind), *astrology* (study of the stars), *phrenology* (study of the cranium as guide to mental faculties), etc. The *-graphy* suffix (literally meaning 'writing') can be used in a fairly similar way.

Insight

A difficulty with understanding the precise meaning of noun suffixes lies in the comparative wideness of meaning of some suffixes. Not all suffixes have the precise focus of meaning of *-(o)logy*. A famous television commercial of the 1990s had a doting grandmother enthusing over her grandson's less than impressive GCSE results,

'He's got an *ology*.' The suffix is so firmly associated with areas of study and knowledge that, long before that, even the *Concise Oxford Dictionary* defined *ology* as a jocular word for 'any science'. On the other hand, *-is (m) (t)* is just too versatile. Almost no religious faith, social theory or political party can be without its *-ism*: *Catholicism, Anglicanism, Taoism, Hinduism, Conservatism, communism, nationalism, monetarism, utilitarianism*, etc. Beware, however, of thinking of *-ism* as solely a suffix meaning 'a system or principle' and *-ist* as a believer in that principle. Think of words as different as *euphemism, heroism, somnabulis (m)(t), tobacconist, dentist*, etc. And what about *Baptist*? The adjective/personal noun (with capital letter) is indeed applied to membership of a certain religious group, but *baptism* (lower-case letter) is a sacrament of the Christian Church, central to the practices of Baptists, but by no means confined to them.

SUFFIXES FORMING PERSONAL NOUNS AND ADJECTIVES

There is a large group of suffixes which form **agent nouns** – that is, nouns referring to the doer of an action. Among the most common are *-er, -or, -ar, -ant, -ent,* and *-ist* (the last often doing duty for believers, followers, etc.): *runner, actor, beggar, claimant, resident, realist.* All these examples make clear the word (usually a verb) from which the noun is derived, though you will have realised that the root is not always so easy to detect: suffixes can just as often be added to obscure Classical roots as to recognizable English words.

What of the distinction between personal nouns and adjectives? Sometimes none exists in the form of the words. For example:

I was allowed to pass as I am a *resident* (noun) here.
The *resident* (adjective) tutor is responsible for the students' welfare.

A similar situation can apply with many other suffixes, such as:

-ian: The *Australian* (adjective) Prime Minister/Don Bradman was a great *Australian* (noun).
-ary: She volunteered for *missionary* (adjective) work/My great-uncle was a *missionary* (noun) in China.
-ite: Millais was one of the first *Pre-Raphaelite* (adjective) painters/Holman Hunt was also a *Pre-Raphaelite* (noun).
-ist: The Conservatives followed a *monetarist* (adjective) policy/Mrs Thatcher was a *monetarist* (noun).
-ive: We had a *captive* (adjective) audience/After the kidnapping, he remained a *captive* (noun) for some months.

OTHER SUFFIXES

The Oxford Companion to the English Language devotes four columns and at least 300 entries to listing suffixes, while quoting the 19th-century philologist Walter W. Skeat as noting, '...an attempt to exhibit them all would lead to confusion.' This is sufficient discouragement to any attempt to cover suffixes comprehensively. The use of suffixes to form adjectives, adverbs and verbs will thus be dealt with very briefly before examining some individual cases that may be of interest or difficulty.

If a suffix is added to an existing word, the original root word is most likely to be a noun or a verb or both. If we start with the word *help*, that is both verb and noun and, with the addition of suffixes, forms:

▶ adjectives: *helpful helpless*

▶ adverbs: *helpfully helplessly*

▶ agent noun: *helper*

▶ abstract noun: *helpfulness helplessness*

For this reason we may find fewer interesting verb suffixes, though you will probably be familiar with such verb suffixes as *-fy* (*intensify*), *-ise/-ize* (*memorize*) and *-ate* (*infuriate*).

Most adverbs are formed by the same suffix (*-ly*), though you should look at the later note on *-wise*. Adjectival suffixes, on the other hand, are many and varied, but many of the most important have already been covered in the earlier sections.

There is also a whole class of endings, sometimes called suffixes, which have not been considered here. More correctly known as **inflectional endings**, these modify the form of a word to indicate tense, number, etc. To consider endings like *-s* (3rd person singular present tense of verbs or plural of nouns) and -*ed* (past tense of verbs) as suffixes is unhelpful.

▶ -*ice*, -*ise* and -*ize*

The endings -*ise* and -*ice* can both be found attached to the same root: *advice/advise, practice/practise, device/devise, licence/license*. The rule is quite simple: -*ise* for the verb, -*ice* for the noun:

> I asked him to *advise* (verb) me, but she gave the better *advice* (noun).
> Ruth left to *practise* (verb) the piano: she needs to do an hour's *practice* (noun) every day.

In American English, incidentally, *practice* as a verb is normal and correct.

The endings -*ise* and -*ize* give rise to a disputed area of correct usage, though fortunately one in which most authorities accept both alternative spellings. There is, however, a school of thought that insists on -*ize* for certain words. The words in dispute constitute quite a narrow group. The first criterion depends on pronunciation. Only those words ending in –*ise/-ize* with the pronunciation 'eyes' are affected. So words like *practi(s)(c)e* and *licen(s)(c)e*, both pronounced with a soft s sound, need not be considered. On the other hand, while *advice* and *device* require the soft s sound, *advise* and *devise* use a hard z sound (the 'eyes' pronunciation).

The second criterion, however, rules out *advise* and *devise*. This dispute concerns only verbs for which both -*ize* and -*ise* are in use. There are many common verbs where only -*ise* is in use: not only *advise* and *devise*, but also *surprise, revise, disguise, exercise, improvise* and many others. These are excused from the rule either because they are identical to a noun ending in -*ise* or because the stem contains -*is*.

To summarize, some current books on grammar and spelling insist that, for verbs which end in the 'eyes' sound and for which -*ise* and -*ize* are in use, only -*ize* is correct. These words include *authorize, familiarize, agonize, memorize* and *sterilize*. However, for every reference book insisting on the -*ize* ending, there is one allowing -*ize* or -*ise*; most dictionaries give both as alternatives. American and Australian practice differs from British English.

Therefore, sensible advice would suggest that, if you have seen both spellings and are unsure, -*ize* is the safer, but that, if you prefer -*ise*, you may safely ignore pedantic critics.

▶ -able and -ible

Unlike -ice and -ise there is no clear-cut distinction here. It is true that the ending is determined by the original Latin suffix, but such is the only real difference between them. Both are adjectival suffixes meaning 'able to do' or 'able to suffer'. If you are unable to believe something, it is *incredible*; if you cannot put up with it, it is *unbearable*. If you have a reasonable meal, the food is *edible*, the wine is *drinkable*. It is *impossible* to lay down any rules and *preferable* to learn individual words.

The only guide that you have is that -*able* is more often added to words of clearly English original and -*ible* more often to those of Classical origin: e.g. *incredible*, *unbelievable*. There are, however, enough exceptions to make the theory seem *indefensible*. What is certain, however, is that only -*able* can be used as a living suffix to create new words: a rather old-fashioned coinage like *clubbable*, for instance, or *filmable*. If you wished to coin a typically 21st-century word (*a sponsorable event*, perhaps, or *webbable information*), you would turn to -*able*, not -*ible*.

Insight

An oddity among suffixes is -*wise*. It has a perfectly honourable history as a conventional suffix to form an adverb or adjective. *Clockwise*, for instance, can be either adverb or adjective: 'You must move the pieces *clockwise* (adverb)' or 'The *clockwise* (adjective) M25'. *Likewise* and *lengthwise* are other adverbial formations. More recently -*wise* has been used as a living suffix to add to existing words in new formations, often extremely ugly and clumsy, usually separated by a hyphen. '*Corporate-affairs-wise* this is a bad move' is the worst of jargon and even the classier popular songs are not immune:

Weather-wise it's such a lovely day.

For all that -*wise* can be useful as a living suffix, as can -*like* which also gives rise to some hyphenated monstrosities.

▶ -ant and -ent

The suffix -*ant* or -*ent* implies the same meaning as the present participle (-*ing*); in fact you may recognize the present participle form in French. So the adjective *repellent* means something that repels (is repelling to) you; a *dependant* is depending on his/her guardian/benefactor; a *superintendent* is watching over (superintending) his/her staff/place of work. But which suffix should it be: -*ent* or -*ant*?

The absence of rules is well summed up by the fact that another word for *superintendent* is *intendant*, commonly applied to the chiefs of European theatres and opera houses, but increasingly common here.

You should take note of a small, but significant, group of words where *-ent* is the adjective ending and *-ant* the noun ending. The most common of these are *depend(e)(a)nt* and *pend(e)(a)nt*. In adjective form these simply mean *depending* and *hanging*; in noun form they have specific meanings:

> The fête was *dependent* (adjective) on weather conditions. He claimed for two extra *dependants* (noun) on his self- assessment form.
> The house seemed menaced by the *pendent* (adjective) crag.
> Finally we decided on the *pendant* (noun) as a birthday present.

Insight

The outsider in Southport in Lancashire is immediately struck by the name of the local paper, *The Visiter.* Enquiries bring the answer, 'That's the way it's always been spelled.' The newspaper obviously dates back to times when there was less rigidity about spelling. It also points up the futility of attempting to establish rules for the three 'doer' suffixes: *-er*, *-or* and *-ar* (fairly infrequent, but remember words like *scholar* and *liar*). Interestingly there is a small group of words which take both *-er* and *-or* suffixes with different meanings. *Adapter*, *conveyer* and *resister are* all personal nouns referring to a person adapting, conveying or resisting. With *-or* suffixes they become specialist terms for electrical or mechanical devices.

HOW SUFFIXES CHANGE THE FORM OF THE ROOT

You will already have noticed the typical changes that suffixes make in the form of the root or stem of the word:

▶ A silent final *e* disappears before a suffix beginning with a vowel: *argue/arguable*, *intense/intensify*, *late/latish*, *dense/density*, etc. The main exception to this is words where the *e* is necessary to keep the *c* or *g* before it as a soft sound: *peaceable*. In a few cases the final silent *e* is dropped before a suffix beginning with a consonant: *argue/argument*, *awe/awful* (but note *awesome*) and *true/truly* are among the most common.

▶ The loss of an *e* can sometimes result in the elision of an entire syllable. This can happen with a final *e* (*subtle/subtly -whole/wholly* is similar, but without the loss of a syllable) or by eliding a final *-er* (*remember/remembrance*, *enter/ entrance*).

▶ In many cases a final consonant is doubled before a suffix beginning with a vowel. To simplify complicated rules with considerable exceptions, this is mainly done when to use a single consonant would transform a short vowel into a long one. Either the stem is a monosyllable or the final vowel bears the main stress. So the final consonant of *hat* is doubled to make *hatter* (*hater* being something else altogether); *hit* turns into *hittable* to avoid the pronunciation 'high-ta-bel'; *trap* gives us *trapper* rather than *traper* (which would be pronounced 'tray-per'), etc. Note that, if the preceding vowel is not stressed, nothing happens: e.g. *man/mannish*, but *woman/womanish*. In this case *a* is the only vowel in the monosyllable *man*, but the stress in *woman* falls on the first syllable, so the *a* is unstressed.

▶ As always in English, *y* following a consonant is subject to change. If following a vowel, it remains unchanged: *joy/joyful*, *play/playful*, *boy/boyhood*. Following a consonant, it is likely to be replaced by *i* (*happy/happiness*, *psychology/psychological*, *remedy/remedial*) or disappear altogether (*geography/geographer*, *philosophy/philosopher*). Words like *geologist* could be said either to omit the *y* altogether or to replace it with *i*.

▶ Just like the single *l* at the end of the *-ful* suffix, a final *ll* at the end of the root words becomes single before a suffix beginning with a consonant (though, in many cases, not if you are American): *full/fulfil*, *install/instalment* (but *installation* where the suffix begins with a vowel). *Skilful* and *wilful* are good examples to remember: *-ll* at the end of both stem and suffix has been turned to a single *l*.

Insight

For some reason we are uneasy about adding a suffix beginning with a vowel to a root that ends with one. Perhaps the sheer oddity of words like *taxiing* is too much for us. Under no circumstances should you add an apostrophe to cover your unease; hyphens are more harmless (*taxi-ing*), but not necessary. It is perfectly correct (if none too graceful) to write, 'He spent the morning *radioing* home while his *bikinied* girlfriend *sambaed* on the beach.'

11.1 In the following examples the meaning of the root or stem is given. Try to work out the meaning of the full words:

  a The Greek *logos* means 'word', the Latin *loquor* means 'to speak'. What do you think the following words mean?

    soliloquy, monologue, dialogue, duologue

  b The Latin word *dicere* means 'to say'. What do the following words mean?

    predict, contradict, interdict

  c The Latin word *iacere* (also spelled *jacere*) means 'to throw'. What do you think are the meanings of the following?

    inject, dejection, interjection, reject, projectile

  d The French word *poser* means 'to place'. What are the meanings of the following words derived from it?

    propose, impose, interpose, juxtapose

  e The prefix *mono-* means 'one'. A *monolith* is a single block of stone, often used in monuments; a *monopoly* gives rights as the only trader/producer in a commodity; *monogamy* is the practice of having only one mate; *monochrome* means in one colour. What do the following mean?

    megalith, duopoly, polygamy, polychrome

11.2 Each of the following words begins with a prefix. Not all of the prefixes have been mentioned in this chapter. Try to work out the meanings both of the prefixes and the words in which they are used:

  a intermission
  b interminable
  c perimeter
  d transfer
  e peninsula
  f submarine
  g antepenultimate
  h congress
  i compatriot
  j co-opt
  k correlation

    l   geography

   m   trilogy

   n   autograph

   o   pandemonium

   p   octosyllabic

   q   discontinue

   r   polyglot

   s   dodecagon

   t   unicorn

11.3 Choose between the alternative versions in the following sentences:

   a   Three years after it closed down, Mrs Archer was hoping to (reform, re-form) the village drama group.

   b   In front of the offices is a paved (forcourt, forecourt).

   c   I have been appointed to (coordinate, co-ordinate) the efforts of the two groups.

   d   Mr Walpole was inordinately proud of his (forbears, forebears).

   e   In fact, he could not (forbear, forebear) from talking about them constantly.

   f   By resigning the Minister (preempted, pre-empted) the committee's decision.

   g   I am afraid that I can't (ensure, insure) perfect safety.

   h   Margot claims to be an (exdancer, ex-dancer).

   i   Our laws allow the (extradition, ex-tradition) of wanted criminals.

   j   The police (enquiry, inquiry) was expected to lead to an arrest.

11.4 Identify the suffixes in the following words and say what they mean or what function they perform. In some cases there will be more than one suffix in a word:

   a   freedom

   b   physiology

   c   reprographic

   d   scholarly

   e   demonstratively

   f   sameness

   g   technologically

   h   criticism

   i   farmer

   j   recognize

   k   vilify

   l   remembrance

m relation

n graciousness

o obedient

11.5 Transform the following words into different parts of speech by adding suffixes. The part of speech required is given by each word:

a noble (adjective into abstract noun)

b horror (noun into adjective – *not the participle 'horrifying'*)

c infection (noun into adjective)

d collapse (verb/noun into adjective meaning 'able to collapse/ be collapsed')

e meteor (noun into adverb)

f transfer (verb/noun into adjective meaning 'able to be transferred')

g shrewd (adjective into abstract noun)

h fellow (personal noun/adjective into abstract noun)

i act (verb/noun into adverb)

j frantic (adjective into adverb)

k beauty (noun into adjective)

11.6 Choose between the alternative words in the following sentences:

a You should go to a lawyer for (advice, advise).

b She claimed to be the (auther, author) of several best-selling romances.

c I can't say I (benefited, benefitted) from the deal.

d (Basicly, basically) he is just not well enough qualified.

e My latest commission is as (adapter, adaptor) of a Russian play.

f Eventually the (merryment, merriment) became tiresome.

g Miss Wordsworth is a (descendent, descendant) of the poet.

h Dr Stockman spoke out (publicly, publically).

i I'm hoping to form a (geographic, geographical) society.

j You can never mistake the roar of a (classic, classical) sports car.

Gender and grammar

In this chapter you will learn:

▶ *the difference between actual and grammatical gender*

▶ *how non-grammatical forces have caused changes in usage*

▶ *how it is possible to reduce, but not remove, confusion in current usage.*

The gender problem

The difficulty with gender in English arises from the fact that the language does not possess the concept of **grammatical gender**. In this it is unlike Old English and many current European languages. In French the house and the street are as feminine (grammatically) as the girl or the woman. In Italian the meat you eat is feminine, the wine you drink is masculine. In German there is even the word *Mädchen*, meaning 'girl', which is grammatically neuter, simply because all words ending in *-chen* ('little') are. The presence of grammatical gender causes problems and confusions of its own, but the fact that grammatical and actual gender are separate concepts avoids interaction of language issues and social issues – which is where the difficulty lies in English. Inevitably, trying to apply two different standards in this way is likely to lead more to compromise and 'best fit' answers than to the certainty of correctness.

THE HISTORICAL SITUATION

Though having the advantage of comparative clarity, the state of English even a generation or two ago was founded on an unthinking assumption of the superiority of men, reflecting the fact that *man* (or *mankind*) is the name for the species and *man* the term for the male of that species. *He* could be taken to include both sexes: 'Any person leaving the aeroplane should make sure that he takes his luggage with him.' The policy in letter-writing (unless the writer knew the recipient's name) was to use *Dear Madam* where the recipient was certainly a woman (e.g. the Manageress) and *Dear Sir* where the recipient was certainly male, but also when the gender was uncertain, sadly based on the assumption that the Managing Director or the Proprietor was more likely to be male. *Dear Sir or Madam* was reserved for circulars.

The same sense of masculine superiority could be found in vocabulary. On the one hand, *coalman*, *postman* and *milkman* suggested that these physical professions were beyond a woman, just as only a *chairman* could run a meeting. On the other hand, *usherette* and *waitress* emphasized the sort of jobs that were considered suitable for women. On the buses, of course, *conductress* was in common usage, but not *driveress*, this the consequence not of equality, but of the absence of women bus drivers. *Actress* somehow sounds somewhat less grand, less serious, than *actor* (think of the different figures they cut in jokes, always a good guide to social attitudes), and the identification of the little woman even extended to such absurd terms as *poetess* and *sculptress*, doubtless both known for the delightful prettiness of their work.

It is not only understandable, it is desirable, to react against this, silly jokes about *personhole-covers* notwithstanding. The problem is, however, that social and linguistic matters have become entangled. Things are altered not because they are bad grammar, but because they are socially divisive, and the English language does not always adjust easily. So what follows is mostly advice on the best (or, sometimes, least bad) solution to a situation which will always be open to change.

WRITING LETTERS

Increasingly we find it offensive to write *Dear Sir* in a letter to the Sales Director or the Site Manager or the Box Office Supervisor. If there is no other solution, then *Dear Sir or Madam* is preferable, though clumsy and old-fashioned. Fortunately it is used much less often on circulars now, as formal letters become less formal and *Dear Colleague* or *Dear Supporter* becomes more frequent.

Business letters (both individual and circular) now make much more use of names. There are two main reasons for this. Firms wish to give a sense of personal service: even on the telephone, the operative will give his or her first name before taking your order or solving your problem. Also, before word-processing and computer systems, firms sending out a series of letters (particularly circulars) used identical wording; now letters can easily be personalized with the recipient's name. For all these reasons the problem of gender in letters is solving itself. Even in business letters, we are now far more likely to write *Dear Sally* or *Dear James*.

Note that *Dear Sirs* is often acceptable in writing to firms, many of which bear the names of their (usually male) founders: George Green & Co., J.B. Harper & Sons.

Insight

The etiquette of letters is losing its strictness, not only in matters of gender, and this can only be accelerated by the growth of emails. A business correspondent may end the letter *With very best wishes* or *Kindest regards*, but, if you wish to observe the old niceties, remember the rule: *Dear Sir* or *Dear Madam* is followed at the end by *Yours faithfully*, *Dear Richard* or *Dear Mrs Morrison* by *Yours sincerely*.

VOCABULARY AND TERMINOLOGY

As a basic principle it is preferable to use the same word for men and women performing the same role or job. In some cases the perception of the job has changed and with it the terminology.

For instance, *air hostess* conjures up an old-fashioned decorative image that has less to do with efficiency than with glamour. Men and women alike no doubt feel that *cabin crew* (by analogy with air-crew) more accurately reflects their work. *Schoolmasters* and *schoolmistresses* (reflections of single-sex schools and didactic methods) have been absorbed in *schoolteachers*.

Using *actor*, not *actress*, or *manager*, not *manageress*, is straightforward, though there are a few words that exist only in the feminine form and suggest traditional roles. Probably *seamstress* is harmless, little enough used these days and with no sign of male *seamsters* necessitating a new word. In the same way *shepherdess* is archaic and belongs to an unreal traditional world: no one could believe that Dresden shepherdesses or Arcadian shepherds serenading their shepherdesses have any bearing on the role of women today.

Insight

Old conceptions about which jobs are for men and which for women can also suggest that there are jobs that men do not do. Hospitals give rise to many of these. Has the term *male nurse* disappeared yet? If not, it should have. *Sister* and *matron* also suggest that men should be consultants or porters, never part of the nursing staff. Fortunately terms like *charge nurse* are eroding the distinction.

The greatest oddity is to find chain restaurants claiming *waitress service* even though some of the waiters are male. What this shows about current gender stereotypes is difficult to interpret.

The -*man* words are more problematic. All that can be said as a generalization is that variants using -*person* (*spokesperson*, for instance) are showing no sign of becoming an idiomatic part of our language, though sometimes there is no alternative. Otherwise each case has a different solution (or lack of one):

▶ After an uneasy attempt at establishing *chairperson*, *chair* is a settled alternative to *chairman*, probably because its use as a verb (Who is *chairing* the meeting?) outweighs the fact that it is also an item of furniture.

▶ Redefining the role of *linesmen* in football brought a solution (*assistant referees*) just as women were first appointed to games at the highest levels.

▶ The fact that women have found difficulties gaining equality in the Fire Service and the Police makes it particularly important to use terms like *Fire Officer* and *Police Constable* rather than *-man* or *-woman*. Perhaps the increased use of *postie* for *postman* has something to do with equality.

▶ It is difficult to see alternatives to terms like *groundsman* and *binman* (not *refuse operative*, please!). Given the use of the verb *man* to mean fill or operate (as in '*manning* the till' or '*manning* the lifeboats'), these can probably be seen as inoffensive.

▶ When the only known term for a precise job ends in '*-man*', like '*draughtsman*', there is a choice of two unsatisfactory alternatives: to use the term regardless of sex or to use a word, '*draughtswoman*', that sounds as if it is only on loan to the English language.

Insight

It is surprising that, when so many of the *-ess* and *-ette* words are now being actively discouraged, such unflattering coinages as *ladette* (a young woman with many of the social habits of *the lads*) and *hackette* (a young female tabloid journalist) seem to be accepted. The roles identify the desire for equality, but the terms are unfortunate. *Ladette* and *hackette* have crossed over from slang into journalistic use: by 2002 *ladette*, but not *hackette*, had reached the Concise Oxford Dictionary.

HE OR *SHE*?

Our ingenuity is most tested in finding alternatives to *he*, *him* and *his* when the personal pronoun refers to both genders (see Chapter 4). Perfectly correct at all times is to replace *he* with *he or she*, but, though correct, it can be clumsy and unidiomatic. In a document (a contract, an insurance policy, a hire purchase agreement), where there is no need to hold the reader's interest or to write entertainingly, *he or she* (or *(s)he* or *s/he*) fits the bill perfectly. In a serious newspaper article, the use of *he or she/him and her* is fine, so long as it is not frequently repeated: most of us are happy enough to read, 'The responsible shopper must make up his or her mind about the continuing use of plastic', but not to read it throughout the article. So how do we balance interest and correctness?

HAS *THEY* A FUTURE?

The two most acceptable methods are to recast the sentence totally or to transfer it into the plural (where there is no gender distinction), so that the above example becomes:

The continuing use of plastic is an issue that must task the mind of every responsible shopper.

or

Responsible shoppers must make up their minds about the continuing use of plastic.

A more radical measure which is being used with increasing frequency is to employ *they, them* and *their* as singular terms, as in 'Every floating voter must make up *their* own mind' or 'Has your child decided which school *they* prefer?'

They is, of course, incorrect: *voter* and *child* are singular and must be used with a singular personal pronoun or possessive adjective. But it is also useful: the only 3rd person singular pronoun we have that is not specifically masculine or feminine is *it/its* and that clearly will not do. So are we witnessing a change in the definition of *they/them/their*? After all, *you* was once only a plural and slid into singular use via the polite form: *they* could do the same over a different question of manners.

It is impossible to say whether *they/them/their* will appear in dictionaries of 2030 as '3rd person plural personal pronoun; also applied to 3rd person singular if gender is not implied'. For the moment, if you use it, you will be grammatically incorrect, but in good company – the BBC, for instance.

12.1 In this section it is nearly impossible, for all the reasons stated above, to give correct answers, but it is worthwhile thinking about what problem is presented in each of the following sentences and what you think is the best solution:

a Sheila had never planned to become a milkman.

b I want each pupil to check that he has the right examination paper.

c We are hoping to cast several well-known actors for *Macbeth*, plus an established actress in the role of Lady Macbeth.

d Whoever is appointed Sales Manager will take up the post as soon as is convenient for him – or her, if we appoint a Sales Manageress.

e A parent has the right to choose a suitable school for his child, one that will suit his abilities.

f Who is the spokesman for the Townswomen's Guild?

g He applied for a job as a male nurse.

h Mrs Harrison is the first woman chairman we have had.

i The passenger asked the driver if the bus stopped near his house.

j Anyone needing assistance should raise his hand.

Register: formal and informal

In this chapter you will learn:

▶ *how standards of formal correctness are always subject to change*

▶ *the meaning and importance of register in language*

▶ *how political correctness has a role in effective communication.*

Received by whom?

Received Standard English is not the only 'correct' form of English any more than Received Standard Pronunciation is the only 'correct' way to pronounce the language. The concept of the Queen's English can hardly be current when Her Majesty's pronunciation (though perfectly understandable and in no way offensive) is decidedly different from that of the national newsreaders and reporters whose purpose is to communicate with the entire nation.

Even the Queen's English is not a fixed point of reference. A survey in December 2000 came to the following conclusions about how the Queen's manner of speaking had changed in Christmas broadcasts from 1952 onwards:

> It has been 'influenced by the standard southern British accent of the 1980s which is more typically associated with speakers who are younger and lower in the social hierarchy'; 'the vowels...are still clearly set apart from those of the standard southern English accent' – this standard accent has, of course, also changed.

So the Queen's English is still different from the norm, but it is subject to change and influence – interesting, but a survey of her vocabulary and speech patterns as well would have been even more interesting.

Insight

Changes in spoken English over even a fairly short period of time can be well illustrated by British films of the 1930s–50s. Two linguistic points are immediately obvious:

1 No romantic heroine (except when a 'character' like Gracie Fields was cast in the role) was allowed to speak with a regional accent or use regional vocabulary or constructions, no matter how broad the Yorkshire or cockney accents of her parents – a demure touch of Scots or Irish might be permitted;

2 The received 'correct' pronunciation sounds strange and highly affected half a century later.

It is worth noting that some of those actresses whose 1940s-style Received Standard Pronunciation jars so much today can be heard using a much more class-less (and, to our ears, more attractive) delivery in later plays/films/interviews.

CORRECTNESS IN AN INFORMAL AGE

The concept of 'correctness' is more fluid than in the first part of the 20th century or in the 19th century. This is not to say that the English speech has deteriorated in correctness. Look at Charles Dickens' (no doubt somewhat exaggerated) depiction of the speech patterns of the uneducated, such as the country blacksmith Joe Gargery in *Great Expectations*:

> ...*when (my father) were overtook with drink, he hammered away at my mother, most onmerciful. It were a'most the only hammering he did, indeed, 'xcepting at myself. And he hammered at me with a wigour only to be equalled by the wigour with which he didn't hammer at his anvil.*

Sam Weller (or, as he would say, Veller)'s cockney in *Pickwick Papers* almost reinvents the language, to exuberant effect:

> *I worked down the wery day arter the night as you caught the rheumatiz, and at the Black Boy at Chelmsford – the wery place they'd come to – I took'em up, right through to Ipswich, where the man servant – him in the mulberries – told me they was a goin' to put up for a long time.*

However, Dickens, other Victorian writers and educated real-life Victorians carefully separated the formal and informal in language. Dickens' narrative voice is that of an educated and abundantly articulate man and, however personal the language in which a Victorian businessman conducted his private life and intimate affairs, his business letters never lost their dignified and orotund formality. Now, in a world where, for instance, forenames are commonly used in important correspondence and call centres deliberately feature regional accents to suggest honesty, the question of **register** is of great importance.

What is register?

Despite (or perhaps because of) the blurring of divisions suggested above, it is essential to set your language within the context in which it is being used. The word **register** is a comparatively recent term for language's adaptation to this context. The British linguist Michael Halliday contrasted language defined by the user (for which he used the term dialect) and language defined by the context or situation (register). Thus there are certain features of your language use which are always present and some which are determined by where and how you are using it. Such features as breadth of vocabulary, richness of imagery and (particularly in the case of speech) regional origin will affect everything you say or write. However, it is highly unlikely that you will use the same language for writing a formal report for head office and persuading your young son to eat his tea.

WHAT DETERMINES REGISTER?

Register can be determined on three grounds affecting the discourse (what is being said or written):

1 **Field of discourse:** This refers to the subject matter with which you are dealing. Partly this relates to jargon or technical language. Each field of work or study has its own technical language which is employed within that field, but should be avoided or explained when writing for the layman who may not understand, for instance, the vocabulary of advertising or film production. However, in less technical situations, the subject matter will still affect the register.

2 **Mode of discourse:** What medium you have chosen to put over the information, ideas, imaginative fiction, etc., will affect the register. The most obvious distinction is between speech and writing, speech generally being less formal. However, the mode involves much more subtle distinctions than this. If the mode you are employing is speech and we then narrow it down to speech on radio, the register associated with Radio 1 is far different from Radio 4 – as are making a point one-to-one and addressing a gathering of several hundred. In books, think of the difference in register between Mills and Boon romances and multi-volume histories of the Crusades; in newspapers, the variety of registers in the daily press.

3 **Manner of discourse:** This is the social relationship between the participants. You are more formal speaking to a superior at work than to a colleague in the same workplace. This does not solely apply to speech: there is at least an implied relationship between writer and reader in written English. Think of election addresses, newspaper columns, cookery books, even novels. Such matters as difficulty of language, assumed similarity/ difference of interest, assumed knowledge/ignorance/opinions/ prejudices of the reader and intended effect on the reader all affect the register chosen. All writing (this book, for instance) implies a target readership.

THE APPLICATION OF FIELD, MODE AND MANNER

A group of people wishes the local council to make improvements to playing fields, including better changing facilities and an increase in the number of football pitches. It is highly unlikely that a phone call to the Parks Department saying 'Why don't you do something about the playing fields?' will be of any use. So how is the concept of register set out above likely to increase the possibilities of success?

A successful approach requires expertise which will be reflected in the use of language (**field**): the chances of success will no doubt be enhanced by the presence in the group of the secretary of the local football league or a surveyor, builder, groundsman or architect.

The **mode** will dictate a detailed report, laid out not in continuous writing, but with subheadings, paragraphs and sub-paragraphs, and diagrams. This will be written in quite a different style (factual, detailed, analytical) from the persuasive letter which will accompany it.

The **manner** will reflect the fact that, though the writers are sure that they are right, the council has the right to be right. Persuasion, politeness, even flattery, must mix with reason and confidence. A wheedling, aggressive or too forthright style will be a failure of register – and of application.

In a case like this it is essential to be able to use language in a way that suggests that you are in the right, but have every respect for the person(s) being addressed:

We are certain that you must be aware of the need within the community for these facilities and will wish to do everything possible to bring about an improvement.

On the other hand you must be capable of the clear and firm presentation of facts and figures:

At the moment the borough owns ten full-size football pitches of which four at the Gresley Road site are subject to severe flooding in winter. As recently as 2010 the number was 17.

Most important of all, the different registers should not be confused: a heartfelt appeal on sociological grounds should not interrupt a detailed summary of the negligible provision of changing facilities.

INFORMALITY IN BUSINESS

Informality in business can only go so far. A business letter is now quite likely to begin *Dear Alan* and end *Best wishes* or *Kind regards* rather than the strictly correct *Dear Sir* or *Dear Madam* and *Yours faithfully.* This is perfectly acceptable, even welcome, but the letter itself must reflect its field of reference and the relationship between sender and recipient. The register suitable for writing to a friend about visiting may well be highly unsuitable for enquiring about possible employment or the availability and cost of mechanical parts.

ALL THE DIALECTS

Halliday defines what the speaker or writer brings to the form of language (which includes his/her regional origins) as **dialect**. In the common use of the word dialect is specifically regional. Modern books on English grammar, which tend to be descriptive, not prescriptive, may place spoken regional speech at the heart of their description and claim (correctly) that English is the sum of all its dialects, including standard English.

The truth of the matter is that all dialects are equally valid, but also equally subject to the needs of register. Educated Scots or North-Eastern speech, reassuring, harmonious and straightforward, may be ideal for call centres, but a strongly accented Glaswegian running a training course for the unemployed in Hackney must modify his speech patterns to make himself understood. Similarly supporters' notes in football or rugby programmes may be written, say, in a version of Yorkshire speech:

Mooast times it pays ter wait an' watch action replays on telly afoor mekkin judgements on such matters, an' i' these two instances, 'ave got ter say at officials gorrit reight, even if it wa'r moor good luck than mannidgement. (from Barnsley FC match programme)

Great fun, but not a suitable register for an advertisement in Caernarfon.

The greater the flexibility of register you have in your speech and writing, the more effective your use of English. This applies equally to those who might claim to speak and write 'correct' English. You can probably remember some teachers at school who could never find the correct register of communication, who were incomprehensible or 'talked down' to pupils. Similarly it is a strength in an academic historian that he or she can write very learned volumes, but also put across his or her message to the 'general reader'.

Insight

In Yorkshire there is a widely believed story, though probably not true, that, when level crossings with lights and half-gates were introduced, the area witnessed an upsurge in accidents. The problem was signs which read, 'Wait while the lights flash', meaning that during the time the lights were flashing no cars should cross. Unfortunately, in Yorkshire dialect, *while* means *until* and rumour has it that drivers waited until the lights flashed before driving dutifully in front of the East Coast express. A cautionary tale, even if untrue, which demonstrates that it can sometimes be the official register which commits errors of manner.

PC AND EMAILS

Communication in the first part of the 21st century has been, and still is, subject to rapid change. We might think that the spread of emails, texts and social media might be the death-knell for correct grammar, orthodox spelling and punctuation, capital letters and normal spacing of words. It is wiser, however, to see these simply as the chosen modes of discourse. If, for instance, unspaced lower case is the norm, that is no different from the fact that old-fashioned telegrams were full of the word *stop*.

Modern electronic communication does not make any change to what is correct in certain situations; it simply creates a new register where some of the normal rules do not apply. Clearly, Twitter, with its 280-character rule, is a medium where writing full sentences is not to be recommended. Texting is also a means of instant communication where abbreviations are the norm. Apart from such established terms as 'u r' for 'you are', such graceless contractions as 'tomoz' are not incorrect; ironically, the spelling 'tomorow' could be considered incorrect.

It is all a matter of situation and context. Emails, for instance, are now commonly used as the medium for holiday bookings, insurance contracts, job applications and other documents, written in formal, sometimes over-formal, style. Now that texting is often the chosen method for notifying us of hospital appointments, vehicle services and so on, we expect a terse, but fundamentally accurate, form of English.

It seems odd after (or, more likely, during) such a revolution in communication and acceptable modes of discourse to assert that English grammar remains unchanged, but it is more or less true. It is certainly fair to say that the communication revolution has accelerated existing tendencies towards informality. Changes of fashion in the layout of letters (including the removal of punctuation in addresses) may also be boosted by the coming of emails which help to suggest that there is no one correct model and that punctuation varies with the mode of communication. Essential language rules, however, remain unaffected.

Language changes occasioned by political correctness are more profound. Even if largely confined to vocabulary, these changes represent a notable (and generally very welcome) shift of manner. The terminology used has something to say about the relationship between the speaker and the person addressed, described or commented on. The question of gender applies, but there are many more cases of political correctness.

It is easy to mock political correctness and phrases like *follically challenged* (bald), *more mature citizens* (what used to be called pensioners) and *senior moments* (caused by the fading memories of the extremely mature) have their ludicrous side, together with the egregious *personhole-cover*. Comedians and writers create their own PC terms, with the ....-*challenged* field particularly rewarding.

However, what lies at the heart of the more sensible PC creations is a willingness to take a group of people on its own terms: to create a register based on a manner of respect. This has to be a good thing. To take a simple example, the indigenous people of North America were long known as *Indians*, a term which reflects only what the European invaders thought they should be. By the end of the 20th century the argument was whether they should be called the Indigenous Peoples, Native Americans or the Native Peoples, the last one apparently being preferred by the native peoples. However footling the differences may seem to us, the expression of identity does matter; after centuries of being called what the conquerors wanted them to be called, the Native Peoples' own choice of name expresses the fact that they are still there, unconquered.

These politically correct (a particularly ungenerous phrase, incidentally) changes of register can make similar changes to attitudes to disability, mental illness or incapacity, age, youth, colour, race, etc., a reminder that the term **register** was first applied in sociolinguistics, the study of language within society and social groups.

CONSISTENCY OF REGISTER

The selection of register is most often a matter of avoidance or inclusion of technical language and a choice of the level and type of formality or informality. For instance, informality in letters to your brother might involve cheerful insults which would be totally inappropriate in a friendly letter to a business acquaintance or former colleague.

It is equally important to maintain a consistent register unless you wish to gain some effect (shocking, perhaps, or possibly comic) from a switch of register. In a technical handbook we would not expect to find among *upper flange bracket (C)* and *universal connector pin (G)* a reference to *that curly thing that looks a bit like a corkscrew*, even though some of us might find it easier to understand – which also raises the question of whether manuals adopt a user-friendly register.

You will sometimes find an author struggling for an appropriate register. Think, for instance, of historical novels that attempt, often in vain, to reflect the language of the period (or, at least, vaguely old-fashioned language) and employ present-day English, yet at the same time present a consistent register. Changes of register can be deliberate. The politician who suddenly uses the word *gobsmacked* amid the formal phrases of politics wants to shock us with his amazement or pose as 'man of the people' or both.

A sudden change in register can create **bathos**, a ludicrously comic anti-climax, as when Alexander Pope described Queen Anne's palace:

Here thou, Great Anna! whom three realms obey,
Dost sometimes counsel take – and sometimes Tea.

The first line and a half is full of words of grandeur and politics: *great*, *realms*, *obey*, *counsel* – suddenly brought down to earth with *Tea* (pronounced 'Tay' in the 18th century). The ludicrously comic effects that Pope deliberately creates are likely to befall by accident those who find a consistent register difficult to sustain.

13.1 Read each of the following paragraphs and see if you can describe the register being used: bear in mind the **manner** of discourse, the implied relationship with the hearer or reader. Correct any words or phrases which you feel do not fit in with the overall style adopted:

a I wish to propose that we make an appeal to the Lottery Commission for a grant to facilitate the design and construction of a new Village Hall. The present building is a focal point for village activities, an essential part of our social life and one of the few remaining centres for community life. Unfortunately, it is now structurally unsound: you get half drowned if you hold a meeting there in a rainstorm. If we are to retain our identity as a village, this project is a major priority.

b The by-election, due to take place next Thursday, is stirring up intense feeling locally on the matter of planning permission for a vast out-of-town shopping precinct. Joan Hobday, striving to keep the seat for the Conservatives, is cautiously supportive of the project, but Alan Brigshaw for Labour fears for its catastrophic demographic impact in a structurally underemployed area of marginal investment. Local opinion is divided: buxom 35-year-old barmaid at the Red Lion, Suzy Fairclough, said, 'It will reduce town centre trade.'

c So what it comes down to is I think I might be up your way at the end of June, but, if I don't get to see you then, I'll try and get something organized about the time of Len's birthday – but you know what he's like – it takes him half an hour to decide what he wants for breakfast. Anyway, I anticipate your response to these proposals.

d Well, Mrs Kershaw, I'm not really sure about your son's suitability for 'A' Level Maths. He works hard, there's no doubt about that, can't fault him on doing his homework, his work is always neatly laid out – very good generally – but he's the first to admit he has problems understanding difficult concepts. He's bright and enthusiastic, popular with the rest of the class, but he gets pushed around a bit – don't you think he's a bit of a wimp?

e Eventually, after a second-half onslaught, City drew level. A hanging cross from Meadows on the right was met with Morgan's fierce near-post header and, though Ford got a hand to the ball, the United keeper couldn't keep it out of the net. Morgan's celebrations of his 14th goal of the season proved too much for the referee who administered a caution to the City striker which really was a bit silly.

Spelling and punctuation

'Correct' spelling

For many people the idea of 'correct' English centres on being able to spell and punctuate accurately, but in fact these are not central to the structure of good English. We are all familiar with the oddities of Shakespearean spelling and the capital letters scattered wantonly through 17th and 18th century texts, but even so it comes as something of a surprise to read about Jane Austen's eccentric spelling that made its way into the published versions of her novels.

Insight

The introduction to the 1996 Penguin Classics edition of *Pride and Prejudice* refers to retaining 'variant spellings ... acceptable in the period' and gives an extended list of oddities of punctuation, among them, commas between subject and predicate and parentheses opened with a dash and closed with a comma. Thirty years earlier the 1966 Penguin Classics edition of *Emma* opted to retain 'inimitable Jane Austen spellings' which were then listed as including *scissars* and *stopt*, as well as such recognizable archaisms as *receipt* for *recipe*. Learned scholars approved these departures from the norm first published in the early 19th century: would they have been so tolerant of a new book with eccentric spellings and punctuation?

If Jane Austen, correctly regarded as an extremely polished stylist, can get away with oddities of spelling and punctuation, why can't we all do the same? The answer is that, up to a point, we can: if we have sufficient genius (to take two disparate examples, James Joyce and Spike Milligan), we can bend the language to suit ourselves.

In small ways we all have choice. Nobody is really sure about – *ise/-ize* and *-isation/-ization*. Do you prefer *connection* or *connexion*, *judgment* or *judgement*? American spellings are so acceptable that occasionally, for trade reasons, a book by a British writer will be published by a British publishing house with American spellings. If you prefer *color* to *colour*, go ahead and use it. Nobody can say that you are wrong, though some may think that you are somewhat pretentious, like people favouring the archaic *shew* for *show*.

The important point about spelling and punctuation is that they are only conventions, though very important conventions, that enable language to work as written communication. They are not part of the essential structure of language. So the common protestation, 'I'm no good at English; I can't spell for toffee', simply does not hold water.

SOME NOTES ON SOUND AND SPELLING

Clearly how you pronounce a word is not a certain guide to how you spell it, nor is it possible that it could be, with differences in regional pronunciation. However, the sound of a word can be either a useful guide to spelling or the cause of confusion.

▶ *i* **before** *e* **except after** *c*

Perhaps the best-known rule in English spelling is also one of those with the fewest exceptions so long as you add the last clause *when the sound is* 'ee'. There is no problem with *field, siege, hygienic*, etc., all with *i* before *e*. There is no problem either with *ceiling, conceit, perceive*, etc., all with *e before i after c*. There have to be one or two exceptions: *seize* and *weird* are the most common.

But how do you pronounce *counterfeit* or *heinous*? If you say *counterfit* and *haynous*, you will expect *e* before *i*. Perhaps, though, you say *counterfeet* and *heenous*. Most controversial of all is the case of *either* and *neither* (in the words of Ira Gershwin, 'You say *eether* and I say *eyether*'). Those of us who say *eyether* find that the spelling rule holds good, but must feel sympathy for those generations of school pupils who, pronouncing the word *eether*, have to be coaxed away from the spelling *iether*.

▶ Double c and double s

When we double a letter, we usually make only one sound. The letter *c* is unusual. It has two distinct sounds (what we may call *k* and *s* sounds) and, when doubled, sometimes makes each sound in turn: *succeeds* the pronunciation of which as *suck-seeds* leads to many a laboured pun. *Eccentric* (*eck-sen-tric*) is another example of the same practice. Thinking about the sound can help you distinguish the spelling of several series of similar words:

> *access* (*ack-sess* – approach); *assess* (*ass-ess* – estimate) *excess* (*ecks-cess* – too much)
> *accent* (*ack-sent* – way of speech); *assent* (*agreement*)/*ascent* (climb) (both *ass-(s)ent*)
> *accept* (*ack-sept* – take); *except* (*ecks-cept* – omit or apart from)

▶ Soft and hard c and g

The reason why double *c* does not always make two separate sounds (*k* followed by *s*) is that it only applies when it is followed by *e* or *i*, usually the former. The rule is that *c* and *g* are hard (as in *cat* and *go*) when followed by *a*, *o* or *u* or a consonant or when they fall at the end of a word, but soft when followed by *e* or *i*. It is a rule that holds good for most of the time (*get* is a major exception, as are *gig* and *giggle*). Interestingly enough, the *gg* sound in words like *suggest* is rather blurred (the hard *g* barely sounded) compared with *cc* in *accept*.

▶ Ways of making vowels long

We can all distinguish between long vowel sounds (which are essentially the same as the names of the letters) and short vowel sounds (which are probably what we learned in infant school). This is one of the areas where knowing the sound of the word can help spelling the most. For instance, a single consonant follows a long vowel and a double consonant a short one. *Caning* is corporal punishment, *canning* is placing in a metal container. *Fury* is great anger, *furry* is an adjective applied to rabbits.

▶ Silent letters: a help and a mystery

Other ways to lengthen vowels involve silent letters: most notably *e* following a single consonant to lengthen the preceding vowel. A *rat* is a rodent; the extra *e* in *rate* is not in itself sounded, but creates the long *a* in *rate*, meaning speed or level. The *i* in *rapid* is short, in *provide* it is long. Diphthongs (two vowel sounds merged) also lengthen vowels. Sometimes the vowel sound changes (*fond/found*), but sometimes the second vowel is silent and simply lengthens the sound (*god/goad*).

Among the most mysterious of silent letters are *-gh-*. This combination is useful for lengthening the *i* sound (*fit/fight, sit/sight*), but often, following a diphthong which is already a long vowel, *-gh-* becomes absolutely silent: *fought, though, height*, etc. As for silent letters to begin words, there is no system short of knowing the origins of the words to explain the *g* in *gnat* or the *k* in *knot*. The silent *p* usually (not always) precedes *s* and it is worth remembering that some rather similar Greek sources give rise to a large number of English words: e.g. *pseudes* (false), *psukhe* (usually *psyche* – life or soul) and *psalmos* (song). The words from *psyche* must not be confused with those from *phusis* (usually *physio* – nature): *psychology* as compared with *physiology* – those hybrid words beginning *phs* simply do not exist!

▶ **ex- and *exc-*, *-ceed*, *-cede* and *-sede***

You may be able to distinguish between the first sounds of words like *except* and words like *exercise*, an extra sibilant consonant, but here we are in territory where sound is a very limited guide to spelling. By the time we reach *proceed, precede* and *supersede*, there is nothing to fall back on except learning which is which: even knowing the Latin origins is no guarantee!

HOW TO SPELL CORRECTLY

Ultimately the only way to spell correctly is to learn the spelling of all the words you need! Of course this is not a matter of starting from scratch every time: most words are made of reusable building blocks (see Chapter 11) which usually do not change their spelling. For instance, the many people who spell adverbs like *correctly* with *-ley* are making only one mistake, but committing many misspellings. Matters such as the change of *-y* to *-ie* before the addition of *-s* or *-d* and the changes to the stem when *-ing* is added are dealt with elsewhere in Chapters 5 and 6.

You must not expect consistent logic in a language that rhymes *though* with *go, sew, snow* and *beau*, but not with *through, thought, thorough* or *trough* – and none of the last four words rhymes with any of the others! Therefore the section on spelling in a book of this sort has to be limited in its scope: the only alternative is a huge, but still incomplete, list of spellings.

TEN PAIRS OF CONFUSABLE WORDS

It is, however, worthwhile examining some words which are easily confused and can be learnt in pairs:

▶ counsel(lor)/council(lor)

Counsel is an old-fashioned noun for 'advice' which has become more common as a verb: to *counsel* people involved in a tragedy, for instance. This is *counselling* done by *counsellors*. A *council* is some sort of controlling group or assembly (perhaps a Town *Council*) and a *councillor* is a member of it. To confuse matters a barrister in court is known as *counsel* and *counsellor* is also used (rather archaically) as an adviser to a king or suchlike.

▶ principal/principle

It is worrying to see these so often confused in 'quality' newspapers. A *principle* is a moral truth or guide to existence: *a man of principle, the principle of equality*. *Principal* can be used as noun or adjective, but always means 'chief' or 'main': *principal of a college, principal witness*.

▶ complement(ary)/compliment(ary)

Complement has been much used in this book as something that completes; you will also find it in phrases like *ship's complement* and people whose qualities or characters fit together are *complementary*. A *compliment* is a favourable comment; *complimentary* is also used for something that is not charged for: *a complimentary buffet*.

▶ program/programme

The American spelling of the word, *program*, is used in computing parlance in Britain. In all other meanings *programme* is used in Britain, *program* in the USA.

▶ capitol/capital

Capital can be used as noun or adjective with many meanings to do with 'chief' or 'head': *capital punishment, a capital idea, capital funding, the capital of Romania*, etc. The Roman *Capitol* was the chief temple and now the term is used throughout the USA for state or federal legislature buildings: *Each state capital has its Capitol*.

▶ review/revue

These are particularly confusable since both may well be used in the same area (theatre) and a writer may well write both. A *revue* is an entertainment, usually made up of songs and sketches, often satirical, while a *review* is literally 'another look', which can have many applications: from a display of troops for a senior officer to a 'write-up' on the previous night's television. If New Year television promises *A Review of the Year*, it looks back on important or interesting events; if it promises *Revue of the Year*, it uses those events to entertain via songs and satire.

▶ roll/role

A *role* is a part in a play or, by extension, a part played in real life: 'The Opposition Leader took on the *role* of defender of national sovereignty'. *Roll* has many meanings, from bread to lists of workers, and the two are sometimes confused in the latter area: 'Mr Walker is on the *roll* of candidates for promotion.' If he is successful, you could then write, 'Mr Walker was looking forward to his new senior *role*.'

▶ martial/marshal

Like various others in this list, *martial* and *marshal* can easily find themselves in the same context, thus adding to the possibilities for confusion. *Martial* is the easier to explain: an adjective meaning 'to do with war or fighting', as in *martial arts* or *court martial*, an old-fashioned reversal of noun and adjective. *Marshal* is a verb meaning 'to assemble or arrange' or a noun as in US marshal. You might *marshal* the troops for a court *martial* and, of course, a Field *Marshal*'s career is at the highest level of *martial* affairs.

▶ straight/strait

Both are adjectives, with nouns of similar meaning derived from them. *Straight* is direct, without deviation and can also be an adverb ('Come *straight* home') and as a noun might be the *straight* of a racetrack. *Strait* means 'narrow', but is rather archaic as an adjective. We find it in the Bible ('*Strait* (narrow) is the gate') and as a noun in the *Straits of Dover*, etc.

▶ meter/metre

Again there are similarities of meaning to spread possible confusion. Both deal with measuring, but, whereas *meter* is a measuring device (as in *electricity meter*), *metre* is a measured distance (or the rhythmical form of a piece of poetry). Both have many compounds: *barometer/thermometer, kilometre/millimetre*.

▶ And one extra...

The fact that *there* and *their* are short, commonly used words does not prevent errors of spelling. The guidelines are simple and clear-cut. *Their* comes from *they* (the *y* doing its usual switch to *i*). It means 'belonging to them' and the *e* precedes the *i*, the sound not being *ee*. *There* relates to *here* and is its opposite in meaning; it is also used in phrases like *there is/are…* And, finally, of course, the abbreviated version of *they are* is *they're*.

Punctuation: terminal points

Punctuation, it is worth repeating, is a convention to aid clear communication. A writer's style and preferences may be indicated in his/her ways of using such punctuation marks as semicolons and dashes. However, unless you are so distinctive a stylist as to be able freely to ignore the rules (or, perhaps, a poet), it is as well to found any idiosyncrasies on the basic principles of punctuation. These are much more clear-cut than those concerning spelling and, unlike the section on spelling, the following makes an attempt to be comprehensive. However, it is far from being detailed: very little explanation is needed of the functions of some of the major punctuation marks, so the briefest of reminders will suffice.

Each sentence ends with a terminal point, followed by a capital letter at the beginning of the next sentence. It is hardly necessary to point out the differences between **full stop**, **question mark** and **exclamation mark**, but you might like to note:

▶ A **question mark** is used when the form of the sentence is a question, not when the speaker is expecting an answer. *I wonder if you can tell me the time.* is followed by a full stop although an answer is expected whereas *Would you mind being quiet?* keeps its question mark although it is an implied command, answerable by silence.

▶ Most of the full sentences ending in **exclamation marks** do so by the choice of the writer: the tone of voice or the style of the article determines whether *Now we are going to swim with the dolphins* ends with full stop or exclamation mark.

Insight

It is in the nature of exclamation and question marks that they occur more often in speech and in writing that reflects speech. Exclaiming and questioning are part of the give-and-take of conversation. Therefore the basic rules tend to be bent somewhat, not only in questions like *You what?* or exclamations like *Gercha!* For instance *You expect to win tomorrow?* is perfectly normal in writing that quotes or imitates speech. It is as well to keep in mind the basic format, however; writing scattered with exclamation marks or question marks mid-sentence needs to have a good justification.

COLONS (:) AND SEMICOLONS (;)

The role of colons and semicolons in dividing clauses has been touched on in Chapter 9, but their functions extend more widely than that. The interesting point is that colons have clearly defined functions whereas a semicolon is a much more flexible punctuation mark, one that you never need to use, but which can give precision to your writing.

▶ The semicolon

It is probably as well to see a semicolon as occupying the territory between a full stop and a comma. In other words, if a full stop seems too terminal or a comma too temporary a pause, there is a role for the semicolon. Two main clauses may not be linked by any conjunction, yet seem too close in meaning to be separate sentences:

In the morning the Geography paper was really hard; the English in the afternoon was much better.

It is, of course, a matter of choice: a full stop would also be correct and there is scope for a subordinate clause, perhaps using *whereas*.

The other use is when a comma seems inadequate. A list is punctuated by commas, but what if each item in the list is lengthy, with various commas in use?

We took with us to the party a bottle of white wine, though we failed to find their favourite Chablis; all the presents, including those Jane had sent from Scotland; a couple of CDs we thought would interest them; the birthday cake we had promised and a special bottle opener to add to Steve's collection of gadgets.

You could punctuate that solely with commas, but it would be very difficult to follow. With such long and clumsy phrases, some writers would even favour inserting another semicolon after '...we had promised'.

▶ The colon

The **colon** has two specific purposes. Placed in the middle of a sentence, it introduces a section that explains, amplifies or completes what has gone before: this may be in terms of a reasoned account (as in this present sentence) or simply a list. As so often, the function of a colon is best illustrated by examples:

Rovers were playing with a back four: Bell, Miller, Jones and Doyle. (first half amplified by list)

Seville Cathedral is a dominating structure: it is said to be bigger than St Paul's. (first half amplified by clause adding extra facts)
Eric was worried about his health: a check-up proved negative. (first half completed by clause)
I decided not to go to Australia after all: the prospect of such a long flight put me off. (first half explained by clause)

If you use the colon in this way, do not insert a subordinating conjunction. The alternative to the last example would be:

I decided not to go to Australia after all because the prospect of such a long flight put me off.

The second purpose of a colon could be defined as introducing speech, although that is not quite accurate. For ordinary speech, though a colon is acceptable, a comma is preferable. However, colons are rightly used for examples or extended quotations, perhaps from a newspaper or a work of literature, as in the following example:

Hamlet at this stage appears to be contemplating suicide: 'To be or not to be, that is the question…'

The addition of a dash to the colon is not encouraged.

DASHES AND HYPHENS

Unfortunately these can appear identical (correctly the dash is longer than the hyphen) although they have very different, almost opposite functions. A *dash* is essentially a piece of sentence punctuation, dividing parts of a sentence, whereas a *hyphen* usually links single words.

▶ Dashes

A major function of the dash (or, usually, of a pair of dashes) is to separate a **parenthesis** (or **parenthetical phrase**) from the rest of the sentence:

Our itinerary includes a visit to Dubrovnik – the ancient walled city has now undergone successful restoration following the civil wars – before resuming the cruise through the Adriatic.

A parenthesis is an insert which does not form part of the grammatical structure of the sentence. Sometimes a phrase which could be absorbed syntactically is treated as a parenthesis because it seems like an insert or afterthought:

The problem with dashes – and also with brackets – is knowing when to use them.

A parenthesis can also be indicated with **brackets** (properly, but confusingly, known as parentheses). This is a matter of preference, but consistency helps to improve your English style: perhaps brackets for short phrases, dashes for clauses or non-finite clauses. Remember that, once opened, brackets must be closed; dashes must also be repeated, unless the end of the sentence intervenes.

Dashes also have a useful function as the most informal of punctuation marks: to indicate a gap or interruption, to hold the tension for a pause before a comic or dramatic resolution:

> 'I need to see you to talk about –' Suddenly the line went dead. The main speaker slowly stepped forward, surveyed the audience with a patronizing smile, placed his speech on the lectern – and knocked the water jug all over the first page.

▶ Hyphens

The main function of hyphens is to join two words or sometimes prefix and stem, to form a word that may exist as a dictionary entry or may be created for the occasion. For instance, *anti-personnel* (meaning 'intending to harm people') exists as a word; movements to outlaw pugilism or beauty contests would be termed *anti-boxing* or *anti-Miss World*.

Insight

The insertion of a hyphen can affect meaning even though words are unchanged. Let us imagine a film critic writing about one of those comedians who work hard to make us feel sorry for them: what you might call the Chaplin tradition. What is the difference between writing *X cuts a comic, pathetic figure*, and (forming his own compound) *X cuts a comic-pathetic figure*? The difference is slight, but definite: the first states that X is comic and he is pathetic, the second bases his style on the fusion of the two.

This fusion of words via hyphens can take various forms, including, of course, names (*Anne-Marie* or *Lloyd-Roberts*) and set phrases, often of more than two words (*out-of-date*, *happy-go-lucky*). A pair of words might make a progress over the years from being two separate words to being hyphenated to being one word and it is often difficult to be sure where along that journey any word is. Inconsistencies abound: we are *hardbitten*, but *hard-hearted* and *hard up*. Hyphens are often used when a noun or adjective phrase is used before the noun: we use *common sense*, but take a *common-sense attitude*.

It is interesting to note what happens to nouns based on **phrasal verbs** of two or more separate words. The nouns are hyphenated (occasionally even single words):

> This meant we could not *run through* the play on stage until Sunday.
> The first *run-through* was a disaster.

In print a dash rather than a hyphen can be used between names to indicate movement or opposition rather than unity (A *driver-mechanic* (hyphen) combination may go on the *London–Brighton* (dash) run), but this is a nicety that need not occupy the minds of most students of English.

APOSTROPHES AND QUOTATION MARKS/INVERTED COMMAS

Like dashes and hyphens these are similar in appearance, quite different in function. **Inverted commas** or **quotation marks** are considered in the section on **direct speech** in Chapter 10. The main points to consider are:

Some guides to English write that single quotation marks are used for the main speech and double for a quotation inside the speech. A preference for double quotation marks is, however, generally acceptable, but it is important to reverse the form for a secondary quotation:

> The new trainee said, 'I'm sorry I missed what you said. Did you say, "Turn right at the double doors"?'

or

> The new trainee said, "I'm sorry I missed what you said. Did you say, 'Turn right at the double doors'?"

The example above illustrates the important rule about punctuation marks (most noticeably exclamation and question marks) in speech. If the question/exclamation is within the speech, the punctuation mark is inside the quotation marks. In the example the trainee is asking a question, but the other speaker did not ask a question: hence the placing of the question mark.

Remember that quotation marks surround **only the words actually spoken**. For *she said* or *he remarked*, the quotation marks close and re-open:

> 'I remember that holiday in Greece,' she said, 'where we all suffered with sunburn.'

Quotation marks can be used to suggest that the word you are using may not be true (the equivalent of 'so-called') or is a title not yet proven. Generally nowadays titles of books, films, albums, etc., are indicated by italics, but quotation marks are equally common for the titles of chapters, articles, songs, etc. So you might refer to the song 'With a little help from my friends' from the Beatles' album *Sergeant Pepper's Lonely Hearts Club Band*.

▶ **Apostrophes**

The basic purpose of apostrophes is to indicate the omission of letters in the middle of a word: *we'll, didn't, Hallowe'en, it's* (only when it means *it is* or *it has*).

Occasionally an apostrophe will be used for an omitted letter at the beginning of a word (*'cello* for *violoncello*), but this is not necessary. Omissions at the end of a word are indicated by a full stop: *Co.* for *Company*. Also such abbreviations as *Mr.* and *Mrs.* (for *Mister* and, originally, *Mistress*) traditionally employ a full stop when an apostrophe might seem more logical. The current tendency to economize on punctuation in titles and addresses means that it is now common to omit the full stops, certainly in print (as in this book).

It is widely thought that the other use of apostrophes (to indicate **possession**) stems from a misunderstanding of the omission rule. Formerly possession was simply indicated by an *s*, but the belief that this was short for *his* led to the inclusion of the apostrophe. When indicating singular possession, *'s* follows the noun. Plurals in *s* form possession by adding the apostrophe after the *s*:

The missing girl's school has not been disclosed.
Most schools are mixed, but there is a girls' school in the town.
The bank's policy is not to give unsecured loans.
The banks' merger should strengthen their financial base.

THE COMMA

Left until the end, the comma is the punctuation mark with either the least or the most functions of all. If you attempt to define the different functions of a comma, the list seems almost endless: adjectives or nouns in a list, introducing speech, dividing many forms of subordinate clause from the main clause or each other, following written salutations, etc. On the other hand the role of the comma can be defined as making a necessary short pause or division between elements that are nonetheless closely linked. A comma asks the reader to distinguish between the elements on each side of it, but not to make a fresh start.

The main weakness in use of the comma is, in fact, overuse, especially where a full stop, semicolon or colon is needed. Though a pair of commas can mark a parenthesis, this is advisable only in short parentheses; otherwise sentence structure disappears beneath the various different applications of commas. The two following sentences are good examples of the use of the comma for a parenthesis:

> The car, incidentally, has had to go in for service.
> The path by the beach, the 'prom' as we called it, was under several inches of water.

but not:

> When it became obvious that the fire was out, the chief officer, with a wry smile, his good temper had been undisturbed throughout, congratulated us on our good luck.

The parenthesis, 'his good temper…throughout', needs dashes or brackets.

A FEW FINAL NOTES

An ellipsis (…) can be useful:

▶ as above, to indicate a section of sentence or speech omitted;

▶ to indicate an unfinished sentence: generally dashes are better for a sudden interruption, dots for a fading away.

Square brackets have a specific function in formal academic works. You may find them of use in the difficult 'brackets-within-brackets' situation. This can be equally well done by changing one set of brackets to commas or dashes:

> The rescue party eventually caught sight of the survivors – by this time the water levels (a record for the river at the time of year) were alarmingly high – but could not reach them as yet.

Above all punctuation should be used to aid clarity of communication: rules are fairly clear-cut, but form a basis that should be used constructively, rather than slavishly.

? Test yourself

14.1 A 'spelling test' would not really be appropriate in this book and would have to run to many pages to be really effective. However, you can examine the following choices of spelling and decide which is right. Not all have been dealt with in this chapter:

a   Vanity was the (principal/principle) cause of his downfall.

b   The *Mirror* published (exerpts/excerpts) from his autobiography.

c   I am sorry you took offence at a (humorous/humourous) comment.

d   The climbers prepared for the (assent/ascent) of Everest.

e   She was hoping to be elected to the borough (counsel/council).

f   Our problems seemed to (receed/recede) into the distance.

g   If you are not careful, spelling rules can (decieve/deceive) you.

h   The inspector (accepted/excepted) Jones from his criticism.

i   I always enjoy (marshal/martial) music.

j   The Prime Minister suffered a (fierce/feirce) attack in the Commons.

k   Is (phsycopathology/psychopathology) an interesting study?

l   The (consensus/concensus) of opinion is on our side.

m   Working together, Claire and Emma had (complementary/complimentary) skills.

n   The (siege/seige) of Ladysmith was one of the major events of the Boer War.

o   The traffic was (stationary/stationery).

14.2 Insert the punctuation of your choice in the following passage. There is no intention to confuse you about the meaning, so the end of every sentence is marked. However, as you have a choice of terminal points, each is marked with*, not a full stop.

If you are doing this as the final exercise in the book you probably feel a sense of relief fourteen chapters on grammar and the English language may be considered more than enough* As you come to the end some of you of course may be approaching the chapters in a different order you will we hope have derived some benefit from the book* What you may be asking yourself did you hope to gain from it and has that been achieved* Some of you may have been seeking purely practical assistance some may have been interested in the forms of English some students ambitions may have extended to pursuing advanced study* Possibly some of you may be discouraged* why you may say to yourself did I bother to start* We hope you are not so down hearted and may be thinking Ill carry on studying English* Its really interesting* There was quite a bit I didnt know* Whatever your feelings and reactions are bound to be different you will certainly have appreciated the kind heartedness involved in finishing with such a straightforward exercise*.

Test yourself answers

1 THE HISTORY OF THE ENGLISH LANGUAGE

▶ **1.1**

a *This King stayed at Camelot at Christmas, with many noble lords, the best of princes, graciously (or, perhaps, reputedly) all the high-ranking brothers of the Round Table, with rich revelry in the right fashion and carefree mirth.*

b *Murder will out, we see that every day. Murder is so loathsome and abominable to God, who is so just and reasonable, that he will not allow it to be concealed, though it may stay for a year or two or three. Murder will out, that's my conclusion.*

It would be surprising if you did not find the first one more difficult, despite a straightforward first line (allowing for the thorn at the beginning). Therefore you probably decided to place it at an earlier date than the second. In fact, both belong to the last quarter of the 14th century. *Sir Gawain and the Green Knight* was probably written in Lancashire. The second extract is from Chaucer's *Canterbury Tales*, written in the East Midland dialect, the forerunner of modern English.

Apart from spelling (*wlatsome* for 'loathsome' being the oddest) and the occasional change in meaning *(heled* means 'hidden') there is very little difference from modern English, mainly word order and the use of the double negative (*ne wol nat*). It is easy to see the 15th century, the time of Chaucer's influence, as the date when the English languages became the English language.

▶ **1.2**

a *The skies began to scowl, overcast with misty clouds, when (as I rode alone towards London, cloakless, unclad/unclothed) I sang and spoke as follows.*

The poet is George Gascoigne and the poem was published in 1573. You will note that essentially it is normal modern English. The differences lie in the spelling and the use of the capital letter. The main difficulty is a social matter, not one of language. We know that *unclad* is an old-fashioned version of *unclothed*, but what did an Elizabethan gentleman mean by *unclothed*?

b *The most senior answered him, the leader of the band unlocked his word hoard.*

The lines come from the famous Old English poem *Beowulf* (date disputed – maybe 800). Note some familiar words, but also the fashion in Old English poetry for using repetition and metaphorical set pieces for simple acts: 'to speak' is often *to unlock the word hoard*, probably accompanied by *speak* or *answer*.

c Translation not needed. The extract is from the 19th-century American novel *Huckleberry Finn*. Mark Twain is imitating the speech of Mississippi folks.

d Translation not needed, except to insert the date: 1764. Edward Gibbon's *Decline and Fall of the Roman Empire* is a fine example of the rolling cadences and structured sentences of 18th-century academic writing.

e *In summer when the sun was warm, I dressed myself in rough clothes as if I were a shepherd. Dressed like a hermit who does not do holy things, I went out into the wide world to hear of wonders.*

William Langland was Chaucer's contemporary, probably dying in the same year: 1400. His *Piers Plowman* is written in a more northerly and western dialect than Chaucer; it is set on the Malvern Hills in Worcestershire. Note that he still uses thorn. The pattern of alliteration (for instance, *s* in the first line) is also like Old English poetry. In general, the vocabulary seems very 'English' compared to Chaucer.

f *– But is this the law?/ – Damn right it is, coroner's inquest law./ –D'you want to know the truth? If she hadn't been a gentlewoman, she would never have got a Christian funeral.* This is Shakespeare, the gravediggers in *Hamlet* discussing Ophelia's death. Note that slang is subject to most change. These are 'Clowns', rough comedians, and 'of it' turns into *an't*, etc. *Marry* is a mild oath, referring to the Virgin Mary, for which *damn right* gives the tone, but not the meaning.

g Translation not needed. This is *Great Expectations* by Charles Dickens (mid-19th century). When Dickens is difficult to follow, it is usually due to the complications of his sentences or, as here, his love of metaphor: education becomes a dangerous journey, beset by brambles and thieves who dog his steps in disguise.

h *I know a bird in a bright bower, that is very fair to see, a graceful and powerful maiden, fair and free to take.*

This is a rather conventional 14th-century carol in praise of the Virgin Mary. You may have noticed the alliteration again and the use of phrases like *on syht* and *of myht* as rhyming 'fillers'. The most interesting feature is *Ichot*. *Wot* meant 'know' (linked with the current word, *wit*). *Ichot* is short for *Ich wot* (I know), so we find the Germanic (and Old English) *ich* for 'I' as late as the 14th century.

2 DIVIDING THE WORD

▶ **2.1**

The following are compounds. The hyphen is inserted to show the join between the original words; it is not part of the normal spelling: head-strong; house-wife; time-keeper; foot-man; milk-maid.

▶ **2.2**

in-digest-ible: derivational morpheme (prefix) *in-*, free morpheme *digest*, derivational morpheme (suffix) *-ible*
turn-ed: free *turn*, inflectional morpheme *-ed* (past)
prune-s: free *prune*, inflectional *-s* (plural)
oral: free morpheme.
re-call: derivational (prefix) *re-*, free *call*
embarrass-ment: free *embarrass*, derivational (suffix) *-ment*
dis-taste: derivational (prefix) *dis-*, free *taste*
fly-ing: free *fly*, inflectional *-ing* (present participle)
cobra: free morpheme
fore-man: two free morphemes
forest: free morpheme
mis-direct-ion: derivational (prefix) *mis-*, free *direct*, derivational (suffix) *-ion*
weari-ly: free *weary* (i), derivational (suffix) *-ly*
condens-ation: free *condens(e)*, derivational (suffix) *-ation*
elephant: free morpheme

▶ **2.3**

syllables	morphemes
de-part-ure	depart-ure
in-ac-cess-i-ble	in-access-ible
post-script	post-script

post-er	poster
in-firm	in-firm
dis-arm	dis-arm
dis-eased	dis-ease-d
un-app-eal-ing	un-appeal-ing
dread-ful	dread-ful
wick-ed-ly	wicked-ly
att-empt-ing	attempt-ing
ket-tles	kettle-s
walk-ing	walk-ing
re-fresh-ing	re-fresh-ing
re-col-lect	re-collect

3 NOUNS

▶ **3.1**

Proper: Edison, Clarendon, Suite, Regency, Welcome, List, Oak, Tree, Restaurant, Grapes, Bistro.

Common: hotel, site, rooms, standards, comfort, television, telephone, minibar, luxury, style, rates, firms, meals, residents, menus, wine, discrimination, breakfast, risers, discretion, management.

Collective: set, groups, parties, list, team.

a A case could be made for *management* and *firms* being collective nouns.

b All words of an individual name or title have been listed as proper nouns. Of course words like *oak*, *tree* and *restaurant* are familiar common nouns, but here they are used as part of an individual name.

c *Welcome List* is particularly interesting. If the hotel had used lower case, that would imply that there was a *welcome list* which had not been given a specific name. Firms could equally well refer to a *priority list*, for instance. In that case *welcome* and *list* would be common nouns. The capital letters show that the management has named it *Welcome List* just as they have named the *Grapes Bistro* – hence proper nouns.

d Some of the nouns here (e.g. *Regency* and *management*) are used as modifiers to other nouns, normally the function of an adjective. If you have left them off your list for this reason, consider your answer correct.

e The phrase *en suite* seemed too French for *suite* to be included in the list!

▶ **3.2**

comfort; luxury; style; discrimination; discretion.

▶ **3.3**

friends	matches	fish *or* fishes
cargoes	valleys	enemies
memorandums *or* memoranda	spoonfuls	ladies-in-waiting
	brasses	elephants
bonuses	moose	armies
trousers*	reefs	censuses
journeys	sopranos	hoofs *or* hooves
catches		
toys	theories	ditches
swine	lice	brothers**
auditoriums *or* auditoria	monkeys	taxes

*exists only in plural/the singular is *pair* of trousers
**archaic *brethren*

▶ **3.4**

a adjectival

b apposition

c apposition

d adjectival

e adjectival

f apposition

g apposition

h   adjectival (tricky to distinguish these two – remember the rule about the sentence making sense without one part of the apposition)

i   apposition

j   adjectival.

4 PRONOUNS

▶ **4.1**

a   I presented *my* report at the same time as the secretary and treasurer presented *theirs*.

b   When my friends and *I* went to the zoo, we took my brother with *us*.

c   He enjoyed his day out with my friends and *me*.

d   Yesterday the team met *its* new manager.

e   We need at least two phones, so, even if Jane brings *hers*, you'll have to bring *yours*.

f   We'll play doubles: you and your sister against my brother and *me*.

g   The dog wagged *its* tail.

h   Mr and Mrs Brewer resisted every attempt to direct *them* towards *their* destination.

Note: any use of apostrophes in the personal pronouns is incorrect.

▶ **4.2**

a   *His* before *first novel* has to be changed. You could use *his or her* or turn the whole thing into the plural, being careful to put everything into the plural: 'Novelists (or all novelists) are bound to find that their first novels are difficult to place with publishers.'

b   *He* needs to be changed. This sounds like an instruction or memo, so the rather awkward *he or she* is quite suitable.

c   Unless you wish to rewrite completely, this is one of the comparatively few cases where *one* sounds idiomatic: 'Attending one's first interview…'

d   This is very much like b, a formal instruction, and you could choose the same solution.

▶ **4.3**

Your version may be very different from the one below and still be correct. You may simply have made different decisions about who did what. But this is one of the versions that makes sense:

As Marion was turning the corner, she saw Kate who called out to her. Marian caught up with Kate just as she reached the Market Hall. At this moment Jamie and Chris came out of the burger bar: they looked amazed to see the girls. They waved to them, but Marion and Kate were in a hurry and, calling out 'See you later', ran to the bus station.

Note: There are still examples of doubling personal pronouns – 'They waved to them' –, but in the context all becomes clear.

▶ **4.4**

a Playing in the park, the children really enjoyed *themselves*.

b The General *himself* took responsibility for the prisoners' safety. (You could leave out *himself*, but the General is probably important enough to justify some emphasis!)

c David cut *himself* on the broken glass.

d My family and *I* enjoy giving our opinions on radio phone-ins. ('My family and *myself*' would be ungrammatical as well as pompous.)

e We needed no second invitation: we helped *ourselves* to the drinks and snacks.

f You're so conceited you're always praising *yourself*. (This answer assumes that you are addressing one person. Perhaps it could be more than one – if so, *yourselves*.)

g It was Sue who raised the alarm. (Unless in your story Sue is a very important character, perhaps someone very afraid of fire, perhaps the person who started the fire. Then you would put, 'It was Sue *herself* who raised the alarm.')

▶ **4.5**

There are usually two variants, depending on which clause you make the main sentence. The following versions choose the likelier variant; if you have chosen the other, it is not wrong, though probably more awkward.

a The dog which we bought was a German shepherd.

b The girl whom we met on holiday came to see us yesterday.

c The shopkeeper whose premises had been raided went to the police.

d We wanted to see the church the tower of which dated back to Saxon times. (That is the strictly correct version; many people would be happier with 'whose tower'.)

e I arranged to photograph the model who had been featured in the new magazine.

f The police arrested the woman whom they found at the scene of the crime.

▶ **4.6**

a brings

b an

c a

d those

e is

f are – a bit of a trick because, although *either* is usually singular, here the alternatives are plural, so the verb has to be plural too.

g what

h that

i the driver of which

j was

5 VERBS

▶ **5.1**

a *lay*: doing – intransitive.

b *was*: being; *brought*: doing – transitive.

c *did appear*: doing – intransitive.

d *questioned*: doing – transitive.

e *appeared*: being.

f *laid*: doing – transitive; *sighed*: doing – intransitive.

g *did tell*: doing – transitive (an awkward one: the object is the noun clause 'that Sue became the area supervisor last year' – it answers the question, 'Tell you what?' so it is the object); *became*: being (another awkward one as it implies something happening, but 'the area supervisor' is the same as Sue and thus the complement).

h *have found*: doing – transitive (noun clause as object like g); *are*: being.

i *seems*: being.

j *whispered*: doing – intransitive ('they whispered secrets' would be transitive).

k *said*: doing – transitive.

l *has applied*: doing – intransitive; *have*: doing – transitive.

m *were*: being; *went*: doing – intransitive.

n *is*: being; *have had*: doing – transitive (again tricky: the object is 'the best day' before the verb).

o *can tell*: doing – transitive (noun clause again); *is growing*: being.

p *kick*: doing – transitive.

▶ **5.2**

a Each of the brothers *has* a job with the Post Office.

b I *was* sure that he *had taken* the key.

c The goods *would arrive* on Tuesday. (This would be used in connection with statements made in the past – 'He assured me that...')

d I *thought* that she *went* to her night class on Mondays.

e The machine *was working* perfectly.

f Britain *has opted* out of the treaty.

g The band *has* a gig in Warrington.

h Your father *has spoken* to you about it.

i The window *was smashed* last night.

j The 100 metres record *will not be broken*.

Simple past	past participle
a defined	defined
b tried	tried
c ran	run
d treated	treated

(The old strong form *tret* is still common in regional speech, but is not formally correct.)

e swam	swum
f sawed	sawn

(another example of the -*n* past participle in a seemingly regular verb)

g led	led
h scanned	scanned
i paid	paid

(note the spelling: the same applies to *say*)

j hung or hanged	hung or hanged

(the form depends on the meaning: game is hung in a shop, men were hanged on the gallows)

k smote	smitten
l went	gone
m sowed	sowed
n chose	chosen
o founded	founded

(no connection with *find/found/found*)

p bent	bent

▶ 5.4

a *has*: used with past participle to form present perfect.

b *is*: used with past participle to form passive.

c *should*: modal verb used with infinitive and suggesting correct situation; *be*: used with past participle to form passive.

d *would*: both *woulds* are conditional (what would apply under certain conditions). The first also suggests will (wanting or planning to do something).

e *is*: used with present participle to form continuous tense.

f *do*: used with infinitive to divide verb for a question.

g *have*: used with past participle to form present perfect; *can*: modal verb expressing permission (*may* would have been more formal, but *can* is acceptable).

h *had*: used with past participle to form past perfect.

i *does*: used with infinitive to divide present tense verb with *not*; *has*: used with past participle to form present perfect.

j *do*: used with infinitive to contradict or give emphasis, possibly in response to 'You don't even know where India is!'

k *have*: used with past participle (*been*) to form present perfect; *been*: used with past participle (*imprisoned*) to form passive.

l *am*: used with past participle to form passive.

m *shall*: used with infinitive to form future; *are*: used with past participle to form passive.

n *would*: used with infinitive to form future in the past.

o *might*: modal verb used with infinitive to express possibility (*may* equally acceptable).

p *ought* (*to*): modal verb used with infinitive to express moral conviction; *are*: used with past participle to form passive.

▶ **5.5**

a	was	g	is
b	were	h	be
c	were	i	were
d	was	j	was
e	see	k	was
f	was	l	were

▶ **5.6**

a *To find*: infinitive, part of noun phrase, subject of sentence.

b *hoping*: present participle, part of adjectival phrase modifying *Dr Jamieson*; *interesting*: present participle used as adjective to modify *lecture*.

c *Driving*: gerund, part of noun phrase, subject of sentence; *to get*: infinitive, part of complement; *arrested*: past participle, used to form passive voice.

d *receiving*: gerund, part of noun phrase, object of sentence.

e *Snoring*: gerund used as noun, subject of sentence; *irritating*: present participle used as adjective to modify *habit*.

f *snoring*: present participle, used to form present continuous.

g *Elated*: past participle, used as part of adjectival phrase modifying *Amy*; *depressed*: part participle, used as part of adjectival phrase, complement; *to find*: infinitive, part of noun phrase, object of *failed*.

h *fixed*: past participle, used to form perfect tense. *broken*: past participle, used adjectivally to modify *window*.

i *battered*: past participle, used adjectivally to modify *yacht*; *towed*: past participle, used to form passive.

j *climbing*: present participle, part of adjectival phrase modifying *we*.

k *climbing*: gerund, part of noun phrase as subject of sentence.

l *climbing*: gerund, part of noun phrase, object of sentence.

m *been*: past participle, forming perfect tense; *climbing*: present participle forming continuous tense (past continuous).

n *To err*: infinitive as subject of sentence.

o *To forget*: infinitive, part of noun phrase as subject of sentence; *shocking*: present participle, used adjectivally as complement modifying subject (the entire noun phrase).

▶ **5.7**

a The Ambassador, coming to meet the Prime Minister, nearly tripped over.

b Each of the answers is right.

c The Bishop, with acolytes, servers and members of the choir, is due to enter at any moment.

d Here are the Bishop and the choir.

e The choir has joined the Bishop.

f If we had got up earlier, we might have caught the train.

g Haven't you eaten your tea yet?

h If I had been notified in time, I would have prepared the room.

i There are two reasons for leaving early.

j I was dreading meeting the Lord Mayor.

6 MODIFIERS

▶ **6.1**

Adjectives	Participles	Nouns	Phrases
front	fascinating	theatre	in the 19th century
empty	peace-keeping	car	at the back
red	warring	wine	on the stage
other	separated	combat	
new	advanced		
large			
small			
preliminary			
new			
this			

▶ **6.2**

a All are modifying nouns: *bus* or *gear*.

b *In the valley* modifies *house*; *lonely* and *desolate* (which can be regarded as two adjectives or joined together as a phrase) form the complement.

c *Sure* and *green* are both complements.

d At *his last gasp* is complement. *Last* is also an adjective modifying *gasp*.

e All words and phrases modify nouns: *sun* or *problems*.

f A bit of a trick: the complement is *the successful applicant*, a noun complement, not an adjectival complement. Within that *successful* modifes the noun *applicant*.

▶ **6.3**

a *Less than last year*: when you are dealing with a quantity, the comparative of *little* is *less*.

b Correct.

c *More* comfortable: only two contenders, so use comparative.

d Correct.

e *More desperate*: *desperate* is far too long to take the *-er* ending, unless you want a comic effect.

f 'The *last*': *the latter* (comparative) refers to the final one of two; here there are three.

g Probably correct (unless there are only two chairs!).

h *Fastest*: using *more* and *most* for a short word like *fast* sounds silly. *Younger*: only two of them.

▶ **6.4**

Many different alternatives. Here is one:

> I was suffering from a *painful* knee, so it was *pleasing* that Sue should offer me a lift. *(Probably better to recast sentence: 'I was pleased/relieved/delighted when Sue offered me a lift.')* There was *heavy* traffic in the city centre and we were afraid we would be late which would have been really *embarrassing*, but we hit a *clear* stretch of road and kept up a *high* average speed until we reached Sutton. There's a *dangerous* turn just before the college where they have set up temporary traffic lights, but a *helpful* man waved us through. At the gates we had some difficulty because the direction signs were *very confusing*, but we found a *convenient* parking place and got into the lecture in *good* time. *(Probably better to recast as 'We had plenty of time' or some construction using 'early'.)*

▶ **6.5**

Adjectives		modifying	Adverbs	modifying
a	crucial	document	evidently	*Whole sentence*
b	afraid	*complement*		
		– I	violently	angry
	angry	mob		
c	new	model	very	well
			well	worked
d	attractive	picture	never	*whole sentence*
e	slow	service	when	*interrogative*
			dreadfully	slow

f	superficial	*complement*		
		– charm	only	superficial
g	chief	minister		
	present	*complement*		
		– minister		
h	longer	*complement*		
		– road		
i			longer	waited
j	final	– stage	dangerously	fast
	fast	*complement*		
		– stage		

▶ **6.6**

happily	subtly	well	helpfully
finally	hard	basically	friendlily
incorrigibly	gaily	shrilly	definitely

▶ **6.7**

a *Suddenly* (adverb – time) and *for no good reason* (phrase – reason) both modify verb *withdrew*.

b *Indeed* (adverb) modifies whole sentence; *when the news broke* is an adverbial clause of time; *incredibly* (adverb of degree) modifies participial adjective *unprepared*.

c *If I take the job* is an adverbial clause of condition; *each day* is an adverbial phrase of time. Both modify verb *travel*.

d *Tomorrow* is an adverb of time modifying verb *start*.

e *Regularly* (adverb) and *on the 15th* (phrase) – or put together as one phrase – modify verb *receive* as adverbial phrase of time. *Monthly*, despite the *-ly*, is an adjective, not an adverb.

f *In the event of fire* (phrase – condition) and *immediately* (adverb – time) both modify verb *gather*.

g *Slowly* is an adverb of manner modifying verb *returned*. *Home* is very interesting: it is here used as an adverb of place – you could define it best as a noun used adverbially.

h *Where the Ml meets the M25* (adverb clause – place) and *often* (adverb – time) modify verb – since the verb is *is*, better to say the verb/complement (*is...a hold-up*).

i *Desperately* is an adverb of manner (or, perhaps, in this case, degree) modifying adjective *close*.

j *From the balcony* (phrase – place) modifies verb/complement (*is...a view*); *much* is an adverb of degree modifying adjective *better*.

These are quite detailed statements of function; if your answers contain some, but not all, of the details given here, please consider them correct.

▶ **6.8**

a Some might object to the split infinitive, but this is probably all right.

b Substitute *badly* for *bad*: it is an adverb modifying verb *played*.

c Correct: *bad* is an adjectival complement relating to *group*.

d Don't use *at the end of the day* in this sense. This sentence is obvious nonsense.

e An awful example of split infinitive: please move *despite the opposition* to the beginning or the end.

f This is perfectly acceptable; those who (for no particular reason) dislike this use of *hopefully* are fighting a losing (maybe even lost) battle.

g This could be right. This means that she acted as if she were (pretended to be?) stupid, probably to deceive the police. 'She acted *stupidly*' would mean she did stupid things: tried to escape through a window, perhaps, or confessed to things she didn't do.

h The placing of *only* means that you did nothing else to these articles except find them: you didn't, for instance, steal them or fight a gang of hoodlums to get them back. What you are probably trying to say, though, is that these were the only things you found: the scarf, perhaps, is gone for ever. This should be, 'I found *only* the handbag and the umbrella.'

7 FUNCTION WORDS

▶ **7.1**

to: preposition. *to*: could be termed preposition – part of infinitive *to use*. *about*: preposition. *of*: preposition. *but*: conjunction, its normal usage, but it can be a preposition in sentences like 'Nobody *but* an optimist would believe that.' *during*: preposition. *about*: preposition, even though at the end of the clause. *after*: subordinating conjunction. *down*: adverb, *of*: preposition. *before*: adverb. *at*: preposition. *in*: preposition. *up*: adverb. *by*: preposition. *In*: preposition. *in*: adverb. *across*: adverb. *at*: preposition. *down*: adjective (admittedly rather slangy!)*. *up*: adverb*. *to*: preposition. *to*: part of infinitive. *on*: preposition. *out of*: preposition. *at*: preposition.

*Note: *down* describes Jamie and is an adjective; *up* refers to what he did (cheered up) and is an adverb.

▶ **7.2**

a	from	k	to
b	to	l	with
c	against	m	for
d	on	n	to
e	to	o	of
f	on	p	to
g	of	q	with
h	on	r	of
i	to	s	for
j	from	t	of

▶ **7.3**

a 'Different *from*' is the safe choice, though it is not easy to be dogmatic.

b You could recast this sentence in several ways, even leaving out *who*, but, if it is included, it should be *whom*.

c 'Sue and *me*.'

d Correct in *colloquial* or dialect English which is what this sentence is: a formal piece of writing is unlikely to include this sentence except as a quotation. The formally correct version would, of course, be *to* or *down to*.

e   This is correct: *free from* would be equally correct. As the note on *free from/of* stated, there is overlap between the two.

▶ **7.4**

a   *When* introduces an adverbial clause of time.

b   a slight trick: *after* is an adverb here; *that* introduces a noun clause.

c   *Unless* introduces an adverbial clause of possibility.

d   *If* introduces an adverbial clause of possibility.

e   *where* refers to place, but this is a noun clause, object of the verb *have found out*.

f   *Where* introduces an adverbial clause of place.

g   Sorry, no conjunctions: *since* is a preposition here.

h   *Since* introduces adverbial clause of time.

i   *since* introduces adverbial clause of reason.

j   *lest* introduces adverbial clause of cause.

k   *If* introduces adverbial clause of possibility.

l   *when* introduces adverbial clause of time.

m   *as* introduces adverbial clause of time.

n   no conjunction: *until* is a preposition here.

o   *Until* introduces adverbial clause of time.

▶ **7.5**

The following answers are merely suggestions. You may have thought of different answers, equally good or, possibly, better:

a   The obvious ones are *until* and *unless*, preceding Ms Christophers. *When* in the middle would make some sense. *Because* seems unlikely at first, but move words round a little and you have: 'Because Ms Christophers planned to look for a new job, she received a rise.' Her employers are clearly making a desperate effort to keep her! '*If* (or *when*) Ms Christophers received a rise' suggests that she needed status to help her application.

b The likeliest are *before, as, when* and *after,* at the beginning or in the middle. *Until,* placed in the middle, suggests that they stopped their interviews as the new break-ins meant that he/she was no longer suspect.

c *Because, when* or *before* at the beginning would make sense. Perhaps puzzling over a delayed take-off, you would find 'The aeroplane was due for take-off *if* the cabin crew went through safety procedure' also makes (quite different) sense. *Although* at the beginning would suggest that the cabin crew were late in doing their duty.

d *Until* or *unless* in the middle would be obvious company policy, but you can suggest a customer-unfriendly company by using *if, although* or *when:* 'Don't open up a new till *even if* there are more than five in the queue.'

e Your conjunction can tell us whether Mandy likes Craig: 'Mandy decided to go to the party *because* Craig was supposed to be there.' '*Though* Craig was supposed to be there, Mandy decided to go to the party.' She loves him, she loves him not! You can introduce variations with words like *if* and *unless.* You can even plan a whole new scenario of Mandy changing her mind at the last minute because of Craig's absence: '*When* Mandy decided to go to the party, Craig was supposed to be there.'

8 PHRASES AND CLAUSES

▶ **8.1**

a Adjective phrase or participial clause – either is a correct description.

b Adverbial clause (time).

c Adverbial phrase (place).

d Main clause, one of two in the sentence (see Chapter 9).

e Noun phrase (direct object) or non-finite clause (not participial clause as *to do* is the infinitive).

f Participial clause or adverbial phrase (time).

g The same, but this is an example of a poorly constructed sentence: the participle has no noun to relate to, so who is doing the collecting?

h Adverbial clause (purpose – result is acceptable).

i Noun phrase (direct object) or non-finite clause using the gerund.

j Main clause.

k Appositive noun clause (equivalent to *announcement*).

l Adverbial clause (possibility/condition).

m Main clause.

n Adverbial clause (possibility/condition).

o Adverbial phrase (time).

p Noun phrase (for all its length, the basis is the noun *display*).

q Adjectival phrase (though it relates to place, it modifies *display*).

r Adverbial clause (reason).

s Noun clause (intensive complement).

t Noun phrase (direct object) or non-finite clause using infinitive.

▶ **8.2**

   a

      i   I/put

      ii   Did you put the cat out for the night?

      iii   Put the cat out for the night, please. (In syntactical terms *please* is optional!)

      iv   *the cat* direct object *for the night* adverbial qualification (time)

   b

      i   Jeff/showed

      ii   Did Jeff show you his new book?/Has Jeff shown you his new book?

      iii   Show me your new book, Jeff.

      iv   *me* indirect object, *his new book* direct object

   c

      i   we/close

ii Do you close the outdoor pool in the winter months?

iii Close the outdoor pool: it's winter. (Using *winter* as an explanation sounds better.)

iv *in the winter months* adverbial qualification (time); *the outdoor pool* direct object

d

   i The town/is

   ii Is the town very quiet?/Is it very quiet in town?

   iii *very quiet* intensive complement

e

   i You/must stand

   ii Must we stand for the Royal party?

   iii Stand for the Royal party!

   iv *for the royal party* adverbial qualification (reason)

▶ **8.3**

a Relative referring to whole sentence (sentential relative clause).

b Relative referring to antecedent noun *hold-up* (adnominal relative clause – or adjectival).

c Appositive – in apposition to *the news*.

d Adnominal (adjectival) relative clause – antecedent noun *news*.

e Nominal (noun) relative clause – subject of sentence.

f Adnominal (adjectival) relative clause – antecedent noun *film*.

g Sentential relative clause – referring to whole sentence.

h Appositive clause – in apposition to *policy*.

i Appositive clause – in apposition to *claim*.

j Nominal (noun) relative clause – subject.

The following are suggestions, not answers – your answers may be quite different and just as good (better?):

a while the burglars explored upstairs (time)
   wherever he found himself (place)
   as if there was nothing to worry about (manner)
   as he wished to reassure the children (reason)
   so that the interrogators would be discouraged (purpose)
   so that the interrogators left him alone (result)
   if (or unless) we had been very badly behaved (possibility/condition)
   although he had a violent temper (contrast/concession)

b after the ship set sail (time)
   where the headland could just be seen (place)
   as if the Flood had come again (manner)
   because global warming had started to have an effect (reason)
   so that we refused to travel (result – purpose is only apparent to God!)
   if we ever decided to sail across the bay (possibility/condition)
   though the weather forecast was favourable (contrast/concession)

c after her cat went missing (time)
   wherever she found a sympathetic listener (place)
   as you would expect from a former headteacher (manner)
   because she was determined to find a sponsor (reason)
   so that she could set her mind at rest (purpose)
   so (diligently) that people began to avoid her (result)
   if there was the chance of any scandal (possibility/condition)
   unless her husband persuaded her otherwise (negative possibility/condition)
   although the rest of the villagers gave up (contrast/concession)

d after the Christmas break had ended (time)
   where the generator failed (place)
   as completely as during the strike (manner)
   since management decided that there was no demand for their products (reason)
   in order that the workers should moderate their demands on pay and conditions (purpose)
   so that we had to look for new work (result)
   if there was any difficulty with safety requirements/unless there were perfect safety conditions (possibility/condition)

although the demand for heavy machinery revived (contrast/concession)

e after I've eaten my dinner (time)
wherever I happen to be after dinner (place)
as quickly as I did today (manner)
because I find the meetings so boring (reason)
so that no one can ask me ridiculous questions (purpose or result)
if I drink too much/unless I turn the television up (possibility/condition)
although the television is far too loud (contrast/concession)

9 KINDS OF SENTENCE

▶ 9.1

Where an explanation is needed a number directs you to a note underneath.

Simple: b i k[1] n[2]
Compound: f
Complex: a h 1 o p q r s[3]
Compound-Complex: d j t[3]
Non-sentence: c e[4] g m[2]
Notes:

1 A compound sentence looks likely, but *standing up* and *losing out* are not finite verbs and so there is only one clause.
2 This depends on punctuation. The words can either make a relative clause ('the cad *who took the wine from the fridge*') or be a sentence as a question.
3 The difference between s and t is what follows *and*. In s it is only a noun linked with *government*; in t it is a co-ordinate clause.
4 You may have thought that this was a compound sentence; it is certainly a compound clause, but a subordinate clause. It may have *and* in the middle, but it also has *If* at the beginning and no main clause to follow.

▶ 9.2

These are simply preferences, by no means the only right answers:

a *When* and *because* are fine: or you could simplify it to 'The French farmers' blockade of the Channel ports last year caused lorry drivers in France and Britain severe problems.'

b *When* is again suitable. So are 'Nancy Astor *who* took...was the first...' and 'Nancy Astor, the first woman to take her seat in Parliament, did so in 1919.'

c *As* or *because* is probably best, but again you can turn it into a simple sentence: 'A protection order has been placed on the few black bears left in the wild.'

d The two things your niece did are an obvious opportunity for a straightforward *and*, leaving out *she*. The first clause could be preceded by *after*, *as* or *when*.

e There are many ways of joining the first two (e.g. 'As it was…' or 'On a fine sunny day'), but the second link is the more interesting as you can turn round the speaker's personality in a word: '*but* I only stayed' (he/she likes crowded markets), '*so* I only stayed' (he/she hates crowds).

▶ **9.3**

a The Managing Director resigned.

b Go to Prague.

c Will it go all through the estate?

d Try, try again.

e John and Eric are brothers.

f The whole sentence: two co-ordinate clauses.

g The Prime Minister resigned the leadership and became active in industry (co-ordinate).

h Mr Chitty eventually saw (noun clause – object).

i (Noun clause – subject) is love.

j Mary and Martha lived in Bethany.

▶ **9.4**

a When the treaty, which was drawn up in Paris, was agreed, it seemed that what the smaller nations who had played a considerable part wanted had been forgotten, while the interests of the Powers were safeguarded until their ambitions brought further conflict.

b There are plenty of new industries which help the economy of an area which is showing signs of reviving, but we still remember when the pit had to close and how much hardship there was among men who had relied upon it for employment.

c If you lose your way on the moors, is it best to stand still and hope for rescue or go looking for assistance which might tire you out, but which could lead to safety if you approach it sensibly?

10 DIRECT AND INDIRECT SPEECH

▶ **10.1**

Note that there is scope for variation on the answers in both the following versions, but especially in indirect speech:

Slumping back in his chair, Ernest said wearily, 'I still don't see why it's so important.'
'How many times do I have to explain?', exclaimed Amy.
'If we can't raise some money for ourselves, the local Arts Association will refuse to help.'
'Which means there's no chance of staging the concert properly,' interrupted Diana.
'And we'll never get discovered!' wailed Amy.

'Good thing, too, I should think.'
'Leave him alone. He's only doing it to annoy.'
Diana restrained Amy as Ernest got up and went to the window.
'If you two calm down long enough,' he said, 'I'll tell you how to raise £1,000.'

(Note that the speaker is not given for two speeches. The character and actions of Ernest are well enough established for it to be obvious that he was speaking – if you have any doubts, however, it is better to insert 'Ernest replied' or something similar. In the case of Diana, the fact that she then restrained Amy makes it clear that she spoke the calming words.)

Wearily slumping in his chair, Ernest said that he could not see why the matter was so important. Amy, who was losing her patience, explained yet again that, if they could not raise some money, the local Arts Association would refuse to help. Diana pointed out that this meant there was no chance of staging the concert properly which upset Amy who wailed that they would never get discovered. When Ernest was unmoved by all this, Diana had to restrain Amy and insist that she leave him alone as he was only trying to annoy them.

Eventually Ernest, getting up and going to the window, announced that, if the two women calmed down, he would tell them how to raise £1,000.

(This piece would be improved if you departed further from the original dialogue, but indirect speech as such involves reporting, though not quoting, the actual speech.)

▶ **10.2**

a 'If I can get tickets,' Jack said, 'would you like to come to the club on New Year's Eve?'

b 'The most important consideration,' insisted the superintendent, 'is public safety.'

c This is correct. The full stop after 'superintendent' is justified by the fact that each half of the speech is a separate sentence.

d Didn't you hear me say, 'The shop is shut'? (The question is in the main sentence, not the speech.)

e One voice could be heard shouting above the turmoil, 'Keep the road clear!'

▶ **10.3**

a In a whisper Jack asked if we/I/she/he/they had got the torch.

b The managing director announced that job cuts were inevitable.

c Mrs Barnes argued that, as far as she could see (or 'in her opinion'), the council was just ignoring them/us.

d Eventually the Chair of Housing announces that the new development can go ahead. (In the case of a present tense narration, there is no change in the tense of the speech.)

e Margaret asked if she could go next.

f I told Mark I had seen him in the supermarket the previous Friday. (Oddly, if you retain 'on Friday', rather than changing it to 'the previous Friday', it would be more idiomatic to retain 'saw', also.)

g The invigilator stated that, if we/they had finished the paper, we/they could leave the room.

h The holiday firm claimed that they would beat any other price offers.

i The captain asked me/him whether I/he wanted to open the batting now that I/he was feeling better.

j Kath told me that she (had) met him a few years ago in Ibiza.

11 AFFIXES

▶ 11.1

a speech by one character on stage alone (literally, alone-speak); a speech by one person whether alone or in company (one-speak); several people talking (across-speak); two people talking (two-speak).

b foretell the future (before-say); disagree and oppose someone's opinion (against-say); prohibit or ban (more difficult to explain: 'between-say' could, possibly, mean insisting on placing a distance between the person and the prohibited deed).

c to drive something in by a syringe, etc. (in-throw); sadness (a state of being thrown down); interruption (something thrown between); refuse to accept (another difficult one: take *re-* in the sense of 'back', not 'again' – thrown back); missile (something thrown forward).

d suggest (before-place); place on or force (in-place; the meaning has obviously shifted a little); insert or interrupt (between-place); put next to (next-place).

e a very large block of stone; a market in the hands of two firms/individuals; the practice of taking many wives; many-coloured.

▶ 11.2

a a pause, usually in a show or play (*inter-* means 'between').

b endless (the prefix is not *inter-* but *in-*, and *terminable* means 'able to be ended').

c the circumference or outer limits (*peri-* means 'around').

d to convey or move from one place/person to another (*trans-* means 'across').

e a piece of land with water on three sides (literally 'almost an island' – *pen* means 'almost').

f below water or a vessel that can travel below water (*sub-* means 'below').

g the last but two (two prefixes: *pen-* means 'almost' and *ante-* means 'before'; *ultimate* means 'last', so it is 'the one before the almost last').

h meeting, coming together (*con-* means 'with' – so, too, do the next three prefixes, all variations on the same form).

i fellow-countryman (*com-*, 'with', implies sharing).

j invite to join (a committee, etc.) (choose to be with you).

k the mutual relationship between things (literally, the relation with...).

l the study of the world (*geo-* means 'world').

m a sequence of three plays/novels (tri-means 'three'),

n writing your own name (*auto-* means 'self').

o wild uproar, literally, 'all the demons' (*pan-* means 'all').

p with eight syllables, probably applied to verse (*octo-* means 'eight').

q bring an end to (two prefixes: *dis-* means 'not', *con-* means 'with').

r speaking many languages (*poly-* means 'many' – incidentally, *glotta*, not a prefix, means 'tongue').

s a 12-sided figure (*dodeca-* means 'twelve).

t a mythical one-horned beast (*uni-* means 'one' and *corn*, not a prefix, means 'horn').

▶ **11.3**

a re-form

b forecourt

c co-ordinate

d both are right, but 'forebears' is preferred

e forbear

f pre-empted

g ensure

h ex-dancer

i extradition

j most of us would think both are correct; 'inquiry' certainly is!

▶ **11.4**

a -*dom* forming abstract noun.

b -*ology* forming abstract noun meaning area of study (in this case, living things).

c *-graph* meaning 'write', *-ic* forming adjective (also noun in *reprographics*).

d *-ar* forming agent noun (the person who studies at school), *-ly* forming adjective (not adverb!).

e *-ive* forming adjective, *-ly* forming adverb.

f *-ness* forming abstract noun.

g *-olog* (*y* deleted) meaning area of study, *-ical* forming adjective, *-ly* forming adverb.

h *-ism* forming abstract noun.

i *-er* forming agent noun.

j *-ize* forming verb.

k *-fy* forming verb.

l *-ance* forming abstract noun.

m *-ion* forming noun.

n *-ious* forming adjective, *-ness* forming abstract noun (with a slightly different meaning from the original abstract noun *grace*).

o *-ent* forming adjective.

▶ 11.5

a nobility (note the unusual alteration to the final silent *e*).

b horrific (sometimes syllables are added for no obvious reason: why is it not 'horric'?).

c infectious.

d collapsible (note omission of final silent *e*).

e meteorically (via the adjective *meteoric*).

f transferable.

g shrewdness.

h fellowship.

i actively (via adjective *active*).

j frantically (though *franticly* is an alternative: see Chapter 6).

k beautiful (note alteration of final *y* to *i*).

    a advice (noun).

    b author.

    c benefited (*fit* is not the stressed syllable – however, *benefitted* is often seen).

    d Basically.

    e adapter (*adaptor* is an electrical term).

    f merriment.

    g descendant (*descendent* is a little-used adjective, not a noun).

    h publicly (an exception to the *-ally* rule – see Chapter 6).

    i both are correct.

    j classic (*Classical*, usually with a capital *c*, refers to Greek and Latin history and arts or to the style imitated from them; *classic* refers to a first-class example of something such as the five most renowned flat races or widely admired and established literature).

12 GENDER AND GRAMMAR

► 12.1

    a A difficult one: *milkmaid* is most definitely wrong! Perhaps it is best to recast the sentence: 'Sheila had never planned to take a milk-round.'

    b Obviously a single formal announcement: *he or she* would be fine, but you can turn the whole thing into the plural (*all pupils* followed by *they have*) if you like.

    c This makes a distinction between male and female actors: why not insert 'and established' after *well-known* and finish the sentence after *Macbeth*?

    d Once again it suggests that a woman doing the job is somehow different: finish the sentence '...as soon as is convenient *for him or her*'.

    e You could turn the whole thing into the plural, but this is a statement stressing the individual and it is tempting to use the strictly ungrammatical *their child* and *their abilities* while leaving *a parent* untouched.

f You could leave it as it is and pass it off with an embarrassed smile or use *spokesperson* or *spokeswoman*, but it is probably better to recast the sentence: 'Who is speaking on behalf of the Townswomen's Guild?'

g Just leave out *male* or use *a job in nursing*.

h There is something rather sexist about noticing the fact, but, apart from that, all you need do is use *chair* for *chairman*.

i A great temptation to use *their*. Turning into the plural is not possible and *his or her* is unconvincing. Hopefully examples like this will not be common because it reads like part of a narrative and the context would probably indicate the gender.

j You could use *his or her* on what is clearly an announcement, but why not turn it into 2nd person: 'If you need assistance, please raise your hand.'?

13 REGISTER

▶ 13.1

a This is a formal speech, delivered (one would imagine) to a large number of people, many known to the speaker, at a formal meeting. Use of *we* and *our* established that these are people with whom he/she belongs. The suggestion that this is a large meeting comes from the fact that the style is correct and slightly ponderous, though not really pompous. Note the second sentence where the three attributes of the village hall are nearly identical: they are all given simply to create an imposing list of three. In this sort of speech *you get half drowned* is too chatty: it would have been suitable in a similar, but less obviously prepared, speech to a smaller group (a committee?). Something like 'It is extremely difficult to hold a meeting…' would have been better here.

b This newspaper report is sound, clear, factual, non-technical, non-sensational, aimed at the intelligent general reader. There are two failures of register. From *its catastrophic demographic impact* to the end of the sentence is far too technical (economic theory) and should be replaced by '…its impact on jobs in an area of low employment and investment' (if that is what it means!). The details of the *buxom* barmaid are offensive in almost the opposite direction: trivializing the issues.

c The end of a chatty friendly letter: the references to what Len is like show that the writer and reader know each other well and the abbreviations like *I'll* and choppy sentences with parentheses and dashes are perfectly suitable. *Anyway* is a typical adverb to say, 'Let's get on with it' or 'That's enough for now', but the rest of the last sentence comes from a business letter: how about 'let me know what you think'?

d   This is one-to-one (or two or three with Mr Kershaw and/ or the son) at a Parents' Evening/Open Day. It is friendly, informal, but slightly distant compared with c. The register is a mixture of informality (no prepared speeches) and technical (mathematics and education). You will note the unstructured sentences (the second one the best example) which are perfectly suitable. The teacher has the problem of maintaining a friendly register and encouraging tone while dealing with two touchy subjects: the difficulty of A level Maths. for the boy and the fact that he is being bullied. He manages the first one well with *He's the first one to admit...* and *understanding difficult concepts* is good: he is not talking down to his audience, but he is not asking her to understand the concepts. Where he fails is the *wimp* reference: the word itself is too slangy and (here) offensive and the method is unsubtle. 'Does he tell you how he gets on with his class-mates?' would involve Mrs Kershaw gently in a dialogue on the matter.

e   Straightforward football reporting with just a touch of military imagery: *onslaught* and *fierce*. The decent functional style (aimed at a readership which wants the facts with some sense of mood as well) is let down by the section after *the referee* which pursues two opposite directions: *administered a caution* is a touch too formal (*booked, cautioned*, even *yellow-carded*) and *really was a bit silly* is almost childish in a piece that is adopting a grown up, manly style. How about '... who showed the City striker an unnecessary yellow card' or 'who over-reacted by booking the City striker' or many other alternatives?

14 SPELLING AND PUNCTUATION

▶ 14.1

a   principal

b   excerpts

c   humorous

d   ascent

e council

f recede

g deceive

h excepted

i martial

j fierce

k psychopathology

l consensus

m complementary

n siege

o stationary

▶ 14.2

*There are instances where other versions may be as good. Particular talking points are marked with *.*

If you are doing this as the final exercise in the book, you probably feel a sense of relief: fourteen chapters on grammar and the English language may be considered more than enough. As you come to the end – some of you, of course, may be approaching the chapters in a different order –, you will, we hope, have derived some benefit from the book. What, you may be asking yourself, did you hope to gain from it and has that been achieved?* Some of you may have been seeking purely practical assistance; some may have been interested in the forms of English; some students' ambitions may have extended to pursuing advanced study.** Possibly some of you may be discouraged. 'Why,' you may say to yourself, 'did I bother to start?' We hope you are not so down-hearted and may be thinking,*** 'I'll carry on studying English. It's really interesting! There was quite a bit I didn't know.' Whatever your feelings – and reactions are bound to be different – you will certainly have appreciated the kind-heartedness involved in finishing with such a straightforward exercise.

* There is a fair case for using quotation marks here. The reason against is that the use of *you* rather than *I* suggests reported speech: compare with the later 'thinking'.
** If you wish, modestly, to suggest that such is unlikely, use an exclamation mark. As your modesty is probably not well-founded, we have used a full stop.
*** If your thoughts are put into words, they are treated like speech with quotation marks.

Taking it further

The English language today: A publishing phenomenon

The 2009 Fourth Estate paperback of *Eats, Shoots & Leaves* boasts, "Over 3 million copies sold worldwide" – goodness knows how many have been sold by now! Lynne Truss's book (or should that be Lynne Truss' book?) is the standard-bearer for an increasingly popular type of book which could be unflatteringly termed 'old-school learning with jokes'. Her book is better than that, but its split personality is well summed up by the flippant title (it's the old familiar panda joke) coupled with a severe subtitle, 'The zero tolerance approach to punctuation'. It's an entertaining read, with much sound information and a wide range of reference. Depending on their temperaments, readers will find such things as the four pages of individual errors with apostrophes amusing, infuriating or possibly irritating, with its sense of sneering at the errors of the ignorant.

The runaway success of *Eats, Shoots & Leaves* has spawned a whole series of imitators – yet not quite imitators, for Truss's style is distinctive: quirky, personal, witty, emotionally involved and almost anthropomorphic about punctuation marks. Michael O'Mara Books produces a range of clear, informal, economically priced books on old-fashioned learning and forgotten facts. The provenance of *My Grammar and I (Or Should That Be 'Me'?)*, by Caroline Taggart and J.A. Wines, published in 2008, is clear enough. On the Truss model, the title is simultaneously stern and jokey, with a subtitle, 'Old-school ways to sharpen your English', and the publishers quote a favourable review saying that it 'will do for grammar what *Eats, Shoots and Leaves* did for punctuation'. In fact, it's a very helpful selection of lists, rules, examples and explanations, with very little continuous writing (unlike Truss) and the flippancy confined to headings such as 'Swot's Corner' where this book, for instance, uses the more boring 'Insight'. Offering more individuality of approach is the recently published *Have You Eaten Grandma?* (Michael Joseph) by Gyles Brandreth, again exemplifying the current popularity of the jokey title/grammar guru combination.

Browsing the shelves in a bookshop will uncover any number of such books, with titles such as *I Before E (Except after C)*, also on the

O'Mara list, and even *Grammar: Know Your Shit or Know You're Shit*. This is the golden age of helpful guides to aspects of English language which, in the words on one blurb, 'enlighten and entertain'.

The acknowledged master of the language/grammar book is the prolific Professor David Crystal. The author of the cosy *Rediscover Grammar with David Crystal* (Longman), he is also responsible for the excellent and weighty *Cambridge Encyclopedia of the English Language* (Cambridge University Press, revised 2018). This is surprisingly accessible and varied as it moves from Old English to word games via much solid linguistic information. With its own thorough list of further reading, this is highly recommended. Professor Crystal covers most of the bases, in terms of both academic level and areas of knowledge, in his many books, up to 2017's *Making Sense: The Glamorous Story of English Grammar* (Profile Books). He even essayed a study of *Language and the Internet* (Cambridge University Press, 2006), a subject only touched on in most language guides, including this one.

There are plenty of sound textbooks of contemporary grammar which make no attempt at the readability of Crystal's encyclopedia, and anyone wishing to examine English language more fully could consider studying A level English Language. Remember that it is not like GCSE English Language (testing your use of the language), but deals with analysing the language, its structure and form, in a variety of contexts. Sadly, many adult learning classes have fallen victim to educational cuts, but they do exist and there is no shortage of online courses.

There are, of course, other Teach Yourself books on the English language. Particularly useful is *Aitchison's Linguistics* by Jean Aitchison (retitled in 2010 from *Teach Yourself Linguistics*).

Individual views

The popular travel writer Bill Bryson has published *Mother Tongue* (Penguin), a widespread survey of the different forms of English, as well as *Troublesome Words* (from the same publisher). For a challenging and entertaining read, there is Kingsley Amis's quirky *The King's English* (republished as a Penguin Modern Classic in 2011). The classic overview of the English language in use, *Fowler's Modern English Usage*, has proved so indispensable that there is no sign of the flow of revised versions slowing up some 85 years after H.W. Fowler's death. The latest Oxford University edition, updated by Jeremy Butterfield, appeared as recently as 2015. Getting hold of *The American Language* by H.L. Mencken, referred to in the main text, has been a problem in recent years. There is no one definitive version, as Mencken produced many revisions and additions, and for some time it was difficult to find any edition in print. However, in 2009 the University of Michigan brought out a capacious and relatively inexpensive paperback edition, and since then there seems to have been a revival of interest in the sage of Baltimore and different versions of his text have appeared from Coyote Canyon (2013) and Forgotten Books (2017).

George Bernard Shaw's original approach to language and phonetics is difficult to find in printed form now, and there have been inevitable disputes about the correct form of his alphabet. Penguin's Shavian alphabet edition of *Androcles and the Lion* is probably long out of print, but may possibly be found in a second-hand shop or an online second-hand books site. Otherwise the internet (including Wikipedia) has a fair bit of information on Shaw's Universal Alphabet, and *Pygmalion* in all its forms is a bracing presentation of Shaw's views. Widely available in print, DVD and CD, *Pygmalion* can also be seen on stage or screen in its original form or as the musical *My Fair Lady*.

Eric Partridge is another writer whose views on language are always vigorous and well worth reading. Unfortunately, much of his best work was on slang, and the relevance of an outdated book on slang can be limited. Fortunately, 40 years after his death many of his books remain in print, regularly revised, with his key work, *Usage and Abusage* (1942), last updated by Penguin in 2005.

The history of the language

For an overall textbook of the history of the language, Baugh and Cable's *History of the English Language* (Routledge) is recommended, and it is not difficult to find books on individual periods, including Old and Middle English. On the one hand, Laura and Robert Lambdin's *Companion to Old and Middle English Literature* (Greenwood) approaches the subject from a 21st-century perspective. On the other hand, Henry Sweet's classics (dated by their use of 'Anglo-Saxon' instead of 'Old English' and familiar to generations of undergraduates) are still in print in various revisions: remarkably, a new edition of *Sweet's Anglo-Saxon Primer* appeared from Forgotten Books as recently as 2018. As in most areas of study, there is a Teach Yourself guide, *Complete Old English* by Dr Mark Atherton, newly revised in 2019.

There is no lack of editions and translations of the major texts of Old and Middle English. The great epics of *Beowulf* and *Sir Gawain and the Green Knight* have both been served in the last 20 years by a retelling by Michael Morpurgo (both Walker Books) and a poetic treatment by a distinguished poet: the late Seamus Heaney (*Beowulf*) and Simon Armitage (*Sir Gawain*).

A much older translation of *Sir Gawain* was made by a writer more famous in another field: J.R.R. Tolkien. His translation, together with two other 14th-century masterpieces, *Pearl* and *Sir Orfeo*, is still in print at HarperCollins and can also be accessed on an audiobook read by Terry Jones. Tolkien's dual career, as pre-eminent language scholar and as writer of popular fantasy fiction, puts him in a unique position for the student of languages. In the 21st century the Tolkien of *The Lord of the Rings* and *The Hobbit* is everywhere, in the cinema, in games, CDs and DVDs no less than in books. Language formation is always crucial to Tolkien's fantasies: see Ruth S. Noel's *The Languages of Tolkien's Middle Earth* (Houghton & Mifflin). The shadow of the foremost 20th-century scholar of Old and Middle English always lurks behind the creator of fantasies about elves and orcs, hobbits and dwarves.

If you wish to try your hand at reading the earliest 'Modern' English text (late 14th century), Chaucer's *Canterbury Tales* is readily obtainable in the original and you can study original and modern together on the Harvard Geoffrey Chaucer Website. There is no shortage of translations, including a 2010 retelling by Peter Ackroyd, one of several versions in Penguin. Start, for many different reasons, with the Prologue: naturally, it comes first, but it is also a wonderfully vivid depiction of 14th-century society and divides naturally into bite-sized chunks. If you just want to enjoy Chaucer's characters and stories, a 2003 BBC dramatization is available on DVD, with a host of star performers.

A rewarding way to see the development of the language via important and often beautiful documents and recordings is to visit the exhibitions at the British Library on Euston Road, London, next to St Pancras Station.

Glossary

abbreviation   the shortened form of a word, often indicated by an apostrophe (ma'am) or a full stop (Ltd.).

abstract noun   a noun which deals with a principle/quality/emotion, etc., as distinct from a tangible object or person (**concrete noun**).

active voice   the most usual voice of the verb, with the subject the person/thing doing the action or being described.

adjective   a word which modifies the meaning of a noun or pronoun.

adnominal phrase   another term for 'adjectival phrase'.

adverb   a modifier used most frequently, but by no means solely, with verbs. Adverbial qualification often takes the form of phrase or clause.

affix   morpheme with a fixed meaning (or meanings), added to the beginning or end of a word.

agent   usually used in the phrase **agent noun**, the doer or active party.

agreement   matching different parts of a sentence so that all refer to the same number, tense, etc.

ambiguity   the existence of two possible meanings, effective when deliberate, to be avoided in accidental use.

Anglo-Saxon   no longer used for **Old English**, but still used, particularly as a contrast to classical, in defining the origins of words.

antecedent   the word or words in a text to which a modifier or a pronoun refers back.

antonym   a word of opposite meaning.

apposition   the placing of two or more nouns or noun equivalents next to each other when they refer to the same thing/person, though in different terms.

archaism   a word or usage which is out-of-date.

auxiliary verb   a verb that assists in the formation of a tense of another verb: e.g. *are* going.

case   a set form for noun/pronoun/adjective depending on its function, not widely used in English, though pronouns operate in the **subjective** (**nominative**) and **objective** (**accusative**) cases.

classical   derived from, or pertaining to, Greek and Latin forms: often used in connection with origins of words.

clause   a group of words containing a finite verb and (usually) a subject. Clauses can be **main, co-ordinate** (two or more main clauses) or **subordinate**. Modern grammar also admits the **non-finite clause**.

collective noun   a singular noun for a group of people/objects/places, etc.

colloquialism   a word or usage associated with speech.

command   an order, the only form of clause that regularly lacks a subject.

comparative   the form of an adjective or adverb comparing two nouns/verbs, etc., formed with the word *more* or (in the case of adjectives) the ending *-er*.

complement   the traditional term for the word/phrase/clause which completes the sense of a verb of being: now also known as **intensive complement. Complement** is now often used for anything that completes a sentence, including **objects**.

complex sentence   a sentence containing one or more subordinate clauses as well as a main clause; sentences combining qualities of compound and complex are known as **compound-complex sentences**.

compound sentence   a sentence of two or more equal main clauses, usually joined by a co-ordinating conjunction.

compound word   a word made up of two or more other words.

concession/condition   most terms for types of adverbial phrases/clauses are absolutely straightforward; less so concession (contrast – *though*) and condition (possibility – *if, unless*).

conjunction   word joining together clauses (also sometimes smaller groups of words and single words): divided into **co-ordinating** and **subordinating conjunctions** depending on whether the clauses are of equal weight.

context   the surrounding words and sentences, a help to discovering meaning; also the setting in which your writing or speaking is placed.

determiners   words which demonstrate or determine who or what is referred to: including **definite** (*the*) and **indefinite** (*a/an*) **articles** and **demonstrative pronouns/adjectives** (*this/that*, etc.).

dialect   linguistically this can mean the aspects of language use derived from the speaker/writer him/herself, but its regular use is to mean the language patterns of a region or class.

dialogue   speech involving more than one person, conversation; **duologue** relates specifically to dialogue between two people.

diction   the selection of words used in speech or writing: e.g. simple, technical or archaic diction.

diphthong   a vowel sound made up of two vowels.

direct speech   the form of writing speech which uses the exact words of the speaker, marked by **quotation marks/inverted commas**.

ellipsis   a three-point punctuation mark used to indicate that something has been omitted from a sentence or that speech has been interrupted or broken off.

exclamation   can take the form of a set exclamation (often not a full sentence, but treated as such) or an ordinary statement delivered in exclamatory manner.

finite verb   also known as **tensed**, a finite verb relates to a particular subject and has a specific tense. The opposite is **non-finite (non-tensed)**.

formal   the adjective to describe orderly 'correct' use of language or the situations in which you might use such structured language.

function   the role or task of a grammatical unit within the sentence.

function words   words which can be mainly defined by their roles in linking together the sentence (e.g. prepositions, conjunctions, auxiliary verbs).

gender   the indication of the sex of a person or animal; in many languages, not English, **grammatical gender** gives everything (objects included) a gender.

gerund   a verbal noun, the same form as the present participle, but used as a noun.

homonyms   words that are identical in sound and spelling, but not in meaning; if only the sound is the same, the correct word is **homophones**.

idiom   the language typical of a place: hence 'unidiomatic English' does not sound natural.

imperative   the form of the verb used for commands.

indicative   the regular mood of the word, used for statements and questions about what is/was/might be.

indirect speech   the way of presenting speech in narrative which reports (not quotes) the words used.

Indo-European   the family of languages to which English belongs: forms of words similar to other languages may not have come from the language itself, but from common Indo-European ancestry.

infinitive   the basic form of the verb, often preceded by *to*.

informal   the term for language use that is unstructured, though not necessarily incorrect.

interrogative   any reference to **interrogative** (pronouns, etc.) means *as in a question.*

intransitive verbs   verbs that are complete in themselves, without a direct object.

inversion   reversing the normal order, as in questions.

jargon   the technical language of any specific field of work, scholarship, sport, etc.

lexical unit   a word or words that functions as a unit of meaning, i.e. one that can be defined independently in a dictionary.

lexical words   words which have specific meanings in the world in general, not just roles in the sentence (e.g. nouns, verbs, adjectives).

Middle English   the language spoken in this country between the 12th and 15th centuries.

modal verb   a form of auxiliary verb that also establishes mood.

Modern English   the language defined as Modern English is not necessarily very modern, but the language from the time it first became recognizable as English: 15th and 16th centuries.

modifiers   words which modify the meaning of others: **adjectives** and **adverbs**.

morpheme   the smallest grammatical unit within a word, whether **free** (an independent unit of meaning, possibly a word in its own right) or **bound** (modifying the free morpheme: e.g. affixes and verb/noun endings).

neologism   a newly created word.

nominal   the adjective form of **noun**.

non-finite verb   the forms of the verb (**infinitive, participles**) which cannot operate in a specific tense without an **auxiliary verb**.

noun   a word which gives the name of something, whether general (**common noun**) or specific (**proper noun**).

number singular   (referring to one) or **plural** (two or more).

object   the person/thing a transitive verb is done to, either the direct **object** or the **indirect object**, the receiver, sometimes preceded by *to*. Now often known as **objective complement**.

Old English   the language spoken in this country between the 5th and 12th centuries; actually a complex of similar dialects, rather than a single language.

parenthesis   the inserting of a separate phrase, clause, etc., within a sentence, usually with **brackets** or **dashes** – note the plural **parentheses**.

participles   the past and present **participles** are non-finite forms used adjectivally or (with auxiliaries) to form other tenses.

passive voice   the form of the verb used when the sufferer of the action is the subject of the sentence.

perfect   a series of tenses in the past: the **present perfect** relates to a recently completed action, the **past perfect** (*had done*) is one stage further back.

phrasal verb   verb which consists of verb-plus-adverb, with a set meaning: e.g. *lay off* (workers).

phrase   unit of a group of words which fulfils the function of a specific part of speech.

political correctness   often abbreviated to PC, the use of language that seeks to avoid anything that may offend (especially, but not solely, minorities) on grounds of sex, race, size, age, intelligence, etc.

predicate   traditionally all the sentence that is not the subject: verb and all that follows; now sometimes given as **predicator** and referring just to the verb.

prefix   an affix placed at the beginning of a word.

preposition   word which is placed before a noun or noun equivalent to link it to the rest of the sentence.

preterite   another term for the simple past tense.

pronoun   a word which can perform the function of a noun, many, but not all, **personal pronouns**.

prose   the normal form of written language; not verse.

pun   the simultaneous use (usually humorous) of more than one meaning of the same word.

punctuation   this glossary does not list the various punctuation marks; full definitions are in Chapter 14.

qualify   an alternative term for **modify**.

Received Pronunciation   the term used for the generally accepted standard pronunciation of English; sometimes abbreviated to RP.

reflexive pronoun   the form used when action is 'reflected' on to the doer (e.g. *herself*); the same form is used for **emphasizing pronouns**.

register   the appropriate form of the language for a given context or situation.

relative pronoun   a pronoun that joins two clauses and also fulfils the function of a noun or pronoun: e.g. *who* replaces *and he*.

root   the original basis for a word, before affixes are added; also known as stem.

simple sentence   a sentence consisting of one main clause.

slang   diction based on unofficial colloquialisms, not a permanent part of the language, usually dating and disappearing fairly quickly.

split infinitive   dividing *to* from the verb itself by other words.

subject   the person/thing that a sentence is 'about', the doer/sufferer of the verb.

subjunctive   the form of the verb that relates to intentions, wishes, etc., not actual events.

suffix   an affix placed at the end of a word.

superlative   the form of an adjective or adverb comparing at least three things, formed with the word *most* or (in the case of adjectives) the ending *-est*.

syllable   a single sound within a word, consisting of one vowel sound (not necessarily one vowel) and its accompanying consonants.

synonyms   words of the same (or very similar) meaning.

syntax   what might be described as 'the grammar of the sentence'.

tense   the form of the verb that identifies the time to which it relates.

transitive verbs   verbs that take a direct object.

usage   the normal way in which words and other features of language work to create meaning.

verbs   mostly to do with actions (*verbs of doing*), but also *verbs of being*: be, *become*, etc.

vocabulary   the words belonging to a language, a subject, an individual, etc.

vowel   essentially *a, e, i, o, u*, but *y* and, in words derived from Welsh, *w* can be used as vowels; all other letters are **consonants**.

Index

About the author

Ron Simpson has an MA (Oxon) in English Language and Literature and a PGCE from Birmingham University. He taught English for 30 years and during his teaching career was Head of English at King's School, Pontefract and Head of Sixth Form at Campsmount School, Doncaster. He worked with JMB/NEAB/AQA as Review Panel Member/Moderator for the 'O' Level/16-plus/GCSE English and English Literature examinations. Currently he writes widely on jazz, and reviews plays, operas and concerts for various websites. He recently co-wrote *Don't Worry' bout the Bear*, the musical memoirs of his brother, Jim Simpson.

A complete introduction series

Selected titles

Algebra: A complete introduction

Hugh Neill

Anatomy & Physiology: A complete introduction

David Le Vay, revised and updated by Jenny Stafford-Brown

Patrick Moore's Astronomy: A complete introduction

Sir Patrick Moore, updated by Percy Seymour

Buddhism: A complete introduction

Clive Erricker

Calculus: A complete introduction

Hugh Neill

Catholicism: A complete introduction

Peter Stanford

Christianity: A complete introduction

John Young and Greg Hoyland

Criminology: A complete introduction

Peter Joyce

Economics A complete introduction

Thomas Coskeran

Geology: A complete introduction

David Rothery

Jung: A complete introduction

Phil Goss

Kant: A complete introduction

Robert Wicks

Linguistics: A complete introduction

David Hornsby

Literary Theory: A complete introduction

Sara Upstone

Logic: A complete introduction

Siu-Fan Lee

Marx: A complete introduction

Gill Hands

Mathematics: A complete introduction

Trevor Johnson and Hugh Neill

Nietzsche: A complete introduction

Roy Jackson

Philosophy: A complete introduction

Sharon Kaye

Physics: A complete introduction

Jim Breithaupt

Politics: A complete introduction

Peter Joyce

Practical Electronics: A complete introduction

Andy Cooper

Quantum Theory: A complete introduction

Alexandre Zagoskin

Scottish History: A complete introduction

David Allan

Social Psychology: A complete introduction

Dr Paul Seager

Sociology: A complete introduction

Dr Paul Oliver

Sport Science: A complete introduction

Simon Rea

Sports Psychology: A complete introduction

John Perry

Statistics: A complete introduction

Alan Graham

Trigonometry: A complete introduction

Hugh Neill

Volcanoes, Earthquakes and Tsunamis: A complete introduction

David Rothery